MW00721275

CodeNotes® for ASP.NET

Edited by GREGORY BRILL

CodeNotes®
for ASP.NET

RANDOM HOUSE TRADE PAPERBACKS
NEW YORK

A Random House Trade Paperback Original

Library of Congress Cataloging-in-Publication Data
CodeNotes for ASP.NET / edited by Gregory Brill.
p.   cm.
ISBN 0-8129-9220-2
1. Websites—Design. 2. Active server pages. 3. Microsoft.net framework. I. Brill, Gregory.

TK5105.8885.A26 C64 2002   005.2'76—dc21   2002023705

Using CodeNotes

PHILOSOPHY

The CodeNotes philosophy is that the core concepts of any technology can be presented succinctly. The product of many years of consulting and training experience, the CodeNotes series is designed to make you productive in a technology in as short a time as possible.

CODENOTES POINTERS

Throughout the book, you will encounter CodeNotes pointers: AS010101. Notice that the first two letters are A and S (as in ASP) and the remaining characters are numbers. These pointers are links to additional content available online at the CodeNotes website. To use a CodeNotes pointer, simply point a web browser to www.codenotes.com and enter the pointer number. The website will direct you to an article or an example that provides additional information about the topic.

CODENOTES STYLE

The CodeNotes series follows certain style guidelines:

- Code objects and code keywords are highlighted using a special font. For example: `array[3]`.

- Code blocks, screen output, and command lines are placed in individual blocks with a special font:

```
'This is an example code block
```

Listing ChapterNumber.ListingNumber   Some code

WHAT YOU NEED TO KNOW BEFORE CONTINUING

In order to take full advantage of this book, you should be familiar with certain technologies before continuing.

Basic HTML

One of the major advantages to the .NET Framework is that you really don't need to know very much HTML. However, you should still be familiar with basic HTML syntax before reading this book. In particular, you are likely to encounter `<head>`, `<body>`, and various `<table>` and `<form>` tags. For a quick refresher, see ⟜**CN**⟩AS010005.

XML

XML (eXtensible Markup Language) permeates the .NET Framework and is the data format for configuration files, page layout, etc. Despite the marketing hyperbole you are likely to encounter, at its root, XML is nothing more than a specification for the textual representation of data. By itself, there is nothing extraordinary about the XML standard, which characterizes data in a structured and hierarchal format.

Although you do not need to be an expert with XML to understand this book, you should at least have a familiarity with basic XML principles including tags, attributes, and XSLT. If you have never worked with XML, consult *CodeNotes for XML*.

Visual Basic

Most of the examples in this book are developed using the VB.NET language inside of ASP.NET. For the most part, if you are familiar with VB5, VB6, or VBScript, you should be able to follow the code. However, if you wish to learn more about VB.NET, see *CodeNotes for VB.NET*.

About the Authors

SHELDON FERNANDEZ is Senior Developer at Infusion Development Canada located in Toronto, Ontario. He has developed software for Silicon Valley start-ups, as well as financial and medical institutions in the United States and Canada. He has worked with Microsoft technology for many years and has taught numerous aspects of the .NET Framework (including ASP.NET) to a variety of companies, including financial institutions in New York City and software companies in San Jose.

Sheldon, who possesses a computer engineering degree from the University of Waterloo, was also the chief researcher on *Applying COM+*, a definitive work on Microsoft's enterprise component technology. When not glued to his computer, he can be found jogging along the Toronto lakeshore.

Contributing Author

ROBERT MCGOVERN works as a consultant, architect, and trainer for Infusion Development Corporation. He has worked on everything from large mortgage and stock-trading systems to biomechanics data-collection and analysis systems. Rob currently lives in Ohio with his fiancée.

More information about the authors and Infusion Development Corporation can be found at http://www.codenotes.com/do/aboutus.

Acknowledgments

First, thanks to John Gomez who saw the potential of the CodeNotes idea before anyone else and introduced me to Random House. Without John, there would be no CodeNotes. I'd also like to thank Annik La-Farge, who fearlessly championed the series and whose creativity, enthusiasm, and publishing savvy have been instrumental in its creation. Thank you to Mary Bahr, our unflappable editor, who paved the way and crafted the marketing. Thank you to Ann Godoff, whose strength, decisiveness, and wisdom gave CodeNotes just the momentum it needed. And, of course, the production, sales, and business teams at Random House, with particular thanks to Howard Weill, Jean Cody, and Richard Elman.

On the Infusion Development side, thank you to Tom Nicholson for his patient editing. We would also like to thank the CodeNotes reviewers, who gave us feedback and suggestions on our early drafts. A special thanks to Glenn Eide for his proofreading efforts. And thank you to the entire cast and crew of Infusion Development Corporation, who have supported and encouraged this venture throughout, with special thanks to Irene Wilk-Dominique, Jessica Pollack, and DeBorah Johnson, who helped administrate and manage so much of this process. I know Code-Notes was extremely trying, tough to do, and involved an awesome amount of research, writing, and editing. But here it is . . . as we envisioned it.

—Gregory Brill

Contents

CodeNotes® *for ASP.NET*

Chapter 1

—

INTRODUCTION

ASP.NET is Microsoft's new technology for developing web-based applications. The most significant feature of ASP.NET (formerly named ASP+) is that it allows you to develop web applications using the intuitive drag-and-drop methodology that made Visual Basic popular. Simply "paint" your application within an intuitive development environment, and it will look and behave identically when deployed on a client's browser. In addition to this noteworthy capability, ASP.NET boasts a number of improvements over the traditional Active Server Page (ASP) technology that you may be using today. These improvements, which we will examine throughout this book, are listed below.

STRONGLY TYPED AND COMPILED LANGUAGES

The languages used to write traditional ASP applications (VBScript and JScript) have two primary limitations. First, they are inherently typeless, meaning that they have no concept of variable types. For example, in VBScript all variables are implicitly Variants—there is no way to declare a variable as a more specific Integer or String. Second, these languages are *interpreted,* meaning that ASP translates an application's source on a line-by-line basis. If the fiftieth line of the application contains a syntax error, ASP must process the first forty-nine lines before the error will be detected.

With ASP.NET, applications are developed using strongly typed languages such as Visual Basic, C++, JScript.NET, or Microsoft's new language, C# (pronounced "C-sharp"). Furthermore, applications in ASP.NET are *compiled,* which means that the entire source file is quickly examined and converted into machine code before the application is executed. Compiled applications are not only significantly faster than their interpreted counterparts, they are also easier to debug since syntax errors can be caught at *compile time* (while you are developing), as opposed to *runtime* (when the application executes).

SEPARATION OF CODE FROM CONTENT

Another cumbersome aspect of ASP development is the interspersion of source code with HTML. Because ASP scripts contain both code and HTML, source files are often lengthy, difficult to read, and hard to debug. The intermixing of HTML with ASP code is particularly problematic for larger web applications, where content must be kept separate from business logic.

ASP.NET eliminates this problem by keeping the design and programmatic aspects of your application separate. One file contains the application's design (the HTML), whereas another file, called the Code-Behind file, houses its associated logic (the source code). Thus, developers can work on the application's code while designers and graphic artists independently work on its content.

BROWSER NEUTRALITY

Supporting multiple browsers is a recurrent and persistent problem when developing web applications. ASP.NET eliminates this concern through its Web Control technology. A Web Control is a graphical entity very similar to an intrinsic control found in Visual Basic 6 (such as a `Textbox` or `Button`). Like its Visual Basic counterpart, a Web Control exposes a rich event model that you program against (such as a `TextChanged()` event, which triggers when the contents of the control change).

What is important about Web Controls is that they reside entirely on the server and generate client-side and server-side code to render themselves appropriately in a browser. In the eyes of ASP.NET, a browser can be one of two types: An UpLevel browser, defined as Internet Explorer 4.0 or higher; or a DownLevel browser, defined as everything else (including *all* versions of Netscape).

If the browser is UpLevel, then the control generates client-side

JavaScript so that events can be trapped directly on the client. If the browser is of the DownLevel type, then the control generates standard HTML, which requires a round-trip to the server to trigger events. We will examine Web Controls, and this seemingly unfair browser classification, in Chapter 5.

RICH DEVELOPMENT ENVIRONMENT

Microsoft's new development environment, Visual Studio.NET (VS.NET), allows you to develop web applications as you do in Visual Basic 6—by dragging and dropping GUI elements onto a base form and then writing the logic behind the controls. In addition, Visual Studio.NET offers sophisticated debugging features such as breakpoints, variable inspection, compile-time error checking, and code-stepping capabilities.

VS.NET is the development environment not only for ASP.NET applications, but for all applications that leverage .NET technology (such as component libraries that your web applications might utilize). Such uniformity allows you to debug both ASP.NET applications and the components they call from the same environment. As we will illustrate in Chapter 6, you can, for example, "step" into a library component developed in C# from an ASP.NET application developed in Visual Basic. This is considerably more convenient than today's setup, whereby you might be working with numerous develop environments: Visual Inter-Dev for ASP code, the Visual Basic environment for VB components, and Visual Studio for C++ COM components.

DEPLOYMENT AND ROBUSTNESS

In addition to making web applications easier to develop, ASP.NET makes it easier to deploy and maintain them. Application configuration settings are stored in easily accessible XML files, as opposed to the IIS proprietary metabase that housed such information in traditional ASP. As you will see in Chapter 7, the ASP.NET engine is considerably more robust and manageable than its ASP predecessor, which allows one to store client session information in SQL Server, for example. The engine can also be "recycled" (restarted) when its memory usage reaches a prescribed limit, which offers greater reliability.

WHAT DOES ASP.NET MEAN TO ME?

The impact of ASP.NET on your development efforts largely depends upon your background.

If you are an ASP developer, you will be happy to learn that ASP.NET abstracts, to a large degree, the idiosyncrasies of the web with which you have had to familiarize yourself. Rather than worrying about concepts such as HTML tags, POST, GET, and Querystrings, you can concentrate on writing application code. This is not to say that ASP.NET renders your existing skill set obsolete; it simply takes care of many redundant details that you must manually code in ASP. You always have the option of overriding ASP.NET's automation of these details whenever you wish. ASP developers will especially welcome the strongly typed languages that ASP.NET supports, as well as VS.NET's intuitive design environment, which allows one to debug applications using features such as breakpoints and instant watches.

If you program primarily in Visual Basic, you can apply the design methodology you've used for years directly in ASP.NET—by dragging and dropping controls onto a form (a Web Form in ASP.NET) and then writing the logic behind them. ASP.NET exposes an event paradigm that Visual Basic developers will instantly recognize. For example, when a web page loads, it automatically invokes the Page_Load() method, similar to the Form_Load() method in Visual Basic. With ASP.NET, it is entirely possible to develop a web application without any knowledge of HTTP, HTML, or web design. Simply create your application in VS.NET and it will be rendered in a browser by the ASP.NET runtime.

If you come from the world of C++ or Java you will probably develop applications using either C# or J#. As we will see in this chapter's Core Concepts section, C# (pronounced "C-sharp") is similar to C++, whereas J# (J-sharp) is Microsoft's conversion of the Java language to the .NET world. If you are familiar with JavaServer Pages (JSP), you will find that in many respects ASP.NET is more like JSP than traditional ASP. For example, both JSP and ASP.NET use strongly typed and compiled languages. JSP uses Java and compiled Servlets (server-side applets). Architecturally, you can think of a Servlet container as the equivalent of the ASP.NET runtime. Both the Servlet container and the .NET runtime interpret the compiled code and provide the necessary services for connecting to the Web Server.

Like JSP, both ASP and ASP.NET have built-in objects (Request, Response, Session, etc.) and similar syntax for web tasks (redirect, forward, etc.). However, it is not necessary to use these built-in objects in ASP.NET; you can simply write web-based applications as you would write a desktop application. More on this in the upcoming example.

If you are responsible for infrastructure and deployment in your organization, then you will be happy to learn that existing ASP applications will not be affected when one installs ASP.NET—applications from both frameworks will run side by side. Furthermore, ASP.NET offers numerous options that increase application reliability, fine-tune performance, and simplify maintenance. One of the biggest headaches with traditional ASP was the necessity to shut down the entire Web Server whenever you wanted to update a component being used by an ASP application. In Chapter 7, we will see that .NET components do not suffer from this annoying limitation.

Book's Contents

In this chapter we will examine the fundamentals of ASP.NET and the .NET Framework upon which ASP.NET is built. The Core Concepts section of this chapter lays the groundwork for the more advanced topics in later chapters. This chapter concludes with a simple example that contrasts application development in ASP with ASP.NET.

Chapter 2 provides installation instructions for ASP.NET. Because .NET was still in Release Candidate revisions at the time of this writing, these instructions may be out of date and readers are encouraged to consult the online instructions at ᴄⁿAS020001.

In Chapter 3, we examine the .NET Framework, emphasizing the portions that are relevant to ASP.NET. The .NET Framework is the foundation for all .NET applications, languages, and services, ranging from VB.NET to ASP.NET.

Chapter 4 discusses ASP.NET's new design paradigm, which will be unfamiliar to many developers. In this chapter we examine the framework's web form paradigm and the VS.NET environment that allows you to employ it.

One of the most significant differences between ASP and ASP.NET lies in the area of Windows Forms and Web Forms. Using VS.NET, you can build complicated forms that will automatically generate HTML code appropriate for your target browser. As a developer, you simply have to drag and drop controls. You don't have to worry about writing HTML or checking for compatibility issues. In Chapter 5, we will examine several of the Web Controls and Web Form components that are available in ASP.NET

As discussed in Chapter 6, one of the advantages of using the .NET Framework is that you can leverage features such as cross-language debugging and tracing. Not only can you debug your ASP.NET applications, you can seamlessly maneuver into code developed in C#, J#, VB.NET, or any other .NET language. You can also use the .NET engine to cache the various components of your web page, greatly enhancing performance.

Once you have built your ASP.NET application, the next challenge is to deploy it onto your server and configure it properly. In Chapter 7, we examine many of the deployment issues and configuration strategies. In particular, we will look at building and deploying assemblies and configuring IIS for various conditions.

Chapter 8 discusses security issues. In any significant web application, security will always be a primary concern. With ASP.NET, you have to consider two different aspects of security. First, you must know how to configure the security settings in IIS. Next, you can refine your security settings through the various methods built into ASP.NET. By combining these two independent security systems, you can create complex, fine-grained, and robust security polices to protect your web application.

ASP.NET would not be as exciting if you were forced to rewrite your entire existing code base on the .NET platform. Although Chapter 9 does cover migration from ASP (and other HTML systems), it also covers the mechanisms for executing and working with legacy code, such as COM objects and Enterprise Services.

Core Concepts

One of the fundamental challenges in writing a succinct yet thorough explanation of a technology is the varying knowledge level of the readership. To this end, this Core Concepts section defines many terms you may or may not be familiar with. This section is broken into three parts: the .NET Framework, which examines the architectural foundation for ASP.NET; Web Concepts, which illustrates the required technologies to host web applications on the Windows Operating System; and Windows Concepts, which explains some of the Windows technologies that you may be currently leveraging. If you want a more thorough introduction to .NET or VB.NET, see *CodeNotes for .NET Component Developers* and *CodeNotes for VB.NET*.

The .NET Framework

To fully appreciate ASP.NET you must realize that it is part of a larger and more encompassing vision—Microsoft's new .NET Framework. Depending upon your interests and development background, you may already have a number of ideas as to what the .NET Framework entails. As we will see in this book:

- .NET fundamentally changes the manner in which applications execute under the Windows Operating System.
- .NET brings about significant changes to both Visual Basic and Visual C++ , and introduces a new language called C#, all of which can be used to develop ASP.NET applications.
- .NET is built from the ground up with the Internet in mind and embraces open Internet standards such as XML and HTTP. XML is also used throughout the framework as a messaging instrument and for configuration files.

These are all noteworthy features of the .NET Framework, which consists of the platform and tools needed to develop and deploy .NET applications. We examine the .NET Framework in detail in Chapter 3, but its essential components are summarized here.

The Common Language Runtime

The Common Language Runtime (CLR) is the execution engine for all programs in the .NET Framework. The CLR is similar to a Java Virtual Machine (VM) in that it executes byte code on the fly, while simultaneously providing services such as garbage collection and cross-language exception handling. All ASP.NET applications run through the CLR. Unlike a Java VM, which is limited to the Java language, the CLR is accessible from any compiler that produces Microsoft Intermediate Language (IL) code, which is similar to Java byte code. Code that executes inside the CLR is referred to as managed code. Code that executes outside its boundaries (such as a VB6 and ASP application) is called unmanaged code.

The Base Class Libraries

The Base Class Libraries (BCL) provide hundreds of prewritten classes that you can use within ASP.NET applications. In traditional ASP, you often use functions such as UCase() and Abs(), which are innate functions of VBScript. Simple functions such as these, as well as more advanced services such as I/O and database access, have all been moved into the BCL. Those familiar with Java will find the BCL analogous to the Java Class Libraries.

The BCL is significant because it offers a consistent set of functions and services to any language that targets the CLR. Traditionally, every language had its own supporting libraries that were accessible only from that particular language. In ASP, you can draw upon any function supported by either JScript or VBScript. C++ developers, on the other hand, have an entirely different set of libraries to choose from. For example, whereas ASP developers could use the Mid() function to manipulate a string, C++ programmers would likely utilize the Standard Template Library (STL) for similar functionality.

With the BCL, developers can leverage a common library from any programming language. Thus, a BCL function written in C# is also callable from C++ or Visual Basic. What's more, ASP.NET is itself accessed through the BCL. For example, a web page in ASP.NET is abstracted via a Page class in the BCL.

ASP.NET applications can be developed in any .NET language (there is one important caveat concerning this statement, which the following topic will explain).

The .NET Languages

Writing ASP.NET applications (as well as .NET desktop applications and components) requires a compiler that translates source code into IL code. The .NET Framework contains three standard compilers: Visual Basic.NET, C#, JScript.NET. In addition, Visual Studio.NET ships with a managed C++ compiler, and you can purchase a separate J# compiler. Other companies are in the process of porting additional languages to the .NET Framework. Two noteworthy efforts are COBOL, by Fujitsu Software, and Perl, by Active State. For more information see ℃ℕ AS010002.

The VS.NET Interactive Development Environment (IDE) allows you to develop applications in any language for which you have a compiler. You can, for example, program in C#, J#, VB.NET, and managed C++ without switching development environments. This powerful IDE also provides significant cross-language debugging and compatibility features.

In addition to language compilers, the .NET Framework contains a large assortment of command-line utilities. Some of these utilities are incorporated directly into VS.NET's development environment, while others are exclusively stand-alone. We will examine some of these utilities throughout this book. One particularly interesting point is that the

.NET Framework contains command-line compilers for each language. In other words, you can build your entire application and compile it without using VS.NET.

It is worth noting that although you cannot develop ASP.NET applications in the VBScript language used in traditional ASP, VBScript is syntactically similar to Visual Basic.NET. Moving existing ASP/VBScript code to ASP.NET is possible and will be investigated in Chapter 9. As we will see, however, there are many advantages to developing applications with the strongly typed languages .NET has to offer.

Caveat—Developing in Any Language

You will frequently hear that ASP.NET applications can be developed in *any* language that can be compiled to IL code. Although this is true, to write applications in a Visual Basic–like manner (i.e., by "painting" them within VS.NET), you are currently restricted to VB.NET, C#, or J#. As we will see in Chapter 3, this limitation exists because the Web Forms Designer in VS.NET, which drives the automation process, only supports these languages.

Thus, if you wish to develop ASP.NET applications by using languages such as managed C++ or JScript.NET, you must do so programmatically without the benefit of VS.NET's intuitive design environment. This more laborious approach is demonstrated in o⟨CN⟩AS010003.

Visual Basic.NET

VBScript is a subset of Visual Basic (VB), a language Microsoft introduced in 1991 to rapidly develop Windows Desktop Applications. As its name suggests, Visual Basic.NET is the latest version of Visual Basic for the .NET Framework. In addition to introducing new features into the language (e.g., true object inheritance and structured exception handling), VB.NET brings about some syntax changes that break compatibility with old VB source code. For example, procedure parameters are now passed by value (`ByVal`) by default, not by reference (`ByRef`). Certain syntax elements such as `GoSub`, `IsNull`, and `IsMissing` have been removed from the language altogether. If you want a thorough introduction to VB.NET, see *CodeNotes for VB.NET*. However, a brief discussion of the most important differences can be found at o⟨CN⟩AS010004, and examples throughout this book will also highlight new VB.NET characteristics.

If you are an ASP or VB6 developer, you will likely use this new version of VB to develop ASP.NET applications because of its similarity in syntax.

C#

C# is a new language that Microsoft has touted as a simplified version of C and C++. In this respect, C# hides some of the more complex features of C++, such as pointers and unbounded arrays (they are only accessible if one marks code using the `unsafe` keyword). Like Java and C++, C# is an object-oriented (OO) language that contains requisite OO features such as inheritance, polymorphism, and interfaces.

As of this writing, C# can be used only to produce managed code (i.e., it cannot be used to write code that executes outside the CLR). In this sense, C# can be considered the "intrinsic" language of the .NET Framework, as it was developed solely for the managed world of the CLR. This is in contrast to both C++ and Visual Basic, which had to evolve into their present .NET manifestations. If you plan on doing a significant amount of development in the .NET Framework, it is worthwhile to at least familiarize yourself with C#, as a large portion of .NET sample code on both the Internet and the MSDN is written in C#.

C# will be a logical language choice for C++ and Java developers moving to ASP.NET, although those familiar with Java might also want to consider Microsoft's Java offering for the .NET Framework (see the following J# section). A few examples in this book will be written in C# (ASP developers unfamiliar with Java or C++ need not worry—we will explain C# during the examples). In addition, C# source code for many other examples in the book can be found on the CodeNotes website. For a full examination on the topic consult *CodeNotes for C#*.

Managed C++

Unlike Visual Basic or VBScript, C++ does not "clean up" after the developer. When you allocate memory in C++, there is no runtime to ensure that it is properly released. As a result, C++ developers have always been responsible for managing memory themselves. In addition, C++ allows the use of "low-level" memory manipulation techniques such as pointers and unbounded arrays. Although such latitudes can be dangerous when used incorrectly, they are invaluable for computationally intense operations such as image manipulation and numerical calculations.

Moving C++ to the .NET Framework is problematic because of two competing principles:

1. The latitude that C++ gives to developers (direct memory access using pointers, manual memory management, etc.)
2. The CLR's responsibilities of automatic memory management (garbage collection) and code sanity checks (which are difficult to perform in a pointer-ridden language like C++).

Managed C++ is a set of extensions added to the C++ language that enable it to run within the CLR. The most notable extension is the introduction of "managed types," which shift the burden of memory management from the C++ programmer onto the CLR. Placing the __gc extension in front of the declaration of a class, for example, allows instances of the class to be garbage collected. Another extension is that of managed arrays, which allows these data structures to be managed by the CLR. Managed exception handling is another amendment that differs from C++ exception handling in both syntax and behavior. Additional information on managed C++ can be found at ⌐AS010006.

Although you can use managed C++ to write ASP.NET applications, C# is probably a better choice. Remember, from the previous Caveat topic, that Visual Studio.NET does not have design support for writing ASP.NET applications in C++.

JScript.NET

A common misconception is that JScript (Microsoft's equivalent of Netscape's JavaScript) is somehow related to the Java programming language. In fact, JavaScript was misleadingly named by Netscape for marketing purposes. Neither JScript nor JavaScript is based on or has any direct relationship to the Java language. In fact, both JScript and JavaScript are implementations of ECMA-262, a cryptically named specification defined by the European Computer Manufacturers Associates (ECMA). Prior to .NET, JScript was used primarily as a tool for client-side script code.

With the .NET Framework, JScript has evolved into a mature language that offers many improvements over its predecessor. First-class language elements such as classes, inheritance, and compiled code have all been added to this new incarnation of JScript. In addition, JScript.NET can optionally contain typed variables (you can still use JScript in a typeless manner, and it will "infer" a variable's type at runtime).

Unfortunately, JScript.NET suffers from the same limitation as managed C++ when it comes to ASP.NET development—it cannot be used natively in VS.NET. For a closer look at JScript.NET, see ⌐AS010007.

J#

J# is a Microsoft product for those who wish to use the Java syntax in the .NET Framework. It is incorrect to think of J# as a product for writing Java applications, since J# programs do not run within the confines of a Java Virtual Machine. As you might expect, J# applications are instead executed by the CLR (J# converts Java syntax into IL code).

As of this writing, J# is in its initial beta stage. The Java Class Libraries have been converted to BCL equivalents, and the product contains many of the proprietary extensions found in Visual J++, Microsoft's Java development tool before the days of .NET.

Because J# is a stand-alone product and is not packaged with VS.NET, we will not use it in this book, other than to say that you can develop ASP.NET applications with it. For more information on J#, see ⟨CN⟩AS010008.

Additional .NET Services

In addition to the wide variety of development languages, you can also take advantage of several different add-on service sets. ADO.NET and Web Services are both particularly relevant to ASP.NET.

ADO.NET

With ADO.NET, Microsoft's latest database offering, you can communicate with any database from any .NET language using a paradigm that is specifically designed for distributed computing. In specific, the ADO.NET model is built primarily on the concepts of disconnected data islands and XML data exchange. For a more detailed introduction to ADO.NET, see *CodeNotes for .NET Component Developers,* or ⟨CN⟩AS010011.

Web Services

One of the most interesting new uses for ASP.NET lies in the area of developing Web Services. Using the framework provided by VS.NET, you can write ASP.NET wrappers for any code or any function, regardless of its original use, language, or location. Once you have built this ASP.NET wrapper, you can expose the code as a web service that can be accessed by any client capable of working with SOAP and XML. For a more detailed introduction as to how Web Services work with ASP.NET, see ⟨CN⟩AS010012.

WEB CONCEPTS

Although understanding the intricate details of web architecture is not essential when using ASP.NET, a nodding familiarity of the concepts in this section will go a long way in later chapters, when we start examining advanced topics such as Session and security.

HTTP

The Hyper Text Transfer Protocol (HTTP) is the communications protocol for the Internet. When you access a web page, the information is transferred from your client (the browser) to the server (the website) and back using HTTP. This ubiquitous protocol is a standard defined by the World Wide Web Consortium (W3C). The latest version of HTTP, v1.1, offers some significant improvements over the original version (1.0), such as better performance due to its efficient use of multiple communication channels. Most significantly, HTTP is a stateless protocol, which means that each time you access a website, the call is anonymous. To allow for a level of continuity in your applications (i.e., to maintain the client's identification as they browse through multiple pages), you must utilize state-related technologies such as cookies and Session objects, concepts we will examine in Chapter 7.

Web Server

In order for a computer to *host* web applications it must contain a Web Server. A Web Server is a software entity that listens for incoming HTTP requests from other computers, processes them appropriately, and sends back HTTP responses to the requesting machines. On Microsoft Windows Server products (NT 4, 2000, and XP), this Web Server is named Internet Information Server (IIS). Windows Client products (95, 98, and Millennium) contain a less capable Web Server called Personal Web Server. Some examples of non-Microsoft Web Servers are Apache, iPlanet, and Lotus Domino.

ASP.NET requires IIS version 5.0 or later (other Web Servers are not supported), which means it will only run on Windows 2000, Windows XP, and Microsoft's yet-to-be-released .NET Server OS.

ASP/ASP.NET Runtimes

A runtime (sometimes called an engine) is the software entity responsible for processing applications and returning HTTP responses to the Web Server (similar to a Servlet container in JSP). Consider the following simple ASP application:

```
<%
    Response.Write("Hello World!")
%>
```

Listing 1.1   simple.asp—A simple ASP application

In this case, when the browser requests `simple.asp`, the ASP Runtime interprets Listing 1.1 and generates client-side HTML to display "Hello World" in the user's browser. In addition to producing output that is rendered on a browser, a runtime must also take care of details such as maintaining application state and enforcing security. In the next section on IIS, you will discover that ASP and ASP.NET applications are processed by different runtimes. One of the significant differences between these runtimes is that the ASP engine "interprets" applications (interrogates them line by line before executing them), whereas the ASP.NET engine "compiles" them (rapidly converts an entire application into machine code before executing it). As a result, ASP.NET applications typically run faster than their ASP equivalents.

Internet Information Server (IIS)

In order to understand the importance of Internet Information Server in the ASP.NET world, you must understand that before a runtime even sees a request for an application, the request is first processed through IIS. Upon seeing the extension of the requested file, IIS directs the request to the appropriate engine.

If you have installed the .NET Framework (installation instructions can be found in Chapter 2), you can see IIS's routing characteristics by going to your Start Menu → Programs → Administrative Tools → Internet Services Manager. This will invoke the Internet Services Manager, which allows you to peruse and customize various settings, such as security.

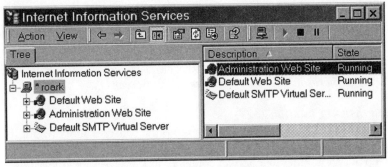

Figure 1.1   Internet Services Manager

Right-click Default Web Site, select properties, and click the Home Directories Tab. Now click Configuration, which will bring up a list of application mappings as shown in Figure 1.2.

Application mappings inform IIS which engine to run when it encounters a certain file extension. If you scroll down the list to aspx (the new file extension in ASP.NET), you will see that its associated engine ("executable path" in IIS terminology) is:

```
\%winroot%\Microsoft.NET\Framework\%sdk_version%\aspnet_
isapi.dll
```

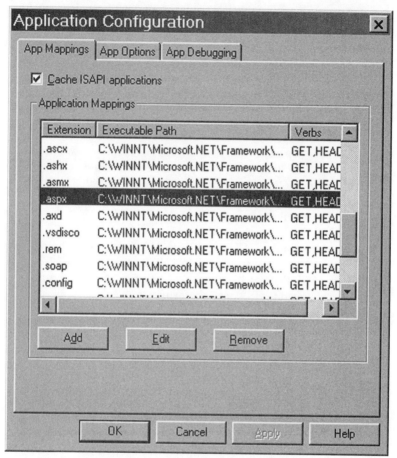

Figure 1.2   IIS application mapping

Conversely, the engine for traditional ASP files (.asp extension) is:

```
%winroot%\System32\inetsrv\asp.dll
```

Based on our investigation we can make a number of observations:

1. ASP and ASP.NET applications are processed through completely different engines. ASP programs are executed by asp.dll, which predates .NET, whereas ASP.NET applications are directed to the newer aspnet_isapi.dll. This realization is not only important from an administrative perspective (installing ASP.NET does not affect

existing ASP applications), but will become significant in Chapter 9 when we consider scenarios where one wants to intermix both technologies in one application.

2. Essential .NET Framework files such as the ASP.NET engine are found in the `\%winroot%\Microsoft.NET\Framework\%sdk_version%\` directory. Look inside this directory and you will find a number of other files required by ASP.NET. We will examine some of these files in subsequent chapters. In Chapter 7, for example, we will see that ASP.NET applications run within the aspnet_wp.exe process, which is considerably more robust than asp.dll, within which ASP applications execute.

3. A number of other file extensions are also associated with the ASP.NET engine. For example, asmx files (which denote Web Services) are also processed through ASP.NET.

In addition to routing HTTP requests to their appropriate engines, IIS provides important infrastructure to ASP.NET applications such as Administration, HTTP error handling, and security. A large portion of Chapter 8 is devoted to IIS's security features.

ASP.NET must run under IIS version 5.0 or later. A byproduct of this requirement is that ASP.NET will only run on the Windows 2000 and XP operating systems. The following table lists each operating system and the version of IIS with which it is packaged:

Basic Operating System	Default IIS Version
Windows NT 4.0 (with the Option Pack) IIS 4.0	IIS 4.0
Windows 2000 Professional, Server, Advanced Server	IIS 5.0
Windows XP Professional	IIS 5.1
Windows .NET Server (not released yet)	IIS 6.0

Table 1.1   Microsoft Operating System and IIS versions

IIS 6.0, which will be available with Microsoft's yet-to-be-released .NET Server Operating System, improves significantly upon existing versions of IIS (particularly in the areas of security and stability). Because IIS 6.0 was still in beta at the time of this writing, this book examines ASP.NET from the perspective of IIS 5.0 and 5.1. For information on ASP.NET's interoperability with IIS 6.0, see ⟳AS010013.

ISAPI

ISAPI (Internet Server Applications Programming Interface) is a specification that allows developers to extend IIS by writing components that process raw HTTP requests. An ISAPI component ends up as DLL that IIS funnels all requests and responses through. Prior to .NET, ISAPI components were often used in performance-critical and functionally esoteric situations where slower, less capable ASP script fell short. The primary shortcoming of ISAPI components is that they can only be written in C++.

The concept of the ISAPI component has evolved into the `httpHandler` in ASP.NET. Like an ISAPI component, an `httpHandler` can capture and interpret raw HTTP requests, which allows you to transcend the capabilities of ASP.NET. Unlike an ISAPI component, however, an `httpHandler` can be written in any of the aforementioned .NET languages, including VB.NET and C#. As we will see Chapter 8, `httpHandlers` play a crucial role in ASP.NET security.

From the previous topic on IIS, you may recognize that the filename of the ASP.NET engine (`aspnet_isapi.dll`) suggests that it is, itself, an ISAPI component.

WINDOWS OS CONCEPTS

As we will see in Chapter 3, the .NET Framework fundamentally alters the way applications execute under the Windows Operating System. In order to appreciate such changes, as well as to understand the many migration issues that will arise as you move existing ASP applications to ASP.NET, it is worthwhile to examine some technologies you may be currently utilizing.

COM/ActiveX

Microsoft's Component Object Model (COM) is the underlying architecture behind component communication in ASP. When you utilize ActiveX components (such the ADO library) from ASP applications using the `CreateObject()` function, COM serves as the communication mechanism between the web application and the external object.

Although COM components were originally written in C++, Visual Basic 5 allowed developers to write their own COM components through its ActiveX-DLL and ActiveX-EXE project options. A common scenario is for developers to write middle-tier logic as Visual Basic COM objects, which are then utilized from the presentation tier written in ASP. For example, a COM component might be used from an ASP script to validate a purchase request and update an underlying database.

Although the concept of a component has evolved into the assembly in the .NET world (as Chapter 3 illustrates), Microsoft does not expect developers to abandon the large number of existing COM components. Facilities exist to call these entities from ASP.NET. In Chapter 9, we will examine the COM Interop technology, which allows you to call legacy ActiveX/COM components from .NET.

Using COM components from ASP applications is frequently cumbersome because they must be registered (using the regsvr32.exe utility) before they can be used. Registering a component often requires shutting down the Web Server (IIS), which is unacceptable in production scenarios. In Chapter 7, we will see how ASP.NET eliminates this problem by means of .NET's assembly model.

MTS/COM+

Windows 2000 introduced COM+, a collection of services that COM components can utilize to improve their performance in the enterprise application setting. Some of these services include transactions (used when a component communicates with a database), object pooling (increases performance by reusing objects to avoid initialization overhead), and queuing (allows a client to communicate with an object asynchronously).

COM+ was the fusion of three existing Microsoft paradigms/products: COM, MSMQ (Microsoft's Message Queue), and MTS (Microsoft Transaction Server). MTS is frequently used by ASP applications and components that run on Windows NT 4.0. In fact, when you use the `<%@ Transaction` directive in traditional ASP pages, you are implicitly using either COM+ or MTS, depending upon the underlying OS.

ASP.NET applications can utilize COM+ components through .NET's COM Interop technology. However, special provisions must be made for COM+ components that access their "object context" (see ᶜᴺ⟩AS090012 for details). In addition, .NET components can leverage COM+ services natively using the Base Class Libraries (also discussed in ᶜᴺ⟩AS090012).

ActiveX Controls

Like a Java applet, an ActiveX control is a software component that runs within the restricted environment of a browser. The difference between an ActiveX *control* (such as a real-time stock-ticker that resides on a web page) and an ActiveX *component* (such as ADO) is that a control runs on the client, whereas a component runs on the server.

Unlike applets, ActiveX controls are a traditional, compiled technology based on COM. Whereas Java applets are downloaded to a browser and interpreted in real time by a Java Virtual Machine (JVM), ActiveX controls are downloaded to the client's file system by the browser, registered, and run as compiled code. The ActiveX strategy is, however, proprietary to Windows and Microsoft Internet Explorer (IE). Because of this restriction (and the security issues they raise), ActiveX controls are most often used in Intranet scenarios where the client browser can be standardized to IE.

Like its predecessor, ASP.NET is a server-side technology that doesn't integrate well with the client-side ActiveX-control paradigm. Although ActiveX controls can be used in ASP.NET applications (as illustrated in Chapter 5), one of the primary design goals of Microsoft's new web technology is to abstract developers from the underlying browser. By using ActiveX controls in ASP.NET applications you immediately restrict the target browser to IE. As we will see in Chapter 5, Web Controls offer much of the power of ActiveX, but are browser-neutral.

Nevertheless, if you want the complete versatility that ActiveX controls provide (i.e., compiled code running within the browser) and can guarantee that client machines will be running both IE and the .NET Framework, Microsoft offers an evolved version of the ActiveX-control paradigm with .NET. This involves running a managed control inside the browser (called a Windows Form control). Because Windows Form controls run within the CLR, they don't have the security issues associated with ActiveX controls. In addition, these new controls utilize the new .NET deployment and versioning schemes discussed in Chapter 3.

Some Simple Examples

To illustrate the virtues of Microsoft's new web technology, we are going to contrast the development and performance of a simple application written in both ASP and ASP.NET. Specifically, we are going to consider an application that times how long it takes itself to sum numbers from 1 to some value entered in by the user. If you haven't already done so, this would be a good time to install ASP.NET using the instructions in Chapter 2, as this example requires that some administrative steps be performed (such as the creation of an IIS virtual directory).

ASP EXAMPLE

Our simple test application is depicted in Figure 1.3.

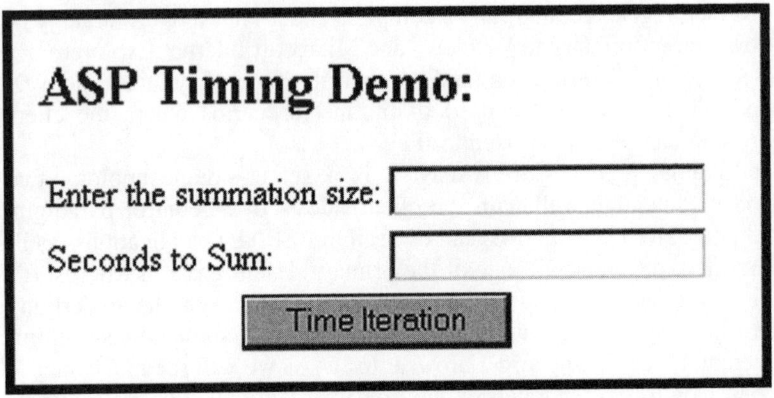

ASP Timing Demo:

Enter the summation size: [   ]

Seconds to Sum: [   ]

[Time Iteration]

Figure 1.3   Simple counting application

There are a number of ways to write this application using traditional ASP. One possible variation is given in Listing 1.2.

```
<%@ Language=VBScript %>
<HTML>
<HEAD><TITLE>ASP Timer Test</TITLE></HEAD>
<BODY> <H2>ASP Timing Demo:</H2>
<%
    dim TimeStamp
    dim i, output, total, count
    If Request.Form("num") <> "" then
    count = Request.Form("num")
       TimeStamp = timer
       for i = 1 to count
          total = total + i
       next
       TimeStamp = CStr(timer - TimeStamp)
    End If
%>
<FORM NAME="timerForm" ACTION="Timer.asp" METHOD="post">
  <TABLE>
    <TR>
      <TD>Enter the summation size:</TD>
      <TD><INPUT TYPE="text" name="num"
          value="<%=Request.Form("num")%>">
      </TD>
    </TR>
    <TR>
      <TD>Seconds to Sum:</TD>
```

```
      <TD><INPUT TYPE="text"
        value="<%=TimeStamp%>">
      </TD>
    </TR>
    <TR>
      <TD COLSPAN="2"><CENTER><INPUT TYPE="Submit"
        VALUE="Time Iteration"></CENTER>
      </TD>
    </TR>
  </TABLE>
</FORM>
</BODY></HTML>
```

Listing 1.2   Timer.asp—ASP timer application

Listing 1.2 is fairly straightforward—when the button is pressed, the form POSTs back to itself and uses ASP's Request object to read the contents of the first textbox (we examine the POST concept in Chapter 4). The block of script code then performs a summation from 1 to whatever number the user has entered, and times the length of its operation by using VBScript's Timer() function. For the sake of brevity, we have omitted error-checking code from Listing 1.2; we would probably want to ensure that the user entered a positive number by using ASP's isNumeric() function.

Listing 1.2 illustrates many of the shortcomings with traditional ASP:

- Script code is intermixed with HTML, which convolutes the source file. Debugging a more complex application would be very difficult, even using a development environment such as Visual InterDev.
- All variables are typeless; ASP determines their types as they are assigned. This not only makes code less readable, but it also degrades performance as the ASP Runtime must do a lot of work behind the scenes.
- Developers must concern themselves with the idiosyncrasies of both HTML and HTTP. For example, HTML controls do not retain their state as a form is reposted. If we wish to maintain the sum size entered by the user when the program reports its operation time, we must manually persist the first textbox during the repost.

Save Listing 1.2 into a file called Timer.asp and place it in the virtual directory you created in Chapter 2. Run the application by navigating to http://localhost/aspTest/Timer.asp in your browser, and enter in a sum size of 5 million. Click the button and Timer.asp will report how long it takes to carry out the summation. Results will vary from machine to machine; on our systems the application took six to eight seconds to perform the computation.

Let us now consider how we would develop this application in ASP.NET.

ASP.NET EXAMPLE

To illustrate the versatility of ASP.NET we will write three timer applications:

- One that we develop outside the Visual Studio.NET environment using VB.NET. This approach is very similar to traditional ASP, where script code is intermixed with HTML. This is not how you normally develop ASP.NET applications, and is not reflective of the power of Microsoft's new web technology. It is meant simply to illustrate some of the underpinnings of ASP.NET.
- One that we develop in Visual Studio.NET using VB.NET. This example is very similar to developing applications using the drag-and-drop approach in Visual Basic 6.
- One that we develop in Visual Studio.NET using C#. This example is identical to the previous one, except that it uses C# as the language.

ASP.NET Application #1—Developing Outside VS.NET

Although you will normally develop ASP.NET applications within the comfortable environment of Visual Studio.NET, you can also write them using a plain text editor such as Notepad. This approach has many disadvantages, most notably the loss of VS.NET's powerful debugging capabilities. Nevertheless, to give you an idea of what happens "behind the scenes" when you use VS.NET, we will illustrate this more arduous approach. Bear in mind that many of the details depicted in this example are abstracted when you develop directly in VS.NET.

The ASP.NET code for our timer application is given in Listing 1.3.

```
<HTML><HEAD><TITLE>ASP.NET Example</TITLE></HEAD>

<BODY>
<H2>ASP.NET First Application/Timing Demo:</H2>
<hr/>
```

```
<form runat="server">
  <table>
    <tr>
      <td>Enter summation size:</td>
      <td><asp:TextBox id="txtSize"
        runat="server" size=20/></td>
    </tr>
      <td>Seconds to Sum:</td>
      <td><asp:TextBox id="txtSeconds"
          runat="server" size=20/></td>
    </tr>
  </table>
  <asp:Button Text="Run Timer Test"
      OnClick="OnSubmit" runat="server" />
  <hr/>
</form>
</BODY>


<script language="VB" runat="server">
  sub OnSubmit (sender as Object, e as EventArgs)
    dim k, count, total as Long
    dim TimeStamp as Double

    TimeStamp = Timer
    count = CLng(txtSize.text)

    for k = 0 to count
       total = total +k
    next
    TimeStamp = Timer - TimeStamp
    txtSeconds.text = CStr(TimeStamp)
  end sub
</script>
</HTML>
```

Listing 1.3   Timer.aspx—ASP.NET timer application

ASP developers will note several features from Listing 1.3 that differentiate Timer.aspx from a typical ASP script. First, note the runat="server" attributes that are highlighted in Listing 1.3. Predictably, this attribute tells ASP.NET to run these lines on the server. If you look closely, you will see that we applied this attribute on two controls that are prefixed with the asp keyword:

```
<asp:TextBox id="txtSeconds" runat="server" size=20/>
<asp:Button Text="Run Timer Test" OnClick="OnSubmit"
  runat="server" />
```

Listing 1.4 ASP.NET controls

It may seem confusing for us to specify that a control (a `Textbox` or `Button` in this case) should *run at* the server. What we are seeing, however, is a Web Control, which does exactly that. When ASP.NET processes `Timer.aspx`, it sees that `txtSeconds` is a Web Control denoted by the `asp` prefix. As a result, the runtime processes this line on the server, and then generates client-side HTML code that renders a textbox on the browser. Thus, the code in Listing 1.3 is sometimes called server-side HTML.

Those familiar with HTML may be wondering why we didn't simply write an HTML textbox in Listing 1.3 instead of having ASP.NET generate one for us. The answer is that Web Controls are more sophisticated than their HTML equivalents. As we will see in the next example, we can do things very easily with a Web Control (resize it as we please, attach event code to it, etc.), which would require considerable skill to accomplish in HTML. By using Web Controls we shift the burden of HTML specifics onto ASP.NET, which automatically converts our control into an entity that the browser can understand. The virtues of Web Controls will be better illustrated in the next example, when we use them from VS.NET.

Turning our attention to the script code in Listing 1.3, we can see that it closely resembles strongly typed Visual Basic code. Variables are declared as specific types (`Doubles` and `Longs`), and Web Controls are referenced in a Visual Basic–like manner:

```
txtSeconds.text = CStr(TimeStamp)
```

Like its ASP counterpart, Listing 1.3 computes how long it takes to perform the summation by using VB's `Timer()` function. Place `Timer.aspx` in the virtual root from the previous example, and run the application by navigating to http://localhost/aspTest/timer.aspx. Enter a summation value of 5 million and click the button, and you will observe some interesting results:

Execution Speed
The application is significantly faster than its ASP equivalent. Again, results will vary from machine to machine, but in our tests, Listing 1.3 took less than a tenth of a second to perform. This improvement in

execution speed is partially a byproduct of ASP.NET's support for strongly typed languages. Because we declared variables as specific types in Listing 1.3, the ASP.NET engine didn't have to determine their contents at runtime. More important, ASP.NET pages are compiled into native code and not interpreted. The first time a page is accessed, ASP.NET very quickly converts it into native machine code (because of this, you may notice an initial delay the first time you access the page, an occurrence we will reexamine at the end of Chapter 3). Admittedly, this is a rather contrived example, but in general, a compiled approach will significantly outperform an interpreted one.

State Maintenance

If you run the example, you will notice that the first textbox (the summation value you entered) retains its value even after the server round-trip. In other words, the textbox can be said to have retained state after the POST completed. Normal HTML controls are inherently stateless. In our original ASP application we had to maintain state manually with extra code (i.e., in Listing 1.2 we had to manually extract the value of txtSeconds and persist with the resulting HTML response). We did not, however, include any state code in Listing 1.3. One of the virtues of a Web Control is that it automatically maintains state between server invocations. But how does a Web Control do this, given that it is ultimately converted into client-side HTML, which itself is stateless? To answer this question we must inspect the client-side code that ASP.NET generated.

Analyzing the Output

Examine the client-side code that was generated (by selecting View → Source from the Internet Explorer menu) and you will notice that it is quite different from the code we wrote in Listing 1.3. First, all of the runat="server" tags have been removed. This should come as no surprise as these lines were executed at the server, and we are inspecting client code. If you examine the client code further, you will note that all of the Web Controls in Listing 1.3 have been converted into HTML equivalents. For example, the line:

```
<asp:TextBox id="txtSeconds"...>
```

has been changed to:

```
<input name="txtSeconds" type="text" id="txtSeconds"
size="20"/>.
```

From this change we see that Web Controls are processed at the server and are automatically rendered as regular HTML on the client. If you look yet again at the client source, you will notice a line similar to the following:

```
<input type="hidden" name="__VIEWSTATE"
value="dDw1NzI3MTUxOzs+"/>
```

This line is a hidden HTML field called VIEWSTATE, which was automatically generated by ASP.NET. The purpose of this field is to maintain the state of Web Controls across server invocations (such as the contents of the aforementioned textbox control).

Don't worry about the details of how ASP.NET uses VIEWSTATE (it is propriety and subject to change). Just realize that the framework is performing some HTML tricks behind the scenes to give your Web Controls characteristics that would otherwise be difficult to obtain in regular HTML. We will reexamine this hidden field and its performance implications in Chapter 5.

Scripts and Languages
Scripts in ASP.NET are declared using the following notation:

```
<script language="VB" runat="server">
```

Listing 1.5   Declaring script

Underneath the <script> tag in Listing 1.3 is our actual ASP.NET code. Note that this script uses the VB.NET syntax (hence the VB language specification). The language attribute of the <script> tag tells ASP.NET which compiler to use when building the ASP.NET page (you can also specify C# or JScript.NET).

Recall that the runat="server" attribute specifies that code should execute on the server. Thus, if you take a look at the client-side source again (View → Source in Internet Explorer), you will notice that the <script> tag does not appear in the client.

If you omit the runat="server" attribute from a <script> tag, ASP.NET will simply persist the script code to the client's browser. As illustrated in Chapter 4, this allows you to add your own client-side script to ASP.NET applications.

One major problem with the weakly-typed scripting language of ASP is that references are not checked at compile time. For example, if we had incorrectly referenced the txtSeconds control in Listing 1.2 as txtSeconds2, our error wouldn't have been caught until a user requested the page. As we will see in the next example, syntactical errors can be caught at compile time when you develop in VS.NET.

ASP.NET Application #2—Developing in VS.NET Using Visual Basic

In this example we will re-create the application that we wrote in Listing 1.2, but we will do it from the intuitive design environment of Visual Studio.NET. Go to the `Microsoft Visual Studio.NET` folder in your Start menu, and then invoke the VS.NET IDE by clicking the `Microsoft Visual Studio.NET` icon. If you are running VS.NET for the first time, you will be asked to choose your preferred keyboard and window layout as shown in Figure 1.4.

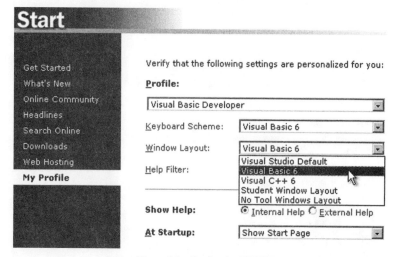

Figure 1.4   Configuring VS.NET

VS.NET houses the development environments for VB.NET, Visual C++, and C#. If you have previously developed in Visual Basic 6 or Visual InterDev, choose the Visual Basic 6 profile, keyboard, and window schemes as we have illustrated in Figure 1.4. Next, go to the File menu and select New → Project. This will bring up the dialog box in Figure 1.5.

As shown in Figure 1.5, choose `Visual Basic Project` under `Project Type`, and `ASP.NET Web Application` under `Templates`. Call your project `TimerApp`, click `OK`, and VS.NET will create a Web Application project for you. Note that VS.NET will place your project in the *localhost* directory, such that it can be processed by IIS when you run it. VS.NET's design environment is depicted in Figure 1.6.

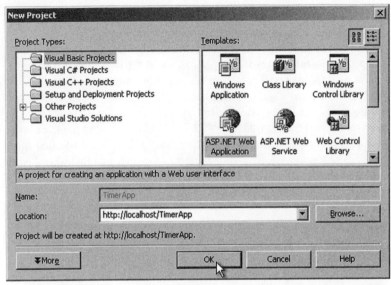

Figure 1.5   New Project Dialogue box

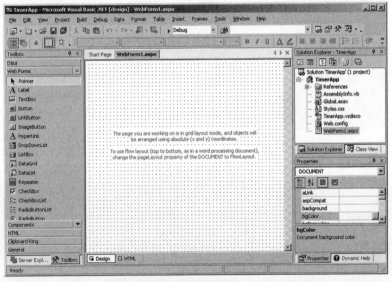

Figure 1.6   VS.NET design environment

Take a minute to explore the VS.NET IDE, and you will recognize several elements from VB6 and Visual InterDev: the toolbox, which contains Web Controls such as buttons and textboxes; the Property Inspector; and the Project Explorer (now called the Solution Explorer). In the center of the screen, however, a blank page exists in place of a form you might expect in Visual Basic. Think of this page as the web equivalent of a desktop Form; you place controls on this page, which represents the viewable area of the web application (this page is sometimes referred to as a Web Form).

Developing web applications in VS.NET proceeds along the same lines as VB6. All you need to do is drag Web Controls onto a page and then write the event logic behind them. To create our timer example, drag two labels, two textboxes, and a button onto the page, and then modify their Text properties such that your application resembles Figure 1.7 (you modify properties by selecting the control and using the Property Inspector to change property values).

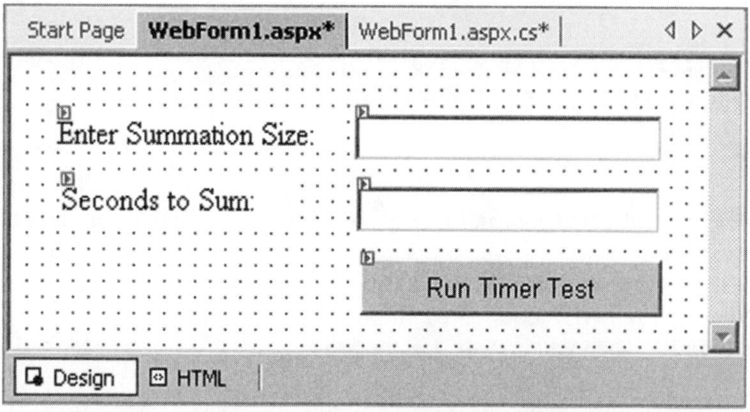

Figure 1.7 Timer application in VS.NET

Double-click the button, which will bring up the CodeBehind file that houses your application's source code. We will examine this file in greater depth in subsequent chapters; but for now, notice that no HTML is present—just a VB-style source code editor. Add the highlighted code in Listing 1.6 to your application.

```
Public Class WebForm1
    Inherits System.Web.UI.Page
  Protected WithEvents TextBox1 As WebControls.TextBox
  Protected WithEvents TextBox2 As WebControls.TextBox
  Protected WithEvents Label1 As WebControls.Label
  Protected WithEvents Label2 As WebControls.Label
  Protected WithEvents Button1 As WebControls.Button
```

+Web Form Designer Generated Code

```
Private Sub Page_Load(ByVal sender As System.Object,
    ByVal e As System.EventArgs) Handles MyBase.Load
End Sub

Private Sub Button1_Click(ByVal sender As object, _
    ByVal e As System.EventArgs) Handles Button1.Click
  Dim k, count, total As Long
  Dim TimeStamp As Double
  TimeStamp = Timer
  count = CLng(TextBox1.Text)
  For k = 0 To count
    total = total + k
  Next
  TimeStamp = Timer - TimeStamp
  TextBox2.Text = CStr(TimeStamp)
End SubEnd Class
```

Listing 1.6   VB.NET timer application code

The highlighted code in Listing 1.6 is almost identical to our previous example (Listing 1.3). Run the application by pressing F5, and VS.NET will spawn an instance of Internet Explorer that points to the program. Note that VS.NET configured the application's directory as a virtual root in IIS when you first created the project (this process is described in greater detail in Chapter 4).

Enter a summation value of 5 million, click Run Timer Test, and you will see the application is functionally equivalent to our previous examples—the program reports how long it takes to perform the operation. Like the previous ASP.NET application, Listing 1.6 takes only a fraction of a second to carry out the computation. If we contrast this example with the previous one written in Notepad, a number of points can be made:

- In VS.NET we are completely abstracted from HTML and server-side tags such as asp and runat="server". In developing this application we simply used Web Controls in an intuitive manner and wrote the logic behind them.
- Developing web applications in VS.NET is similar to developing Desktop Applications in VB6. Note that the code inside Button1_Click() is automatically called when Button1 is clicked, which is similar to the manner in which Command1_Click() is triggered when a button called Command1 is clicked in VB6.

- We are developing in a full-fledged development environment, with features such as compile-time checking and interactive debugging. If you modify Listing 1.6 such that it contains a syntax error (e.g., replacing TextBox2 with TextBox3), VS.NET will detect and report the error when you compile the source and will not run the application.

- In VS.NET there is a clear separation between an application's design and its underlying code; the code in Listing 1.6 is not intermixed with HTML.

- VS.NET generated a lot of code for us behind the scenes—Listing 1.6 contains a declaration for a class called WebForm1, which inherits from the confusingly named System.Web.UI.Page class. Furthermore, this class contains instances of WebControls.TextBox, WebControls.Label, and WebControls.Button. The purpose of this code will be explained in Chapter 3.

- VS.NET also generated a lot of server-side HTML for us behind the scenes, which you can inspect by clicking the HTML box at the bottom of Figure 1.7. Examine the HTML, and you will see it is very similar to the HTML we wrote manually in the previous example. When you drag and drop controls onto a page in VS.NET, an entity called the Web Forms Designer creates the appropriate HTML behind the scenes.

We will investigate many of these points more thoroughly in Chapters 3 and 4, but for now, merely appreciate that with ASP.NET you can develop web applications as quickly as you did in Visual Basic. Try experimenting with more complex applications and using other Web Controls such as the Calendar and Listbox controls, and it will become apparent how intuitive and straightforward ASP.NET web development is. In Chapter 4, we will see how VS.NET performs a lot of this magic.

Remember that with Visual Studio.NET we are not limited to using Visual Basic—we can also use J# and C#. To this end, we will now rewrite the timer application in C#.

ASP.NET Application #3

To write a timer application in C#, create a new Web Application project in VS.NET. Choose Visual C# project under Project Types in Figure 1.5, and click OK, which will return you to VS.NET's familiar design environment. As in the previous example, drag the appropriate controls onto the page such that they resemble the application in Figure 1.7. Next, insert the application's logic by double-clicking the button and adding the following highlighted code to it.

```
public class WebForm1 : System.Web.UI.Page
{
  protected System.Web.UI.WebControls.TextBox TextBox1;
  protected System.Web.UI.WebControls.TextBox TextBox2;
  protected System.Web.UI.WebControls.Label Label1;
  protected System.Web.UI.WebControls.Label Label2;
  protected System.Web.UI.WebControls.Button Button1;

  public WebForm1() {
    Page.Init += new System.EventHandler(Page_Init);
  }

  private void Page_Load(object sender, EventArgs e){
      // Put user code to initialize the page here
   }

  private void Page_Init(object sender, EventArgs e) {
   // This call is required by ASP.NET's Web Form
   // Designer.
     InitializeComponent();
  }

  private void Button1_Click(object sender, EventArgs e)
  {
    long count, total=0;
    long TimeStamp;
    double seconds;
    TimeStamp = DateTime.Now.Ticks;
    count = System.Convert.ToInt32(TextBox1.Text);
    for (int k=1; k<=count; k++) {
      total=total+k;
    }
    TimeStamp = DateTime.Now.Ticks - TimeStamp;
    seconds = (double)TimeStamp /
      (double)TimeSpan.TicksPerSecond;
    TextBox2.Text = seconds.ToString();
  }
}
```

Listing 1.7   C# timer application code

Listing 1.7 is functionality equivalent to the VB.NET code in Fig-ure 1.7. As in the previous example, VS.NET automatically generates some boilerplate code for us, such as the WebForm1 class and its various Web Controls. Those familiar with C++ and Java will find C# syntactically similar to both of these languages. Although it is beyond the scope of this book to review the C# language, Visual Basic and ASP developers will find it different from VB/VBScript in the following respects:

- Loop and control constructs are placed within the '{ }' brackets; they are not terminated with keywords (such as Next, Loop Until, Wend, etc.)
- The majority of statements end with semicolons.
- When a variable type is declared, the type precedes the variable name: long count; (there is no AS in the declaration).

We will delay a full discussion of Listing 1.7 until Chapter 3, when we have a better understanding of the BCL and other concepts such as namespaces. For now, note that the code in Listing 1.7 is more complex than its VB.NET counterpart because C# does not contain intrinsic Timer() and CStr() functions. Instead, we must use the BCL DateTime and Convert classes for equivalent functionality.

Run the application by pressing F5, enter a summation value of 5 million, and you will see that the C# application takes roughly the same amount of time to perform the operation as the previous example (less than a tenth of a second based on our testing). This result illustrates an important point in ASP.NET:

The performance of all languages in the .NET Framework is roughly equivalent, as they all compile to IL code and are executed by the CLR. Your choice of language in ASP.NET will be primarily a function of syntactical preference, rather than any innate advantage of one language over another.

We will examine the language neutrality of the .NET Framework more thoroughly in Chapter 3. The main point of this statement is that you have complete access to all the features in ASP.NET irrespective of the language in which your applications are written.

Multiple Browser Support

Remember that ASP.NET applications are browser-neutral. This means that the program we just developed should be accessible not only through Internet Explorer, but through other browsers such as Netscape and Opera. It may seem confusing and disheartening, therefore, that the application renders itself quite differently on Netscape 4.0:

Enter Summation Size:

Seconds to Sum:

Figure 1.8   ASP.NET application in Netscape 4

The unsightly appearance of the application is not the result of false advertising on Microsoft's part. Rather, it has to do with the project's configuration settings in Visual Studio.NET. By default, VS.NET assumes that you are creating applications for IE 5.0 or higher (a questionable convention, perhaps). To explicitly inform ASP.NET that you wish to target other browsers, you must set the document's targetSchema property by using the Property Inspector as shown in Figure 1.9.

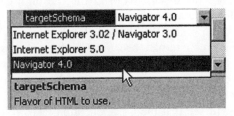

Figure 1.9   Setting the document's targetSchema property

The targetSchema property determines how Visual Studio.NET positions graphical elements. As you can see from Figure 1.9, you can specify one of three target schemas: IE/Netscape 3.0, IE 5.0, or Netscape 4.0. When selecting a target schema you are choosing the lowest version of a browser with which your application will work. For example, if you choose Navigator 4.0, the application will render correctly on Netscape and IE versions 4.0 and greater, but may not translate properly on earlier versions of these browsers.

EXAMPLE REVIEW

The three ASP.NET applications that we have developed illustrate the many advantages of ASP.NET over traditional ASP. In addition to faster execution made possible by strongly-typed and compiled languages such as C# and VB.NET, Web Controls allow you to design Web Application GUIs as you do in Visual Basic 6 by placing and resizing controls graphically onto a page. And, unlike traditional web design tools such as FrontPage and ColdFusion, you can also attach event code to the GUI elements in your application.

HOW AND WHY

What targetSchema Should I Set for the Opera Browser?
If you wish to deploy ASP.NET applications for the popular Opera Browser (developed by Opera Software), then set the `targetSchema` property to Navigator 4.0. Keep in mind that if your applications are going to be accessed over the Internet (as opposed to an Intranet), then you will probably want to set this property to IE/Navigator 3.0 in order to make them accessible to legacy browsers such as Internet Explorer version 3.

Why Do I Get the Following Error When I Try to Run My Application in VS.NET:
```
Error while trying to run project: Unable to start debugging on the
web server. Would you like to disable future attempts to debug
ASP.NET pages for this project?
```
This error (and variations of it) is a document problem with beta 2 of VS.NET (Microsoft knowledge base article Q306165). If you encounter this error, try restarting IIS either through the Internet Services Manager, or by running the `iisreset` utility at the command prompt.

This error should be corrected with the Release version of .NET, currently available from Microsoft.

Chapter Summary

ASP.NET is an evolution of Microsoft's Active Server Page (ASP) technology. With ASP.NET, you can rapidly develop complex web applications using a paradigm familiar to anyone who has programmed in Visual Basic. Simply drag and drop controls onto the Web Form, add code to the various control events, and program in any of the languages supported by the .NET Framework. Such simplicity is made possible through Web Controls, which are graphical controls that convert themselves into browser-appropriate client-side code: DHTML and JavaScript, if the browser supports it, or regular HTML if the browser is less capable.

With ASP.NET, you can write code in strongly typed and compiled languages such as Visual Basic.NET, C#, or J#. ASP.NET's compiled approach is not only significantly faster than ASP's interpreted mechanism; it allows one to catch errors at compile time as opposed to runtime.

ASP.NET offers many additional advantages over ASP, which we will examine throughout this CodeNote. Deployment has been simplified through easily accessible XML configuration files, in contrast to ASP, which stores configuration information in a proprietary format that is difficult to retrieve. The ASP.NET Runtime is also considerably more robust than its older counterpart, which allows one to control its memory usage and easily detect application faults.

In all respects, ASP.NET is a major improvement over ASP and can definitely be considered a viable platform for rapidly developing web-based applications. In Chapter 3, we will see how the improvements in ASP.NET are even more encompassing because of the .NET Framework, which fundamentally changes the way *all* applications execute under the Windows Operating System.

Chapter 2

—

ASP.NET INSTALLATION

The installation requirements for ASP.NET fall into two categories:

1. To *host* ASP.NET applications (to have them execute on a given machine), you must install the .NET Framework (covered in Chapter 3), which consists of the Common Language Runtime, the Base Class Libraries, and the ASP.NET Runtime. As of this writing, the Release Candidate of the framework can be installed as part of the Windows Component Update (which will be explained momentarily).

2. If you wish to develop ASP.NET applications using the intuitive environment illustrated in the example in Chapter 1, you must also install Visual Studio.NET (VS.NET, for short). Visual Studio.NET is Microsoft's new development tool not only for ASP.NET applications, but for all programs that leverage .NET technology (be they traditional Windows Desktop Applications or library components).

Thus, if all you want to do is host ASP.NET applications (on a Web Server, for example), you need only install the Windows Component Update. Infrastructure and Administrator types will be relieved to learn that installing the .NET Framework *will not* affect existing "traditional" ASP applications, as the setup program does not modify the ASP Runtime (asp.dll).

Even though both the .NET Framework and VS.NET are designed to work on all modern Microsoft Operating Systems (with the exception of Windows 95), you will need Windows 2000 or Windows XP to write and deploy ASP.NET applications. This constraint exists because ASP.NET will work only with Internet Information Server (IIS) 5.0 or later. Although early beta documentation claimed that ASP.NET would work with IIS 4.0 (found on Windows NT 4.0), support for NT was eventually dropped in beta 2 of the product. In addition, ASP.NET will not function with Personal Web Server, which is included with Windows 98 and Windows Millennium. If you are unfamiliar with IIS or its interplay with the ASP and ASP.NET Runtimes, it would be a good idea to consult the Core Concepts section in Chapter 1.

INSTALLATION REQUIREMENTS

In order to install the .NET Framework on your machine, Microsoft recommends the following system configuration:

- Processor: Minimum Pentium 133Mhz
- Operating System: Windows 2000 (Professional, Server, or Advance Server), Windows XP Professional
- Memory: 128 MB (256 MB recommended)
- Hard drive: 500 MB free on the drive where the OS is installed (usually C:\), and approximately 2.5 Gigs free on the installation drive (where VS.NET will be installed)

Both VS.NET and the .NET Framework are distributed on four CDs (alternatively, they can be downloaded from the MSDN as one 1.6-gigabyte installation file). The first three CDs contain the VS.NET development tools, and the fourth contains the Windows Component Update. For information on obtaining the CDs either by mail or by download, please see /www.microsoft.com/net/.

Installing the .NET Framework

To install the .NET Framework, run SETUP.EXE, found on the first CD. After a couple of minutes, you will be greeted with the screen in Figure 2.1.

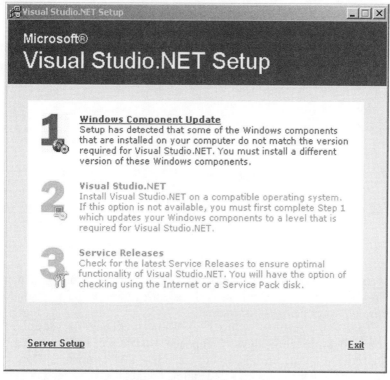

Figure 2.1.   VS.NET setup

As Figure 2.1 indicates, you must run the Windows Component Update before installing VS.NET. After you click Windows Component Update, the setup program will analyze your machine for a few minutes to determine which system files need to be updated. Depending upon the Operating System and the applications that you have already installed, the setup program may have to reboot the system several times during the installation process. Because of this requirement, it offers the Automatic Logon feature depicted in Figure 2.2.

By supplying your password on the screen depicted in Figure 2.2, the system can automatically log on and continue the installation process

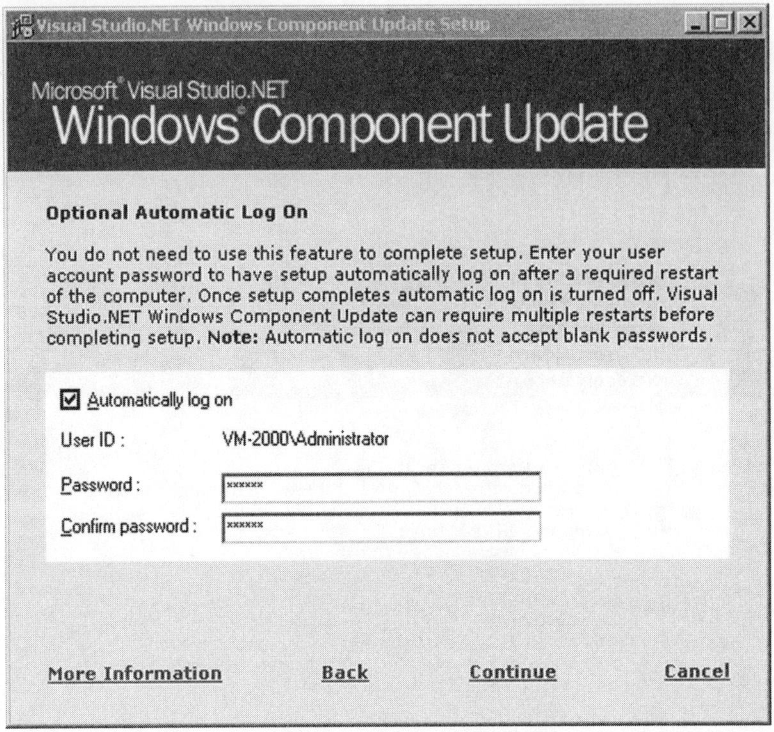

Figure 2.2   Automatic Logon

every time it has to reboot the machine. Because the setup program may have to reboot the machine many times during the installation routine, this option can be a real time-saver.

After either enabling or disabling Automatic Logon, the setup program will begin the Windows Component Update. Depending upon the files it must update, this procedure could take several minutes. During this time the setup program will detail its progress, as illustrated in Figure 2.3. Note that in addition to installing the .NET Framework, the setup program also installs various software components required by .NET, such as the latest OS service packs and FrontPage Server extensions.

After the Windows Component Update has completed, the installation program will proceed to the VS.NET install. Remember, you need only install VS.NET to develop ASP.NET applications. If you are configuring a server that will host ASP.NET applications, you can stop at this point. If you continue, the installation program will ask you to choose which portions of VS.NET you want installed (language tools, MSDN documentation, etc.). The VS.NET options screen is shown in Figure 2.4.

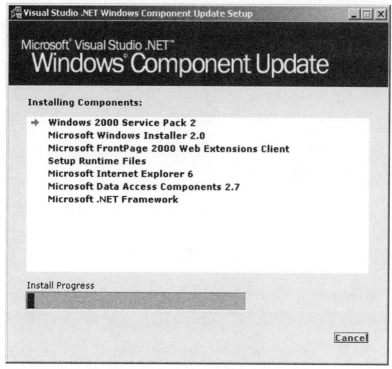

Figure 2.3   Windows Component Update in progress

After selecting those aspects of VS.NET that you wish to install (the ASP.NET module is located under the Server Components tab and is named "Web Development"), click "Install Now." For the purposes of working with the examples in this book, we recommend that you accept the default install options. Note that if the setup program detects that your system does not contain IIS 5.0 or greater, it will not allow you to select ASP.NET from its option menu.

Depending on the options you have selected, installation could take anywhere from twenty to sixty minutes. After the installation has completed, your computer will contain all of the tools necessary to build and deploy ASP.NET applications.

Program Locations

The .NET setup program will append two new items to your Start menu's Program folder. The first item is called Microsoft .NET Framework SDK and contains MSDN documentation and Code samples. The second item is called Microsoft Visual Studio.NET 7.0 and contains links to

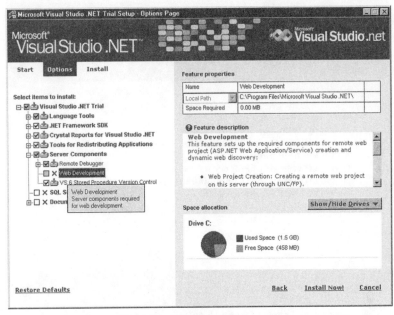

Figure 2.4   VS.NET installation screen

the VS.NET IDE and to another folder called Visual Studio.NET Tools. In this book we will occasionally use utilities from the VS.NET command line, which you can access by clicking the Visual Studio.NET Command Prompt icon shown in Figure 2.5.

Figure 2.5   The Visual Studio.NET Command Prompt

Many of these utilities (e.g., ILDASM.EXE in Chapter 3) are found in the \%Program Files%\Microsoft.NET\FrameworkSDK\Bin directory. If you use the VS.NET Command Prompt in Figure 2.5, this directory will automatically be included in your Path variable, so that you can access the .NET Framework utilities from within any directory.

Ensuring Installation Success

To ensure that ASP.NET was successfully installed, save Listing 2.1 into a file named `test.aspx` and place it in a directory of your choice (we'll use `c:\test` in this example).

```
<script language="VB" runat="server">
  'Output a message when the page Loads:
  sub Page_Load(sender as Object, e as EventArgs)
    Response.Write("ASP.NET is working!")
  end sub
</script>
```

Listing 2.1   ASP.NET test application

Before you can run the application, you must configure `c:\test` as a virtual directory in IIS. Open the Internet Services Manager (Figure 1.1) by going to Start → Settings → Control Panel → Administrative Tools → Internet Services Manager.

Right-click on `Default Web Site`, and then select New → Virtual Directory from the pop-up menu. This will launch the Virtual Directory Creation Wizard. You will be prompted for both a directory alias (enter `aspTest`) and the directory itself (enter `c:\test`). An alias is simply a shorthand mapping to a physical directory that can be referenced in a URL. Next, IIS will ask you to set the access permissions for the directory (whether or not scripts may execute, etc.). Accept the default values by clicking `Next`. You can now access the test application by navigating to the following address in your web browser: http://localhost/aspTest/test.aspx.

Note that when used in a URL, the word `localhost` is used to refer to your machine itself. If all goes well, you should see the words `ASP.NET is working!` inside the browser. If you do not see this message (if the browser doesn't display anything, for example), then ASP.NET was not installed correctly. This could be due to the fact that:

1. You attempted to install the .NET Framework on an incompatible operating system such as Windows NT, 98, or Millennium. Remember, ASP.NET will only work with IIS version 5.0 or greater, limiting target platforms to Windows 2000 or XP.
2. IIS is not processing HTTP requests properly. Restart IIS by invoking the Internet Services Manager (Figure 1.1), right-clicking the computer, and selecting `Restart IIS`.
3. IIS is not properly directing the request to the ASP.NET engine.

Ensure that the application mapping for the .aspx extension has been properly set up (see Figure 1.2 for details).

Last, you may encounter some installation issues if you are attempting to install a later version of .NET over a previous version (installing beta 2 over beta 1, for example). For details on some of these upgrade issues, see ⌖AS020002.

Chapter 3

—

THE .NET FRAMEWORK

The .NET Framework consists of the platform and tools needed to develop and deploy .NET applications. In this chapter we will investigate the following aspects of Microsoft's new software model:

- The Common Language Runtime (CLR), which is the entity that executes all applications in the .NET Framework, including those developed in ASP.NET.
- The Base Class Libraries (BCL), which constitute a collection class that you can utilize from your web applications. The BCL is accessible to all .NET languages in a consistent manner.
- Assemblies, which is the new name for software "components" in the .NET Framework. Assemblies are noteworthy because they eradicate the infamous DLL Hell problem that has plagued Microsoft Operating Systems for the past ten years.

At the end of this chapter we will tie together these concepts and examine how ASP.NET processes incoming application requests.

Although portions of this chapter may not seem directly applicable to web development, understanding the .NET Framework is important because it is the foundation upon which ASP.NET is built. It is not possible to write quality enterprise applications without some understanding of the technology's underlying architecture. Not only will this chapter's contents make you a more productive and resourceful ASP.NET developer; they will also give you a general appreciation for Microsoft's new software strategy. In addition, many of the topics covered in later portions of this book (ASP.NET configuration and security, for example) draw on the concepts in this chapter.

Topic: The Common Language Runtime

At the heart of the .NET Framework is the Common Language Runtime (CLR). In addition to acting as a Virtual Machine, interpreting and executing IL code on the fly, the CLR performs numerous other functions such as type-safety checking, memory management, garbage collection, and security enforcement.

As we will see in this topic, the CLR changes some of the roles of IIS as they existed in traditional ASP.

CONCEPTS

Managed Code

Code that is executed by the CLR is said to be managed. Code that runs outside the CLR is referred to as unmanaged or native. However, there is more to managed code than this semantic classification. For example, what does it mean to "run" within the CLR?

As we learned in Chapter 1, programs you write in the .NET Framework are converted from source code to Intermediate Language (IL) code by a language compiler. The CLR then converts IL code into machine code, where it can be executed by the Windows Operating System. By acting as a buffer between your program and the OS, the CLR can enforce security on the program and ensure that it has the proper resources to run. In other words, it can "manage" the application's execution. This is in contrast to applications authored before .NET, which are executed directly by the Operating System, and are thus unmanaged.

Because managed code is executed by the CLR, the CLR can make decisions (at runtime) as to what it can and cannot do. For example, the CLR can assign certain access rights to code depending on the origin of the code (the local drive, the Internet, etc.). This capability is referred to as Code Access Security (CAS) or Evidenced Base Security; more information about this can be found at ᐅAS010010.

Just-In-Time Compilation

Inevitably, people associate the managed execution of the CLR with slow performance. After all, if the CLR must convert IL code into machine code at runtime, it is reasonable to conclude that some overhead must exist. This line of reasoning derives from a common fallacy first introduced with Java: the notion that because a Java VM interprets Java byte code line by line, Java programs must be inherently slow.

In fact, both the CLR and modern Java VMs rapidly convert an application into native machine code the first time it is run, a process called Just-In-Time (JIT) compilation. What's more, because compilation happens at runtime as opposed to compile time, the CLR can optimize the compilation for the particular processor on which the code is running.

Common Type System

In traditional ASP, variables are typeless—the ASP Runtime determines their types as you assign them. Those familiar with Visual Basic know that typeless variables are the equivalent of the `Variant` data type, which can house any of the allowable types in VB (`Strings`, `Integer`, `Dates`, etc.).

More accurately, a `Variant` encapsulates all the allowable types in Visual Basic. This is all the Common Type System is: a definition of all the permissible types in the .NET Framework. Like a `Variant`, the CTS includes types such as strings and integers, as well as some additional types not found in VB6, such as decimals and chars. And, just as Visual Basic 6 programs can only use types that can be represented by a `Variant`, ASP.NET applications are confined to using types in the CTS.

The important principle to understand about the CTS is that it not only applies to VB.NET, but to *all* languages in the .NET Framework. This means that all .NET languages agree on the types they can use and the representation of those types. In other words, both VB.NET and managed C++ treat an `Integer` as 32 bits; you no longer need to cast your VB6 `Integer` up to a `Long` if you want to pass it to a COM object or the Windows API. As we will see in the Assemblies topic in this chapter, this greatly simplifies the interoperability among languages in the .NET Framework.

Variants in the .NET Framework

ASP languages such as VBScript and JavaScript are ambiguous. For example, you cannot prescribe that a function written in one of these languages return an `Integer` (it simply returns a value). Although in some circumstances this predicament is limiting, it is a blessing in situations where a function may return numerous types (e.g., an integer or string). In Visual Basic 6, such functionality is provided through the `Variant` data type—if you are unsure about the contents of a variable, you can always make it a `Variant`.

With VB.NET, the Variant has been supplanted with the Object type of the Common Type System. All types in the .NET Framework are derivatives of Object. Think of an Object and a Variant as equivalent—no matter what its contents, a variable will always be an Object. Thus, the following ASP code:

```
function Foo(x)
   if x = 1 then
      Foo ="A String"
   else
      Foo = 1
   end if
end function
```

Listing 3.1   ASP script using an implied variant

would be written in ASP.NET as:

```
Function Foo(ByVal x As Integer) As Object
   If x = 1 Then
      Foo = "A String"
   Else
      Foo = 1
   End If
End Function
```

Listing 3.2   ASP.NET script with an object

In both listings, the Foo() function returns either a string or a number, depending on the input value. However, in Listing 3.2, the input value is restricted to an Integer.

Garbage Collection

One of the most useful functions of the ASP Runtime is automatic memory management. Consider the following ASP code that uses the CreateObject() function to create and call an ActiveX component named Comp.SomeComp.

```
<%
   dim o
   Set o = Server.CreateObject("Comp.SomeComp")
   o.DoSomething()
%>
```

Listing 3.3   Creating an object

As responsible developers we should conclude this code with the line Set o = Nothing in order to inform ASP that we have finished using the component. Nevertheless, we can get away with this omission because the ASP Runtime will clean up after us. After the script executes, it will determine that the Comp.SomeComp component is no longer being referenced and it will automatically remove it from memory.

With ASP.NET, it is the CLR that performs garbage collection. Like the ASP Runtime, the CLR determines when objects are no longer being referenced and destroys them appropriately. An important aspect of the CLR's garbage collection is that it is nondeterministic. This is a fancy way of saying that it makes no guarantees as to when objects are collected; it all depends on when the garbage collector next executes.

Nondeterministic behavior is primarily an issue for authors who develop components to be used from your web applications. Specifically, component developers must make special provisions to ensure their objects release resources in a timely manner. In ASP.NET you don't have to worry about such details—simply keep in mind that the automatic memory management services you enjoyed in ASP are now provided by the CLR.

Application Domain (AppDomain)

The Windows Operating System uses processes to protect concurrently running applications from one another. For example, Internet Explorer and Microsoft Word each run in different processes. If Word executes an illegal instruction, Windows can shut down Word's process without adversely affecting Internet Explorer.

Prior to IIS version 4, ASP applications all ran within the IIS process, INETINFO.EXE. This meant that if one ASP application crashed, it could bring down the entire IIS process and any other ASP applications running within it. IIS 4.0 made things more durable by allowing ASP applications to run within their own processes (the *Isolated* setting). IIS version 5 included an additional option by allowing ASP applications to execute within the same process, but one that was separate from the IIS process (the *Pooled* setting). The Pooled setting was thus a balanced approach in that applications could still adversely effect one another, but could not bring down the Web Server (IIS).

Figure 3.1   Application protection settings in IIS

Since processes predate .NET, they must provide robust protection against unmanaged code, making them expensive to create and tear down. Because .NET applications operate within the CLR, they can be afforded the same protection without the costly construction of a process. The .NET Framework saves resources by allowing multiple Application Domains (AppDomains) to exist in a single process. If the CLR must shut down an AppDomain, it can do so without disrupting other AppDomains in the same process. It is proper, therefore, to think of an AppDomain as a "lightweight" process, made possible through the increased protection provided by the CLR.

Your ASP.NET applications all run within AppDomains. As we will see in the upcoming example, the CLR's AppDomain architecture nullifies the IIS settings in Figure 3.1. Although you can still configure ASP.NET applications using IIS's protection options, they will have no bearing on how (or where) your applications execute.

Where Does the CLR Live?

Our discussion of the CLR up to this point has been strictly theoretical; it sometimes helps to see things in a more tangible light. Although the CLR provides services to applications that were previously responsibilities of the Operating System, the CLR *itself* sits on top of the Operating System. It must therefore exist as a tangible entity somewhere on your hard drive.

If you look inside the `\%winroot%\Microsoft.NET\Framework\ versionNum\` directory (where `versionNum` is the particular version of the .NET Framework you have installed), you will find two files: `mscorsvr.dll` and `mscorwks.dll`. These files, each roughly 2 MB in size, represent two versions of the CLR: one for single-processor machines, and one for multiple-processor machines. ASP.NET will load the appropriate version when an application runs, automatically taking advantage of additional processors if they exist.

EXAMPLE

The CLR is ubiquitous in the .NET Framework; virtually any ASP.NET example would demonstrate its usage. We will take a more pragmatic approach in this example, and instead prove that the CLR's architecture influences the role of IIS in ASP.NET.

Application Protection in ASP

For this example you will require the COM component that you can download at ⌐AS030001. Recall from Chapter 1 that a COM component is a software entity that exposes functions callable from ASP. This component exposes one such function, WhatProcess(), which reports the process an ASP script is executing within.

After following the instructions to register the component (⊶**CN**AS030001), save Listing 3.4 into a file named WhereAmI.asp in the virtual directory (aspTest) you created in Chapter 2.

```
<%
    Dim o
    Set o = Server.CreateObject("WhatProc.WhatProc")
    Response.Write("Script is executing in: ")
    Response.Write(o.WhatProcess())
%>
```

Listing 3.4   WhereAmI.asp—determining the host process in ASP

Next, bring up the Internet Services Manager (Figure 1.1), right-click aspTest, and select Properties. This option screen allows you to set various properties for the virtual directory such as security and error routing. Change the Application Protection setting (Figure 3.1) to Low. Run the application by navigating to http://localhost/aspTest/WhereAmI.asp, and it will indicate the process in which it is running:

```
Script is executing in:
%Winroot%\System32\inetsrv\INETINFO.EXE
```

As expected, the Low protection setting causes the application to run within IIS's process (INETINFO.EXE). This is a potentially dangerous situation. If the application misbehaves, it can bring down the entire Web Server. Change the protection setting to Medium, rerun the application, and it will now output:

```
Script is executing in: %Winroot%\System32\DLLHOST.exe
```

The Medium setting forces IIS to run ASP applications in a separate process called DLLHOST.EXE. Because they are isolated from IIS, problematic applications cannot bring down the Web Server. The High protection setting also results in an application being run within DLLHOST.EXE (MTX.EXE, on NT4), but it doesn't share the process with other applications (i.e., it has the process unto itself). Thus, applications configured with the High setting cannot influence either IIS or other ASP applications.

Application Protection in ASP.NET

It should become increasingly apparent that understanding IIS is crucial to web development in ASP and ASP.NET, as both frameworks sit atop the Web Server. Continuing from our previous example, save the code in Listing 3.5 into a file called WhereAmI.aspx in the aspTest virtual directory.

```
<%
  Dim o as object
  o = CreateObject("WhatProc.WhatProc")
  Response.Write(
    "This ASP.NET script is executing in: ")
  Response.Write(o.WhatProcess())
%>
```

Listing 3.5   WhereAmI.aspx—determining the host process in ASP.NET

Recall from our discussion on the Common Type System that the Variant data type has been supplanted with the Object type in ASP.NET, hence its inclusion in Listing 3.5. Also notice that the Set keyword from Listing 3.4 is *not* used in our ASP.NET code. This keyword, which was used to obtain new object instances in VBScript and VB6, has been dropped in VB.NET. Instead, we simply write an equivalent line minus the Set keyword (which has been bolded in Listing 3.5).

Change the protection setting of the virtual directory to Low, run the application, and it will inform you that:

```
Script is executing in:
%winroot%\Microsoft.NET\Framework\vX.xxx\ASPNET_WP.EXE
```

Thus, even though the Low protection setting prescribes that the application should share the IIS process (INETINFO.EXE), the application runs in a separate process named ASPNET_WP.EXE. Change the protection setting to Medium, and the application's host process will remain the same (instead of running in DLLHOST.EXE, as it did in the ASP example).

Based on this example we can make two observations:

1. IIS protection settings have no bearing on the host process of ASP.NET applications; they always run in a dedicated process named ASPNET_WP.EXE. We will examine the role of this process in Chapter 7.
2. ASP.NET applications can utilize COM components through the same CreateObject() function used in ASP (recall, in List-

ing 3.4, that the host process is determined using a COM component). In Chapter 9 we will see that ASP.NET offers a more intuitive way to call COM components. We will also see that special provisions must be made for certain COM components used from ASP.NET.

SUMMARY

All applications in the .NET Framework, including those written in ASP.NET, are executed by the Common Language Runtime. The CLR performs many valuable services such as garbage collection, application isolation, and security checking. The CLR also enforces a Common Type System (CTS) on all .NET languages, which greatly simplifies the interoperability among them.

Applications in the .NET Framework are translated into Intermediate Language (IL) code by a language compiler, which is Just In Time (JIT) compiled into machine code by the CLR the first time an application is run.

.NET applications execute within Application Domains, the CLR's equivalent of Windows processes. This architecture has important implications for certain IIS options, the most important of which is that IIS protection settings have no bearing on ASP.NET applications.

Topic: The Base Class Libraries

In order to understand the Base Class Libraries we must delve, just a little, into the internals of ASP. Although the very word *internal* implies that developers are abstracted from such details, to appreciate the many changes in ASP.NET we must consider the architectural realities of its predecessor.

CONCEPTS

An ASP Tangent
Before examining the Base Class Libraries, consider the following ASP code:

```
<%@ Language=VBScript %>
<%
```

```
dim Name
Name = UCase("Shane")
Response.Write(Name)
%>
```

Listing 3.6   Simple ASP code

As its name suggests, UCase() converts a string to uppercase. Thus, after the code in Listing 3.6 executes, the Name variable contains "SHANE". Although we could have written such a conversion function ourselves, we save both time and space by using an innate function of VBScript.

For years, ASP developers have relied on such intrinsic functions for string manipulation, type conversion, and user input. Although you may not give it much thought, the code for these functions must exist *somewhere* on your machine. For example, there must be some file on your hard drive that houses the implementation code for UCase() so that you don't have to write it yourself.

You are not likely to find this information in an ASP book or reference (these are internal details of ASP), but depending on the language you use, the code for these built-in functions can be found in the following files:

```
%winroot%\system32\vbscript.dll
%winroot%\system32\jscript.dll
```

When the code in Listing 3.6 executes, the ASP Runtime loads vbscript.dll and calls its UCase() function on your behalf. Similarly, when you write ASP applications in JavaScript, jscript.dll is used.

Given this information, we can consider what Listing 3.6 is really doing behind the scenes. Instead of simply calling the UCase() function, it is drawing upon the UCase() "service" found in vbscript.dll. This is all the Base Class Libraries are—a collection of files that expose services and functions that you can utilize in ASP.NET. The difference is that you use the Base Class Libraries explicitly—they are not abstracted by the runtime.

Back to the BCL

In addition to containing functions that were previously intrinsic members of ASP, the BCL contains hundreds of other classes and functions for operations such as File I/O, Remote Messaging, and other technologies you may have used in the past (ADO, for example).

The Base Class Libraries (which are automatically copied to your system when you install the .NET Framework, as shown in Chapter 2) exist as language-independent IL code. This means that they are accessible from all .NET languages. This is in contrast to ASP, where there are different libraries for different languages—vbscript.dll for VBScript and jscript.dll for JavaScript.

Namespaces

In ASP, intrinsic functions such as UCase() and Mid() are globally accessible—you simply use them from your applications by calling them directly. Because the Base Class Libraries contain hundreds of classes and functions, there must be some manner in which to organize them. This is accomplished by using namespaces.

Namespaces provide a scope (or container) in which classes and functions are defined. Several core BCL classes, for example, are found in the System namespace. If the BCL contained a function called Foo(), you would have to *qualify* it by prefixing it with System: System.Foo().

Namespaces can also be nested. The System.IO namespace, for example, contains a number of classes for I/O operations, whereas System.Security contains classes to access the CLR's security infrastructure. It is tedious to have to qualify BCL classes when you use them. Can you imagine writing System.IO.FileStream each time you wanted to use the FileStream class? For this reason, the .NET Framework allows you to reference namespaces implicitly by using either the Imports keyword in VB.NET, or the using keyword in C#. Consider the VB.NET code in Listing 3.7.

```
Imports System
Imports System.IO
Foo()
FileStream.Close()
```

Listing 3.7   Implicitly referencing a namespace

Because of the two Imports statements, we don't have to write the more verbose equivalent:

```
System.Foo()
System.FileStream.Close()
```

Listing 3.8   Explicitly referencing a namespace

As you can see, referencing namespaces implicitly can save you a lot of typing and make your code easier to read. You will use namespaces in the ASP.NET to:

1. Access the BCL classes
2. Access classes authored by other developers
3. Provide a namespace for your own classes that other ASP.NET developers may use.

We will use namespaces in the following Assembly topic, when we write a component and use it from ASP.NET.

EXAMPLE

Now that we understand the BCL, we are in a position to more thoroughly analyze the C# Timer example from Chapter 1. Although we omitted these lines from Listing 1.3, if you reload the C# Timer application in VS.NET you will see the following code at the top of the source:

```
using System;
using System.Collections;
using System.ComponentModel;
using System.Data;
using System.Drawing;
using System.Web;
using System.Web.SessionState;
using System.Web.UI;
using System.Web.UI.WebControls;
using System.Web.UI.HtmlControls;
```

Listing 3.9   Code from the C# Timer application in Chapter 1

VS.NET automatically inserted these lines in the project to reference certain BCL namespaces implicitly. Recall that several core classes and types reside in the System namespace. Two such classes are TimeSpan and DateTime, both of which are used in Listing 1.3 to time how long the program takes to sum numbers:

```
TimeStamp = DateTime.Now.Ticks;
for (int k=1; k<=count; k++)  {
   total=total+k;
}
TimeStamp = DateTime.Now.Ticks - TimeStamp;
seconds = (double)TimeStamp/
     (double)TimeSpan.TicksPerSecond;
```

Listing 3.10   Using the TimeSpan and DateTime classes

Because VS.NET automatically inserts the `using` statements in Listing 3.9 into the project, we can write `DateTime` instead of `System .DateTime`. One of the properties exposed by the `DateTime` class is a method called `Ticks()`, which returns the number of 100-nanosecond intervals that have elapsed since January 1, 0001. By obtaining time stamps before and after the sum operation, we can then use the `TicksPerSecond` property of the `TimeSpan` class to determine how long the summation takes.

The most difficult aspect of using the BCL is figuring out which classes you need to accomplish the task at hand. There are hundreds of classes for many programmatic tasks including data access, GUI design, messaging, and many more. The most complete source for the BCL is the MSDN documentation, although descriptions for some of the more important classes can be found at ᴄᴺ AS030002.

Base Class Library Files

In Listing 3.10 we used the `DateTime` and `TimeSpan` classes by appropriately referencing the `System` namespace that contained them. Where, however, do these classes actually reside (i.e., what files contain their implementation code)?

As of this writing, the BCL classes can be found in the following directory (again, where `versionNum` is the particular version of the .NET Framework you have installed):

```
\%winroot%\Microsoft.NET\Framework\versionNum\
```

If you look inside this directory, you will find several DLLs that contain the BCL classes for a given namespace (some DLLs actually contain numerous namespaces). The following table lists some of the more important files in the .NET Framework.

File	Contents
Mscorlib.dll	Core classes in the System namespace
Microsoft.VisualBasic.dll	Classes/functions for VB6 backward compatibility
System.Data.dll	ADO.NET classes—the new data access mechanism
System.EnterpriseServices.dll	Classes to access COM+ services
System.Web.dll	ASP.NET classes

Table 3.1   Important DLLs containing BCL classes

These files (and hence the .NET Framework) must be installed on a computer in order to execute ASP.NET applications. When you use BCL classes or functions such as DateTime, the CLR determines the file in which the function is located and loads it appropriately when the application executes. In the next topic, we will see that these files are really assemblies, the new way components are packaged in the .NET Framework.

Assemblies and Namespaces

The relationship between BCL files (assemblies) and namespaces can be confusing. An assembly houses executable code, whereas a namespace simplifies the manner in which that code can be accessed. A single assembly can contain multiple namespaces. An assembly that exposes mathematical functions, for example, might partition itself into standard and scientific services and group them into two namespaces called MyCalc.Standard and MyCalc.Scientific. Even though the assembly would contain two namespaces, it would still be packaged as one file.

To use a Base Class Library you must reference the assembly explicitly in VS.NET (and optionally specify namespaces to make your code more concise). We have not referenced assemblies in VS.NET thus far, because the environment references a number of them for us by default. You can see this by opening up the References tree in the Solution Explorer as shown in Figure 3.2.

Figure 3.2   BCLs automatically referenced by VS.NET

Compare Figure 3.2 with the file names given in Table 3.1, and you will see that VS.NET automatically references Base Class Libraries for core BCL classes, ADO.NET, ASP.NET, and a few others. If you want to use additional classes, you have to reference the assembly manually, a process we'll look at in the next topic.

In order to illustrate the power of the Base Class Libraries, we will consider a more useful and complex example. Consider the application depicted in Figure 3.3, which allows the user to add a number of names to a ListBox and then sort it. You can download the source for this application at ☜AS030003.

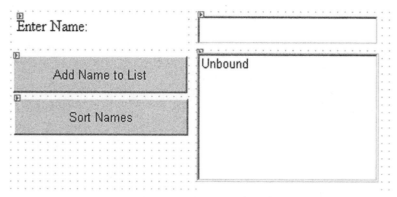

Figure 3.3   ASP.NET sorting example

This example, which would require a reasonable amount of code in ASP, is straightforward in ASP.NET if we use the BCL ArrayList class found in the System.Collections namespace. This namespace contains classes for common data structures such as arrays, queues, lists, hashtables, and dictionaries. The ArrayList class allows us to store a list of objects and access them in an arraylike fashion (by index number). More important, ArrayList allows us to sort its elements.

The important code for the application is given below (the complete source can be found online at ☜AS030003).

```
Private Sub Button1_Click(...)
    'Add the contents of the textbox to the ListBox
    ListBox1.Items.Add(TextBox1.Text)
End Sub

Private Sub Button2_Click(...)
```

```
    Dim aList As New ArrayList()
    Dim k As Integer

    'Read the items of the ListBox into the array:
    For k = 0 To ListBox1.Items.Count() - 1
        aList.Add(ListBox1.Items(k).ToString)
    Next

    'Sort the array and repopulate the Listbox:
    aList.Sort()
    ListBox1.Items.Clear()

    For k = 0 To aList.Count() - 1
        ListBox1.Items.Add(aList.Item(k))
    Next
End Sub
```

Listing 3.11   Code for sorting application

Listing 3.11 looks a lot more like Visual Basic 6 code than ASP code (a theme we will see throughout this book). Again, this is one of the virtues of Web Controls—their ability to be referenced as objects as opposed to HTML entities. When the first button in Figure 3.3 is clicked, Listing 3.11 adds the contents of the Textbox to the ListBox using the Items() property. More interesting is the code attached to the second button, which sorts the ListBox.

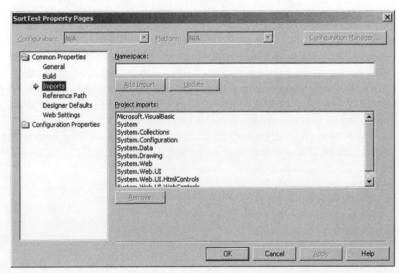

Figure 3.4   Namespace referencing in VB.NET

After reading the contents of the ListBox into an ArrayList class, Listing 3.11 uses the Sort() method to sort the array's contents. Note the Count property, which returns the number of elements in the ListBox, and the Add() method, which adds elements to the ArrayList. Once the array is sorted, the contents of the ListBox are cleared and then updated.

As illustrated by the code in Listing 3.11, using the BCL is simply a matter of understanding the conventions of the classes you will be calling. In the example above, the main functionality of the program (sorting) is provided by the BCL; VB.NET simply acts as a forum to call it.

Namespaces in VB.NET

The ArrayList class in Listing 3.11 is found in the System.Collections namespace. Yet, unlike the C# example in Listing 3.9, there are no automatically generated Imports statements at the top of the source file (recall that Imports is VB.NET's equivalent of C#'s using statement). It might seem puzzling, then, that Listing 3.11 uses the ArrayList class without fully qualifying it as System.Collections.ArrayList.

Like C#, VB.NET automatically references namespaces, but it does so behind the scenes (i.e., not directly in source code). You can see this if you right-click the project name in the Solution Explorer, click Properties, and click the Imports tab, as shown in Figure 3.4.

In VB.NET you can reference namespaces either through this Property window or directly in code by means of the Imports statement. We'll use the latter technique throughout the rest of this book.

The Microsoft.VisualBasic BCL

As Figure 3.4 illustrates, VB.NET automatically references a namespace called Microsoft.VisualBasic. Look back at Listing 3.9 and you will discover that this namespace is not referenced when you use C#.

As you may have guessed, this file contains functions that were previously intrinsic members of the VBScript and Visual Basic languages. In the next topic on assemblies, we will "peek" inside this file and discover that it houses functions such as Mid() and UCase().

The Microsoft.VisualBasic BCL is provided to ease the transition of ASP and VB developers moving to the .NET Framework. Because it is automatically referenced by VB.NET, you can program with the functions you've always used. Simply keep in mind that you are implicitly using a BCL that Microsoft has provided for backward compatibility.

Because C# does not automatically reference this BCL, functions such as Timer() and Trim() are not natively accessible from the language. This is why in the example in Chapter 1, our VB.NET application used the Timer() function, whereas the C# application had to use the BCL DateTime and TimeSpan classes.

Although you can use the `Microsoft.VisualBasic` BCL to call functions such as `Timer()` in VB.NET, the general practice under the .NET Framework is to use the newer BCL equivalents wherever possible. The benefits of doing so are twofold:

1. The BCL contains classes that provide capabilities not found in previous versions of VB and VBScript (for example, the `ArrayList` class we used in Listing 3.11).
2. Understanding the BCL classes is essential when interoperating with other languages in the .NET Framework. Developers writing .NET applications in other languages (such as C#) may not be aware of VB-intrinsic functions like `Timer()` and are likely to use the BCL.

So, try using newer BCL classes wherever possible to replace some of the functions on which you currently rely. For example, instead of using `Rnd()` to generate random numbers, consider the `Random` class found in the `System` namespace.

The BCL—A Universal Library

Before we depart from the BCL, you should know that it houses *all* technologies in .NET Framework. Classes exist to accomplish virtually any task you can imagine, such as reading the system registry, writing traditional Desktop Applications, writing Windows Services, etc.

In fact, as the last topic in this chapter will illustrate, ASP.NET *itself* is housed in the BCL, as are other .NET technologies such as ADO.NET and Web Services.

HOW DO I/WHY DO I

Can I Call Functions in the Microsoft.VisualBasic BCL from Other .NET Languages?

In the next topic, we will see that the Base Class Libraries are packaged as assemblies, which consist of language-neutral IL code. Therefore, any .NET language can access any BCL class.

This means that the functions in the `Microsoft.VisualBasic` namespace can also be called by managed C++ and C#. Thus, if we really want to use `Timer()` in C#, we can do it by explicitly referencing the `Microsoft.VisualBasic` BCL. As we have cautioned, however, the general practice is to shy away from using intrinsic VB functions such as `Timer()` and to use their newer BCL equivalents.

How Do I Use Intrinsic ASP Objects Such as Request and Response?
ASP intrinsic objects such as Request and Response can be used in ASP.NET and are accessible through the System.Web namespace, which is automatically referenced by web applications in VS.NET. ASP.NET also contains a number of additional intrinsic objects, some of which we will examine in the next chapter.

SUMMARY

The Base Class Libraries are a collection of classes accessible to any .NET language. In addition to housing VBScript functions that you used in ASP (such as UCase and Timer), the BCL contains hundreds of classes for common operations such as data manipulation, File I/O, and mathematical computations. Functionality that was traditionally provided by the language environment is now supplied by the BCL. This greatly simplifies the development process, as you only have to familiarize yourself with a common framework rather than a language-specific library.

The BCL is organized using namespaces, which makes it easier to access and syntactically more concise. Core BCL classes are found in the System namespace or nested namespaces within it (such as System.Collections and System.IO). Some of these namespaces are automatically referenced in VS.NET when you write web applications. To explicitly reference a namespace, use the Imports keyword in VB.NET, or the using keyword in C#.

Topic: Assemblies

In order to understand assemblies, you must first understand what a software component is. The definition can vary, but for our purposes a software component is simply an entity that exposes a number of services callable by other applications. For example, the ActiveX Data Object (ADO) library used in ASP for database access is a software component. On the Windows Operating System, software components are usually packaged as Dynamic Link Library (DLL) files, or, in some cases, executable (EXE) files.

Throughout the years a number of standards have emerged as to how components "offer" their services to clients; that is, the means by which clients can discover these services and invoke them if desired. The two prominent standards on the Windows platform are:

1. Win32 DLLs—These originate from the very early days of Windows and are not callable from traditional ASP (however, they can be called from Visual Basic 6). Win32 DLLs are written in either C or C++ and are often used to provide low-level system access to programs (device access, for example). In Chapter 9 we will see that Win32 DLLs can be called from ASP.NET by means of a technology called Platform Invoke.

2. COM, the Component Object Model, was the first evolution of the software component for Windows. The three noteworthy improvements of COM over traditional Win32 DLLs were language neutrality—any language could communicate with a COM component (theoretically); stricter versioning rules—COM tried to improve upon how components evolved; and self-describing components—a client could "query" a COM object to determine if it supported a particular service.

With .NET, the software component has evolved yet again into the assembly. All assemblies in the .NET Framework contain two important entities: Intermediate Language (IL) code, which houses the component's executable logic, and metadata, which describes all the types (classes, functions, etc.) that the assembly exposes. Both of these entities are illustrated in the upcoming example.

Assemblies are noteworthy because they end the DLL Hell problem that has infested the Windows Operating System for many years. The next topic on Shared Assemblies explains both DLL Hell and its elimination from the .NET Framework.

CONCEPTS

Type Library
COM components usually contain a type library that describes the methods they expose. If we examine the type library for the WhatProc component we used in Listing 3.4, for example, we would see that it contained one method named WhatProcess().

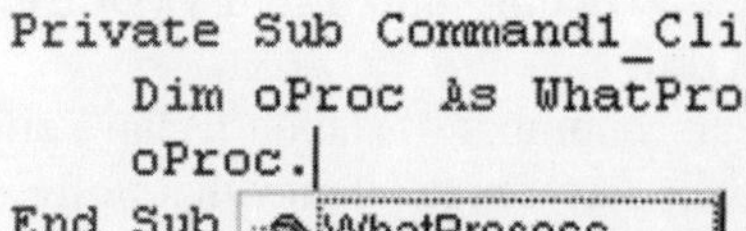

```
Private Sub Command1_Click()
    Dim oProc As WhatProc
    oProc.|
End Sub  ⟨◈ WhatProcess        ⟩
```

Figure 3.5   IntelliSense in VB6

A powerful feature in Visual Basic 6 is IntelliSense, whereby a list of methods appears whenever you press a period following an object in the VB6 environment.

After selecting the particular method you wish to call, the VB6 environment will also list all the parameters the method expects. Behind the scenes, the environment queries the object's type library for information and displays it in an intuitive manner via IntelliSense. With the advent of assemblies, type libraries have evolved into metadata. And, unlike COM components, assemblies *always* house metadata (they are not optional, as in COM). This means that .NET components always support the IntelliSense feature, even directly in ASP.NET.

The Registry

The registry is a database that stores configuration information for the Windows Operating System. The problem with COM (in addition to the versioning problems discussed in the next topic) is that version and type information is stored in two different places, the registry and the component's type library. For this reason, COM components must be *registered* (using a utility called regsvr32.exe) before they can be used. Running this utility populates the registry with the component's type information.

.NET eliminates the need to keep component information in the registry—the metadata for an assembly is stored entirely within the component itself. .NET components are thus self-describing in that they contain both IL code and all of the necessary information needed to execute it.

EXAMPLE

The CLR example in Listing 3.4 uses a COM component to determine the process in which the web application was running. In this example we will write a .NET assembly that does the same thing. Using assemblies (as opposed to COM components) in ASP.NET is desirable for two reasons:

1. As discussed in Chapter 9, calling COM components from ASP.NET incurs a performance hit, as the CLR must transition from managed to unmanaged code.
2. As we will see in Chapter 6, assemblies allow you to "step into" component source code directly from your ASP.NET application.

Writing a Class Library

To create an assembly, open VS.NET and create a new C# "Class Library" project named myAssembly (for demonstration purposes we will use C#, but a VB.NET equivalent can be found online at ⌐ᴺᵞAS030004). A class library is a DLL assembly that exposes a number of functions callable from ASP.NET (or any .NET application).

After you click OK to create the project, VS.NET will create a project file where you can write the methods you wish to expose in the class library. The file already contains some boilerplate code, as shown in Listing 3.12.

```
using System;
namespace myAssembly
{
   /// <summary>
   /// Summary description for Class1.
   /// </summary>
   public class Class1
   {
      public Class1()
      {
         //
         // TODO: Add constructor logic here
         //
      }
   }
}
```

Listing 3.12   Boilerplate code inserted by VS.NET

Recall from the namespace discussion in the previous topic that you access the Base Class Libraries by referencing the namespaces in which they are contained. Similarly, when you author a class library, you place it within a namespace that others must reference. By default, VS.NET places the project in a namespace equal to the project name (myAssembly, in this case). It also gives your project a default class (Class1) that will be exposed to client applications.

As it stands, our class library is useless—the class it exposes doesn't do anything. At the beginning of this example we sought to write an assembly that would report the process in which it was running. Start by renaming Class1 as ProcessInfo, and delete the constructor from the source (i.e., the public Class1 code block in Listing 3.12).

Next, we need a method in this class that determines the process within which it is running. But where can we find such functionality? As you may have guessed, there is a Base Class Library that does exactly what we want.

Referencing a Base Class Library

Recall from the previous topic that in order to use a BCL class you must first reference the assembly that contains it. The functionality we desire can be found in the `Application` class found in `System .Windows.Forms.DLL` (the class is located in this file because such functionality is typically required by Desktop Applications, which use Windows Forms classes).

In the previous topic we also learned that certain BCL files are automatically referenced by VS.NET, such that we don't have to reference them ourselves. Class library projects do not reference the DLL we need, so go to Project → Add References and explicitly select it, as shown in Figure 3.6.

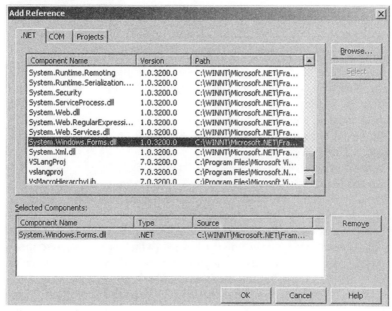

Figure 3.6   Adding a reference to a BCL class

Figure 3.6 illustrates that you can also add references to COM components, an option we will explore in Chapter 9. After selecting the `System.Windows.Forms` DLL, click `OK`. Notice that the file has now been added to the *References* section of your Solution (Figure 3.2). Remember that referencing the BCL file is only part of the process—you must also reference the namespace of the particular class you want to use. With that in mind, add the bolded portions of Listing 3.13 to your project.

```
using System;
using System.Windows.Forms;
namespace myAssembly
{
  public class ProcessInfo
  {
    public string WhatProcess()
    {
      // Use the Application class's ExecutablePath()
      // to determine what process we're running in:
      return Application.ExecutablePath;
    }
  }
}
```

Listing 3.13   myAssembly—reports what process we're running in

Build the library by going to Build → Build Solution, and you now have a class library functionally equivalent to the COM component used in Listing 3.4. The component exposes a function named WhatProcess(), which determines the host process of the application. Before we use the class library from ASP.NET, let us take a look at the resulting DLL file.

The ILDASM Utility

The myAssembly.DLL file you just built is an assembly that contains IL code and self-describing metadata. To look at this metadata we can use a tool provided by Microsoft called ILDASM.EXE [developers familiar with ActiveX or COM will find ILDASM (which stands for Intermediate Language Disassembly) similar to the OLEVIEW.EXE tool that allows one to examine a component's type library].

To use ILDASM, bring up the VS.NET command prompt (Figure 2.5) and go to the directory where the assembly file is located. By default, VS.NET stores the file in your project's bin\Debug directory (..\myAssembly\bin\Debug). Next, execute the following command:

```
ILDASM /adv myAssembly.DLL
```

ILDASM will load the assembly and bring up a screen similar to the one depicted in Figure 3.7.

Figure 3.7   Using ILDASM to inspect an assembly

As illustrated in Figure 3.7, ILDASM lists the types exposed by an assembly, which, in the case of our library, consists of one class named ProcessInfo that contains two methods: ctor and WhatProcess(). Some of you may recognize the .ctor() method as the class's constructor— the method that automatically gets called when the class is instantiated (VB developers can think of this as the Class_Initialize method). Also, note that the class is contained within the myAssembly namespace.

You can also use ILDASM to examine the assembly's metadata by going to its View menu and selecting Metadata → Show!. The metadata listing is quite verbose, but looking through it you will find the following definition:

```
TypeDef #1
----------------------------------------------------------
  TypDefName: myAssembly.ProcessInfo  (02000002)
  Flags      : [Public] [AutoLayout] [Class]
  Extends    : 01000001 [TypeRef] System.Object
  Method #1
  ----------------------------------------------------------
    MethodName: WhatProcess (06000001)
    Flags      : [Public] [HideBySig] [ReuseSlot]
    RVA        : 0x00002050
    ImplFlags  : [IL] [Managed]  (00000000)
    CallCnvntn: [DEFAULT]
```

```
hasThis
ReturnType: String
No arguments.
Method #2
- - - - - - - - - - - - - - - - - - - - - - - - - - - - - - - - - - - - - - - -
MethodName: .ctor (06000002)
Flags     : [Public] [HideBySig] [ReuseSlot]
RVA       : 0x00002068
ImplFlags : [IL] [Managed]   (00000000)
CallCnvtn: [DEFAULT]
hasThis
ReturnType: Void
No arguments.
```

Listing 3.14   The assembly's metadata

The "TypeDef" section of the metadata lists the types exposed by the assembly, which includes our class, ProcessInfo. Recall from our discussion of the Common Type System, at the beginning of this chapter, that all types in the .NET Framework derive from the Object type. Therefore, it should come as no surprise that our class extends (inherits) from System.Object, as shown in Listing 3.14.

The metadata in Listing 3.14 also lists all the methods exposed by our class. This is important, because entities such as compilers, and even the CLR itself, can use this information to ensure that the class is called in a correct fashion. As we will see, this information also fuels IntelliSense inside Visual Studio.NET.

Finally, you can also look at the IL code for a particular method itself. For example, click on WhatProcess() in Figure 3.7 and you will see its underlying IL code. If you are familiar with native machine language (what ASP developer isn't?), you will find IL code similar to high-level pseudo-machine code.

To review, an assembly consists of the two main entities we have examined using ILDASM: IL code, which is converted by the CLR into machine code when the assembly runs, and metadata, which describes all the types the assembly exposes. Now that you understand the internals of assemblies, let us see how you use them.

The Manifest

If you reexamine Figure 3.7, you will see something called the Manifest. This is a special portion of an assembly's metadata that lists all the other assemblies on which it depends. We will revisit the Manifest in the last topic of this chapter.

The Base Class Libraries

In writing our class library (myAssembly), we used the BCL Application class to determine the process in which the application was running. To use this BCL class we had to add a reference to the DLL file that contained it, and also reference the class's namespace.

To use *our* class library, clients would repeat the exact same procedure. This similarity is reflective of an important aspect of the BCL: the Base Class Libraries are themselves assemblies. The only difference between our assembly and the BCL is that the BCL is authored by Microsoft and installed on your system as a part of the .NET Framework. You can, for example, use ILDASM to examine the Base Class Libraries (they can be found in the `\%winroot%\Microsoft.NET\ Framework\versionNum\` directory). Load `Microsoft.VisualBasic.DLL`, look under the `String` class, and you will find functions such as `UCase()` and `Mid()`.

Using the Assembly—the WhereAmI Application

To use our assembly from ASP.NET, create a new VB.NET web application in Visual Studio named `WhereAmI`. Drag a button and textbox onto the Web Form, and then add a reference to the assembly by going to Project → Add References, clicking `Browse` and selecting myAssembly.DLL from the directory in which it is contained (..\myAssembly\bin\Debug). Again, notice that the file is added to the Reference section in the solution window.

Reference the assembly's namespace by adding the line `Imports myAssembly` at the top of the source file. Next, double-click the button and add the highlighted code in Listing 3.15 to its event handler.

```
Private Sub Button1_Click(...) Handles Button1.Click
   Dim oProc As New ProcessInfo()
   TextBox1.Text = oProc.WhatProcess()
End Sub
```

Listing 3.15   Using our assembly in ASP.NET

Run the program by pressing `F5`, and after you click the button the class library will report the process in which the application is running. In agreement with our CLR example at the beginning of this chapter, the textbox will read:

```
%winroot%\Microsoft.NET\Framework\vX.xxx\ASPNET_WP.EXE
```

You will notice some interesting behavior as you type the second highlighted line into your source—the environment automatically lists the methods of the `ProcessInfo` class (IntelliSense). This behavior is made possible by the metadata in Listing 3.14. Behind the scenes, VS.NET consults this metadata in order to determine the methods the class exposes, which it then converts into a user-friendly representation on the screen. The virtues of metadata, however, go beyond the simple fueling of IntelliSense. To understand its importance, we must revisit the `CreateObject()` function you used in ASP.

The Problems with CreateObject()

At the beginning of this chapter we used the `CreateObject()` function to call a COM component from ASP.NET:

```
Dim o as object
o = CreateObject("WhatProc.WhatProc")
Response.Write("This ASP.NET script is executing in: ")
Response.Write(o.WhatProcess())
```

Listing 3.16   CreateObject() in ASP

What is limiting about `CreateObject()` (in addition to the absence of IntelliSense) is that objects created through this mechanism are *late-bound*. This means that there is no way for the development environment to determine, at compile time, whether an object is being called in the correct fashion. If we use the COM component illegally in Listing 3.16 (by writing `o.Foo()`, for example), the error will not be caught until the application is actually executed.

.NET assemblies do not suffer from this limitation. Append the line `oProc.Foo()` to Listing 3.15, try to compile the project by going to Build → Build Application, and VS.NET will inform you that:

```
WebForm1.aspx.vb(30): 'Foo' is not a member of
'myAssembly.ProcessInfo'.
```

During the build, the compiler consults the assembly's metadata and determines that `Foo()` is not a supported member of the class. As a result, such errors are caught during the development period, as opposed to when an application is deployed.

In Chapter 6, we will see that assemblies offer even greater flexibility. Specifically, they allow us to "step into" the `myAssembly` C# component as we're running the VB.NET code in Listing 3.15.

Assemblies—Not Just Class Libraries

Before we depart from the topic of assemblies, we must make an important clarification. Based on this example, you may conclude that only class library files (DLLs) are classified as assemblies. In fact, *any* entity that contains executable code in the .NET Framework is an assembly. This includes traditional Desktop Applications (.EXEs), components (DLLs), and, as we'll see in the last topic of this chapter, even ASP.NET web applications.

HOW AND WHY

How Do I Prevent a Class in My Assembly from Being Used by Other Programs?

Look at Listing 3.13 and you will see that the `public` keyword precedes the declaration of the `ProcessInfo` class. The `public` extension advises the C# compiler that this type should be visible to all programs that access the assembly. With .NET, one can specify the "visibility" of types to the outside world. The `public` extension is the most lenient specification, allowing access to all who want it. There are four other visibility extensions that can be used. (Note that the following keywords are specific to VB. For C# equivalents see ⌀ AS030005).

- `private`—stipulates that a class's method can only be called directly by the class itself.
- `protected`—stipulates that a class's method can only be called by the class and derived classes.
- `friend` and `protected friend`—these two extensions require an understanding of concepts that we will explore in the next topic of this chapter on shared assemblies. Details on these two keywords can be found at ⌀ AS030005.

To make a class inaccessible to the other programs, you would precede its declaration with either the `private` or `protected` keywords.

SUMMARY

Assemblies are the new file format used to house executable code in the .NET Framework. Assemblies are self-describing, as they contain information about the types they expose via their embedded metadata. This metadata fuels VS.NET's IntelliSense feature and allows the development environment to perform compile-time checking on components used from ASP.NET, which greatly simplifies debugging applications. An assembly's metadata can be inspected using the ILDASM utility included with the .NET Framework.

Because an assembly's executable logic consists of language-neutral IL code, interoperability between the .NET languages is greatly simplified; in this topic's example we seamlessly used a C# assembly from VB.NET.

As we will see in the next topic, assemblies solve the problem of DLL Hell that exists with current Windows component technology.

Topic: Shared Assemblies

THE DLL HELL PROBLEM

Microsoft has touted the assembly as the end of the DLL Hell. Although the problem is somewhat removed from web development, if you have practical experience with the Windows Operating System you will recognize that this is a profound claim. To appreciate why, we must understand how the problem of DLL Hell arose in the first place.

The idea behind the DLL was that applications could share libraries for common and useful routines. By sharing executable code, applications would be smaller, conserving hard-drive space.

Problems arose with this model because it became difficult to impose a versioning scheme for these libraries. Installation scripts would frequently and arrogantly update (or downgrade) shared DLLs, unaware (or unconcerned) that numerous other programs depended on them. If the new shared DLL was for some reason incompatible with the old one (i.e., if functions accepted new parameters or behaved differently), many programs would cease to work.

Enter COM
Microsoft's Component Object Model (COM) attempted to tame such versioning problems by declaring that a component's methods (its interface, in COM terminology), once published, could never change. Under this stipulation, components could evolve through new interfaces, but would never cease to be compatible with their older variants. This was a voluntary constraint, however, and developers could (and frequently would) change published interfaces, breaking compatibility with older components.

With .NET, Microsoft has finally eradicated the problem of DLL Hell through the introduction of two types of assemblies.

CONCEPTS

Assembly Versioning

Like existing frameworks such as COM, the assembly infrastructure employs a versioning scheme to prevent developers from updating components in such a way as to break compatibility. Unlike previous technologies, versioning is enforced through public-key cryptography—a rigorous security model that is arguably impossible to foil.

Thus, a developer cannot, either through ignorance or malice, upgrade a component to change its behavior without special permissions and key-based information. There are two types of assemblies under the .NET infrastructure: private and shared.

Private Assemblies

Private assemblies are not designed to be shared. They are designed to be used by one application and must reside in that application's directory or subdirectory. This isolated methodology is reminiscent of the old DOS days, when applications were fully contained within their own directories and did not disturb one another. By default, all assemblies (like the one we created in the previous topic) are private. If you wish to make them shared, you must do so explicitly by *signing* them as the upcoming example illustrates. It is expected that the majority of assemblies you create will be of the private type, as hard-drive space is no longer the issue it was when DLLs were first created.

Private Assemblies and VS.NET

The rules for private assemblies stipulate that they must reside in the directory or subdirectory of an application that uses them. Therefore, it may seem odd that in the previous topic we used myAssembly without explicitly copying it into our web application's directory.

The subtle point worth noting is that when you reference a private assembly using VS.NET's Add Reference option, it automatically copies the assembly to your application's directory. You can see this if you bring up the web project you created in the previous topic. Click myAssembly in the Solution Explorer and then examine the Copy Local property in the Property Inspector as shown in Figure 3.8.

As we will see, when you reference shared assemblies in VS.NET, the Copy Local property is set to False.

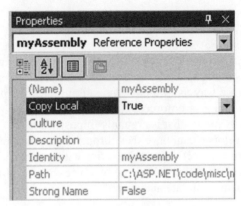

Figure 3.8   VS.NET copies private assemblies

Shared Assemblies

For those components that must be distributed (if, for example, you want multiple ASP.NET applications to use a common component), Microsoft offers the shared assembly. The shared-assembly concept is centered around two principles. The first, called side-by-side execution, allows the CLR to house multiple versions of the same assembly on a single machine. The second, termed binding, ensures that a client obtains the version of the component that they expect. Together, these two principles free developers from having to ensure that their components are compatible with their earlier versions. If a component evolves through versions 1.0, 1.1, and 2.0, the CLR will maintain separate copies of each version and deliver the appropriate version to each client.

Security and the Global Assembly Cache

What differentiates the shared assembly model from COM or Win32 DLLs is that the versioning policy is not voluntary or based on considerate programming practices, but is enforced through public-key cryptography. A full discussion of cryptography and its use by the CLR would quickly plunge us into the cryptic world of hashing, tokens, digital signatures, and other topics beyond the scope of this book. These subjects can quickly become overwhelming, but all you have to understand is that to enforce versioning, the CLR must ensure that:

1. shared assemblies can be updated only by authorized parties.
2. if a component is updated, clients expecting the older version receive it.

These requirements are facilitated by two entities. The first is a private key, which you obtain to "sign" an assembly, allowing you (and only you) to update it. The second is the Global Assembly Cache (GAC), which can house multiple copies of a shared assembly based on your "signature" and the version information used to build it. This information (signature and version) is stored in the metadata of all clients who wish to access the assembly, which allows the CLR to load the appropriate version at runtime. Shared assemblies are best illustrated through the following example.

SHARED ASSEMBLY EXAMPLE

In this example we will consider how we would use the .NET Framework to share the myAssembly component that we developed in the previous topic.

Creating a Private Key

In order to deploy myAssembly as shared, we first create a private key in the assembly's directory by using the SN.EXE utility that ships with the .NET Framework—to call this utility you must invoke the Command Prompt using the VS.NET Command Prompt icon from your Start menu and then type:

```
SN.EXE -k myKey.snk
```

The previous line instructs SN.EXE to store a globally unique private key into a file called myKey.snk (private key files in the .NET Framework end with the snk extension). The term *globally unique* means that our key is guaranteed to be different from any other key created by another individual (or subsequent keys that we might generate). It is very important that we keep the private key in our sole possession. If someone else gained access to myKey.snk, they could produce (and update) assemblies that looked like they were authored by us.

Having generated a private key, we must associate it with the assembly. When you create a class library project in VS.NET, the development environment automatically inserts a file into the project named AssemblyInfo.cs. If you open this file (load the myAssembly project we created in the previous topic), you will find numerous lines of code that specify information about the assembly. The two lines we are interested in are:

```
[assembly: AssemblyVersion("1.0.*")]
[assembly: AssemblyKeyFile("")]
```

These lines of code represent an important entity in the .NET Framework called attributes.

Tangent—Attributes

An attribute is a declarative statement in your code that embeds metadata into an assembly. This metadata can then be extracted at runtime in order to characterize aspects of an application or to influence its behavior. The previous two attributes embed version and key information into the assembly's metadata. When an application uses the assembly, the CLR extracts this section of the metadata to determine whether the versioning requirements of the application have been met.

Attributes are used throughout the .NET Framework. The CLR uses them to determine how objects are serialized, whether or not objects utilize COM+ services, and so on. Attributes are also employed when you write .NET Web Services, which allow assemblies to communicate via open Internet standards such as XML and SOAP.

As the previous lines illustrate, attributes are enclosed within the square bracket characters ([ ]) in C#, and angle brackets (<>) in VB.NET. By convention, attribute names end with the word Attribute. Thus, if you look in the MSDN, you will not find an attribute called Assembly Version, but rather AssemblyVersionAttribute. We can use the more succinct AssemblyVersion in our code, however, because both C# and VB.NET are smart enough to convert it into its longer equivalent.

Back to Our Example

To prepare our assembly for shared deployment, modify the two attributes as follows:

```
[assembly: AssemblyVersion("1.0.0.0")]
[assembly: AssemblyKeyFile("myKey.snk")]
```

The two lines inform the compiler that this is version 1.0.0.0 of the assembly and that it will be signed with the key contained in myKey.snk. Build the class library by going to Build → Build Solution, and ProcessInfo can now be deployed as a shared assembly. Before we consider how we can use it from ASP.NET, a few words need to be said about the versioning scheme used by the .NET Framework.

Versioning and Compatibility

Version information in the .NET Framework takes on the following form:

```
<major version>.<minor version>.<build number>.<revision>
```

The versioning rules for .NET (which have changed significantly since beta 1 of the framework), stipulate that a client will always run against the version of an assembly it was built against. Thus, if you build an ASP.NET application with v1.0.0.0 of an assembly, it will always run against this version even if a newer version (1.5.0.0) is available. (You may be wondering whether there are ways to override this behavior—see the How and Why section after this example).

Given the described nomenclature, you may be confused with the 1.0.* version number that VS.NET initially assigned our component. When you place an asterisk after the major and minor numbers, you are telling VS.NET to automatically assign build and revision numbers to your component, according to the following rules:

- Build number will be equal to the number of days since January 1, 2000, local time.
- Revision number will be equal to the number of seconds since midnight local time, divided by 2 (rounded to the nearest integer). This results in 43,200 possible unique revision numbers in each day.

This means that every successive compilation of our assembly will have different build and revision numbers, provided, of course, that you do not recompile faster than once every two seconds. Such a rapidly changing versioning scheme is useful in development and testing scenarios wherein you may be rebuilding a component many times and will want to test the client against the latest component. It is not appropriate for client deployment, however, which is why we changed the version number from 1.0.* to 1.0.0.0.

In addition to specifying the version number of an assembly, you can optionally specify its culture, which can be used when you are deploying multilanguage assemblies. We will not use it in our example here, but consult ⊶AS030006 for details.

Deploying and Using the Shared Assembly

Having released v1.0.0.0 of our shared assembly, suppose we wish to use it from an ASP.NET application. Before we can do this, we must register the assembly in the Global Assembly Cache (GAC) using a utility called GACUTIL.EXE (remember, the GAC houses multiple versions of the same assembly).

```
GACUTIL.EXE /i myAssembly.DLL
```

Listing 3.17   Running the GACUTIL program

As a result of running this utility, the file is now registered and physically copied to the Global Assembly Cache. It can now be used by any application in the .NET Framework.

Create a new VB.NET web application project in Visual Studio named Client1. As in the previous topic's example, draw a textbox and button onto the Web Form and reference the assembly by using VS.NET's *Add Reference* option (Figure 3.6). Remember that the assembly can be found in the project's Debug directory (..\myAssembly \bin\Debug). Notice that because the assembly is shared, ASP.NET does not maintain a local copy of it (i.e., the *Copy Local* property in Figure 3.8 is set to False).

Add the code in Listing 3.15 to the button's event handler, and the application will function as the one developed in the previous topic; when the user clicks the button it will report that it is running within the \%winroot%\Microsoft.NET\Framework\vx.xxxx\aspnet_wp.exe process.

Updating the Assembly

Some time after the Client1 web application has been deployed, we may wish to make a modification to the ProcessInfo class. Specifically, we wish to give the user the option of retrieving the full process name with path, or simply the process name (aspnet_wp.exe). To this end we modify the WhatProcess() method of our class library (Listing 3.13) with the code in Listing 3.18. Note that in C#, a string with a "\" character is prefixed with the at sign (@) so that the backslash is not interpreted as an escape character (escape characters are a carryover from the C language).

```
public string WhatProcess(bool fullPath)
{
  System.String s = Application.ExecutablePath;
  int k=0;
  // Do they want the full path name or just
  // the process name?
  if (fullPath==false) {
    // extract the process name from the full path:
    for (k=s.Length-1; k>=1; k--) {
      if (s.Substring(k,1) == @"\") {
        break;
```

```
      }
    }
  }
  s = s.Substring(k+1,s.Length-k-1);
  return s;
}
```

Listing 3.18   A new WhatProcess() method

This change breaks compatibility with the old component, however, since the WhatProcess() method signature is no longer the same. Realizing this, we inform the CLR that this version of the component is not compatible with its predecessor by assigning it a different version number:

```
[assembly:AssemblyVersionAttribute("1.5.0.0")]
```

Because we also wish to share this new version of the assembly with other applications, we must register it using GACUTIL (after you have built it from VS.NET, of course):

```
GACUTIL.EXE /i myAssembly.DLL
```

As a result of running this utility, there are now two copies of myAssembly.DLL on the system (v1.0.0.0 and v1.5.0.0). You can see this by using the Windows Explorer and inspecting the \%Winroot%\ Assembly directory. Navigating to this area invokes the Assembly Cache Viewer, which is a shell extension that provides a friendly view of all the shared assemblies on the system (a shell extension is a component that extends some aspect of the Windows User Interface, such as Windows Explorer). This is shown in Figure 3.9.

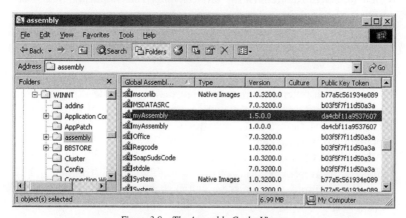

Figure 3.9   The Assembly Cache Viewer

Next to each assembly we see the version number and something called a publickeytoken. We will examine the role of the publickeytoken momentarily. If you examine the other files in the GAC, you will see that the Base Class Libraries themselves are shared assemblies. In addition, some files have *Native Images* listed under their *Type*. Recall from the first topic that the CLR JIT compiles assemblies on the fly before they are executed. It is actually possible to eliminate this step from the equation altogether, by "pre-JITing" assemblies using a utility called NGEN.EXE, to give them "Native Image" designation. Information on NGEN.EXE can be found at ☜AS030007.

We can now write a second application that takes advantage of the new assembly. Create another VB.NET web application (call it Client2), draw a textbox and button onto the Web Form, and reference the assembly (again, located in ..\myAssembly\bin\Debug). Because we are using the new version of the assembly, we must modify the call to the WhatProcess()method, depending on whether or not we want the full path name. Since we want only the process name, attach the following code to the button's event handler:

```
Private Sub Button1_Click(...) Handles Button1.Click
  Dim t As New myAssembly.ProcessInfo()
  'We only want the process name (no path)
  TextBox1.Text = t.WhatProcess(False)
End Sub
```

Listing 3.19   Calling the new component

Run the new application, and it will inform you that it is running within the aspnet_wp.exe process. If you run the first application (Client1), it will run against the old assembly and output the more verbose:

```
\%winroot%\Microsoft.NET\Framework\vx.xxxx\aspnet_wp.exe
```

It is important that you do not run the first application from the VS.NET development environment, but instead execute it by invoking Internet Explorer and manually navigating to http://localhost/myAssembly1/WebForm1.aspx. See the question section after this example for an explanation of this caveat.

We now have two web applications (Client1 and Client2) running against two different versions of our assembly (v1.0.0.0 and v1.5.0.0). Given this example, you can see how the shared assembly model might be practically employed; you could have numerous web applications share an assembly for overlapping functionality. As the assembly and applications evolved, you would deploy new versions of the assembly such that new applications would run against new components, while older applications would run against their older, safe predecessors.

The publickeytoken

Although this example demonstrates two versions of a component working side by side, how exactly do assemblies abolish the problem of DLL Hell? Recall that DLL Hell occurs when another party overwrites our component with an incompatible variant. For example, Mr. X, the evil developer, could write his own myAssembly component that masqueraded as ours but did something malicious (formatted the hard drive, for example).

Thankfully, with .NET, Mr. X's efforts are thwarted via public-key cryptography. Look at Figure 3.9 and you will see that all shared assemblies are associated with publickeytokens. A publickeytoken can be thought of as a portion of our private key that assures applications that they are running *our* code. The interplay between the CLR and the first web application you developed (Client1) would proceed like this:

Client1: I need an assembly named myAssembly, version number 1.0.0.0, with publickeytoken da4cbf11a9537607.

CLR: Let me consult the Global Assembly Cache. Ok, I've found the assembly, here you go . . .

Thus, a client application references both the assembly name (myAssembly) and the publickeytoken, which can only be produced with our private key. Together, these two entities form a *strong name*, which is guaranteed to be unique. Another company could use the myAssembly name, but they could never generate the same publickeytoken.

Similarly, Mr. X cannot populate the GAC with an authentic version of our component because he does not possess our private key. The publickeytoken is actually embedded into your ASP.NET applications (as we'll see in the next topic), which assures component authors that if they don't share their private keys, clients will always call assemblies that *they* themselves have produced.

More Than Just Security

The publickeytoken and metadata also allow the CLR to determine that an assembly's contents (IL code, resources, etc.) have not been corrupted or tampered with. Thus, the CLR assures developers not only that they are running our code, but also that the integrity of the assembly has not been compromised since we signed it.

Similarly, if myAssembly.DLL used an assembly itself, the CLR would ensure that it ran against the proper version. These integrity checks are performed throughout the chain of callers. Developers are not only guaranteed that they are calling our code, but that our code is calling whom it expects and so on. One can see that the versioning provided by the .NET Framework is truly rigorous.

HOW AND WHY

In the Previous Example, After Deploying the New Assembly, Why Did We Have to Access Client1 Directly Through the Browser Instead of the Development Environment?
By default, when you reference a shared assembly in VS.NET, it does not copy the assembly to your application's directory. Instead, it references it from the directory you specify. Consider the sequence of steps in the previous example:

1. We wrote v1.0.0.0 of the assembly.
2. We wrote Client1 and referenced v1.0.0.0 of the assembly from the following directory: ..\myAssembly\bin\Debug
3. We changed the assembly to v1.5.0.0, but in so doing overwrote the DLL found in ..\myAssembly\bin\Debug.

Now, if you reload Client1 in VS.NET, it still references the DLL found in ..\myAssembly\bin\Debug. Unfortunately, this is v1.5.0.0 of the assembly, not v1.0.0.0, which Client1 expects. Thus, if you try to run Client1 from Visual Studio, it will give you the following error:

```
Argument not specified for parameter 'fullPath' of
'Public Overloads Function WhatProcess(fullPath As
Boolean) As String'.
```

There are a number of ways around this problem. First, when referencing a shared assembly, explicitly tell VS.NET to copy it locally by setting the `Copy Local` property (Figure 3.8) to True. The second solution is more of a project-management approach. Store each version of a shared assembly in a separate directory where it cannot be overwritten during the development process (\myAssembly10, \myAssembly15, etc). Now, explicitly reference assemblies from these "safe" directories.

Why Do I Get the Following Error When I Try to Recompile the Class Library (myAssembly):

```
Unexpected error creating debug information file '..\someFile
.PDB' — '..\someFile.pdb: The process cannot access the file
because it is being used by another process.
```

This error results when the ASP.NET Runtime has locked your class library project for debugging purposes. As we will see in Chapter 6, it is possible to debug directly into assemblies called from ASP.NET applications. You get this error when you have previously run a web application that used the assembly.

In order to get the ASP.NET Runtime to release the lock on the project you must restart IIS, either by using the Internet Services Manager or by running iisreset at the Command Prompt.

How Do I Change the CLR's Versioning Rules?

In some situations it may be desirable to change how the runtime determines the version of an assembly that is loaded. For example, we may wish for clients built on v1.0.0.0 of the assembly to use v1.5.0.0 if it is available. This is accomplished either through XML configuration files or the .NET configuration utility, both of which can override the default versioning behavior of the runtime. Details on using both of these methods can be found at ᴼᶜᴺ⟩AS030008.

Are Assemblies with Strong Names Trustworthy?

Although strong names can assure you that an assembly comes from the same person, they make no guarantees about who that person is. Anyone can generate a private key by using SN.EXE and distribute a shared assembly, claiming it originates from company X. Identity is only guaranteed through Microsoft's Authenticode technology, information on which can be found at ᴼᶜᴺ⟩AS030009.

Can I Avoid Signing an Assembly Until It Is Time to Deploy It?

Quite often, numerous developers work together on a project. It may not be desirable to sign assemblies during the development process, because every developer would need a copy of the private key. Sharing the private key is not only a nuisance; it also increases the chances that the key will be compromised. To address these concerns the .NET Framework exposes the delayed signing option, whereby an assembly is signed only immediately before it is deployed. Information on delayed signing can be found at ᴼᶜᴺ⟩AS030010.

SUMMARY

Shared assemblies solve the problem of DLL Hell through the Global Assembly Cache (GAC), which allows multiple versions of an assembly to exist side by side on the same machine, and through public-key cryptography, which ensures that an assembly can only be updated by an authorized party. A shared assembly must be signed using a private key generated with the SN.EXE utility.

You must also give the assembly a version number using the CLR's four-digit versioning scheme: `<major version>.<minor version>.<build number>.<revision>`. By default, clients always run against the version of the assembly they were built against. Thus, an application built against assembly version 1.0.0.0 will always run against this version even if there are newer versions available. This behavior can be overridden by using either XML configuration files or the .NET Configuration utility.

Private assemblies don't really solve the DLL Hell problem so much as they avoid it. They are intended to be called by one application and must reside in that application's directory or subdirectory. Because private assemblies don't reside in a prescribed shared area, there is less chance of these assemblies falling prey to malicious (or negligent) installation scripts that wish to update them. Unlike shared assemblies, private ones are not afforded the luxury of version and signature checking. By default, assemblies created in VS.NET are private.

Topic: Inside ASP.NET

Now that we understand both the Base Class Libraries and assemblies, we can state the following two important facets of ASP.NET's architecture:

1. ASP.NET itself is exposed through the Base Class Libraries found in the `System.Web` namespace (and other namespaces within this one).
2. ASP.NET applications are compiled into assemblies, which the ASP.NET Runtime uses to generate client-side HTML, to process user input, and to respond to user requests.

These details, which will become increasingly important as we delve into advanced ASP.NET topics such as security, are best illustrated by example.

EXAMPLE

To begin our "under-the-hood" look at ASP.NET, load the first example application (Client1) that we created in the previous topic. Click WebForm1.aspx in the Solution Explorer, and then click the HTML tab at the bottom of the page (Figure 1.6). Visual Studio.NET will then bring up the server-side HTML for the project. Recall that this HTML code represents the design of the application (i.e., its graphical representation on the screen).

Look at the top of this file and you will find the following line of code:

```
<%@ Page Language="vb" AutoEventWireup="false"
  Codebehind="WebForm1.aspx.vb"
  Inherits="Client1.WebForm1"%>
```

Listing 3.20   The page directive

What you are seeing is an important entity in ASP.NET called the Page directive, which describes certain characteristics of the Web Form to the ASP.NET Runtime. For example, the Language attribute in the Page directive informs ASP.NET which compiler to use on scripts in the .aspx file. More important is the CodeBehind attribute that tells VS.NET where the application's associated logic is located.

Remember, an important aspect of ASP.NET is the ability to separate code from content. This is accomplished (in part) by the CodeBehind attribute. Flip back to the page's GUI by clicking the Design icon (Figure 1.8), click the application's button, and VS.NET will bring up the Web-Form1.aspx.vb file that contains the page's underlying code. From this exercise, we can see that our web application consists of two main files:

- WebForm1.aspx—the application's design. This file contains the server-side HTML that describes what Web Controls are being used, client or server-side script that you directly add to this file, and any other design elements such as Image references, Cascading Style Sheets, etc.
- WebForm1.aspx.vb—the application's logic. This file uses certain Base Class Libraries that map to each element in the design file. It also houses the code that you write. By convention, this file has the same name as the design file with an added language extension (.vb, in this case).

Thus, by using the CodeBehind attribute, which establishes a relationship between the design file and the code file, ASP.NET can keep these aspects of your application separate.

The CodeBehind File

The application's logic file (WebForm1.aspx.vb) houses some interesting code that we have ignored up to this point. Specifically, consider the three lines given in Listing 3.21.

```
Public Class WebForm1
   Inherits System.Web.UI.Page
   Protected WithEvents TextBox1 As _
      System.Web.UI.WebControls.TextBox
   Protected WithEvents Button1 As _
      System.Web.UI.WebControls.Button
```

Listing 3.21   WebForm1.aspx.vb

Based on our discussion of the Base Class Libraries in the previous topics, you can see that Listing 3.21 uses classes found in the `System.Web.UI` and `System.Web.UI.WebControls` namespaces. Let us consider each class in turn.

The Page Class

ASP.NET applications are built using Web Forms. Recall that a Web Form is the entity onto which you drag and drop controls (the .aspx file). Conceptually, think of a Web Form as the equivalent of a Visual Basic Form.

As in VB, an application can house multiple Web Forms. You could, for example, add a second Web Form to the project by using VS.NET's `Project` → `Add Web Form` menu option. The application would then consist of two Web Forms, WebForm1.aspx and WebForm2.aspx. Also, as in the case of VB, one of these forms is designated the startup form that is displayed when the application runs (you can change the startup form by going to Project → Properties → Configuration Properties).

In ASP.NET a Web Form is encapsulated by a BCL Page class. Thus, if an application contains a Web Form named `Webform1`, its CodeBehind file declares a class that *inherits* from the `Page` class found in the `System.Web.UI` namespace:

```
Public Class WebForm1
   Inherits System.Web.UI.Page
```

Listing 3.22   Inheriting from the Page class

Those unfamiliar with the concept of inheritance can consult the brief online explanation at ⟨CN⟩AS030011. Basically, by inheriting from the `Page` class, `WebForm1` obtains all its functionality, such as the ability to fire an event when the Web Form loads. (Note that VB.NET now contains true object inheritance, a feature omitted from previous versions of Visual Basic.)

Again, we can draw analogies between VB6 and ASP.NET. Just as the VB `Form` object exposes events such as `Form_Load()` and `Form _Initalize()`, the `Page` class (and hence the `WebForm1` class) exposes events such as `Page_Load()` and `Page_Init()`. Thus, if you wanted to execute some code when a Web Form loaded (to initialize database connections, for example), you would place it in the `Page_Load()` event.

The `Page` class is the programmatic backbone for ASP.NET applications. It exposes many methods and properties that we will see throughout the rest of this book. For example, the `Request` and `Response` objects you used in ASP are accessed through this class.

The TextBox and Button Classes

As you can see from Listing 3.21, the `WebForm1` class contains a `TextBox` class (`TextBox1`) and a `Button` class (`Button1`), both of which are found in the `System.Web.UI.WebControls` namespace. (Ignore their *protected* designation for now, as this is an object-oriented concept; see ⊶AS030012 for details).

The point is that these automatically generated classes are accessible from your code and map to the Web Controls in the design file. Thus, when the user enters a value into the textbox on the screen, you can retrieve it via the `TextBox1.Text` property. Similarly, when you modify the `TextBox`'s background color (`TextBox1.BackColor`), it is reflected in the design (the output).

Code Generation and the Web Forms Designer

All three of the classes in Listing 3.21 are found in the Base Class Libraries. Yet how, exactly, did these lines get in the source in the first place? The answer is an entity in VS.NET called the Web Forms Designer that converts your graphical manipulations into code.

When you draw a button or textbox onto a Web Form, the WFD translates your actions into VB or C# code that calls the classes found in the `System.Web` and other namespaces. This code then becomes an integral part of the CodeBehind file, to which you can add your own logic.

Remember that the Base Class Libraries exist as language-neutral IL code. They are thus callable from any language that targets the .NET Framework. However, in order for the WFD to generate code automatically, as it did in Listing 3.21, the language must support special Microsoft "Code Generation" extensions. As of this writing, only VB.NET, C#, and J# are so equipped. Thus, although you can certainly call the

BCL classes in Listing 3.21 from managed C++ or JScript.NET, you must write the code manually and bind it to the design file yourself. A C++ example that does just that can be found at ⟨CN⟩AS030013.

In large part, you can ignore such details and simply program in the VB-like manner we have illustrated. That having been said, it is educational and revealing to consider the trickery that ASP.NET is performing behind the scenes. We will relegate the majority of this discussion to ⟨CN⟩AS030014; however, one practical implementation detail is how ASP.NET compiles your applications.

The Compilation Process

When a user requests an .aspx file, the ASP.NET Runtime performs two important operations:

1. It compiles the CodeBehind file into an assembly (if the file hasn't already been compiled either by you or by VS.NET).
2. It creates a second assembly called a Page class, which is a combination of the design file (.aspx) and the CodeBehind assembly produced in the first step. Think of the Page class as an executable file that accepts incoming requests, processes them according to your application's logic, and returns results to the user. (Don't confuse this compiled Page class with the BCL Page class in Listing 3.21)

An important aspect of ASP.NET's compilation process is that Step 2 is performed only when the application is initially requested; subsequent requests execute against an already existing Page class. This is because ASP.NET caches Page class assemblies (in `%winroot%\Microsoft.NET\Framework\vX.xxx\Temporary ASP.NET Files`) in order to improve performance.

If you develop in VS.NET, the environment will perform the first step automatically (it will compile the CodeBehind file). Remember that the resulting CodeBehind assembly is like any other assembly in the .NET Framework—it contains both IL code and metadata. Therefore, you can use ILDASM to examine it by loading it from your project's bin directory. Note that VS.NET automatically places web applications in the `localhost` virtual root, which usually maps the physical directory `C:\InetPub\wwwroot` (where `C:\` is the drive on which the OS is installed). Thus, if the application were named Client1, the assembly would be found in `C:\Inetpub\wwwroot\Client1\bin\Client1.Dll`.

If you use ILDASM to inspect the CodeBehind assembly for the Client1 project we created in the previous section, you will see that it exposes two classes: `Global` and `WebForm1`. We will ignore the `Global` class for now, but if you expand the WebForm1 class, you will see methods such as Page_Load and Button1_Click. These, of course, are the compiled representations for the code you wrote in the previous topic. Inspect the assembly in detail (look at the underlying IL code), and you'll begin to understand the underpinnings of ASP.NET more intimately.

The Manifest

An assembly's manifest is the section of metadata that contains the configuration and dependency information of the assembly itself. You can examine the manifest by clicking on the "MANIFEST" icon shown in Figure 3.7. Doing so brings up a textual representation of the manifest that is shown below (certain parts of it have been omitted for the sake of brevity).

```
.assembly extern mscorlib
.assembly extern Microsoft.VisualBasic
.assembly extern System
.assembly extern System.Data
.assembly extern System.Drawing
.assembly extern System.Web
.assembly extern System.Xml
.assembly extern myAssembly
{
   .publickeytoken = (DA 4C BF 11 A9 53 76 07 )
   .ver 1:0:0:0
}
```

Listing 3.23   Contents of the assembly's manifest

As illustrated in Listing 3.23, the Client1 assembly depends on numerous other assemblies. In addition to those assemblies that are automatically referenced by VS.NET (such as mscorlib, which contains the core BCL classes found in the System namespace and Microsoft .VisualBasic, which houses intrinsic VB6 elements), the class library we wrote in the assembly topic is also referenced.

Recall that Client1 used v1.0.0.0 of our class library. It is this information (the manifest) that enables the CLR to determine that the first version of myAssembly is required. When the .aspx file is requested, the CLR consults this section of the metadata, determines that myAssembly v1.0.0.0 is required, locates it in the GAC, and delivers it to the application.

SUMMARY

To conclude this chapter and review all the concepts we've learned thus far, let us consider the sequence of steps that occurs when a user requests the Client1 application from his or her browser (http://localhost/Client1 /Webform1.aspx on your machine).

1. The incoming HTTP request is received by Internet Information Server (IIS).
2. IIS, upon seeing the .aspx file extension, uses its application mapping settings (Figure 1.2) to direct the request to aspnet_isapi.dll.
3. The aspnet_isapi.dll (an ISAPI DLL; discussed in Chapter 1) starts the ASP.NET Runtime and forwards the request to it.
4. The ASP.NET Runtime inspects WebForm1.aspx and determines that its associated logic is housed in the WebForm1.aspx.vb CodeBehind file.
5. If the CodeBehind file has not already been compiled, the ASP.NET Runtime compiles it into an assembly (Client1.dll).
6. ASP.NET creates a Page class assembly based on the application's design file (WebForm1.aspx) and the CodeBehind assembly created in Step 5. It stores this file in %winroot%\ Microsoft.NET\Framework\vX.xxx\Temporary ASP.NET Files.
7. The ASP.NET Runtime instantiates the Page class assembly within the aspnet_wp.exe process. This process actually contains multiple application domains (AppDomains), each of which houses a different ASP.NET application (Page class).
8. While instantiating the Page class, the CLR determines and instantiates any assemblies the Page class depends on. This includes certain Base Class Libraries, and the CodeBehind assembly created in Step 5.
9. While instantiating the CodeBehind assembly, the CLR consults its manifest (Listing 3.23) and determines that it requires the myAssembly component in order to run. The CLR retrieves myAssembly from the GAC in accordance with the interplay given in the shared assembly topic (i.e., it requests v1.0.0.0 of myAssembly with publickeytoken da4cbf11a9537607).
10. The Page class, which consists of Web Controls and their underlying logic, delivers client-side HTML to the ASP.NET Runtime.
11. The ASP.NET Runtime adds some additional information to the Page class's response (such as the VIEWSTATE information depicted in Chapter 1).

12. The ASP.NET Runtime forwards the response to IIS.
13. IIS forwards the response to the user.
14. Subsequent requests are forwarded directly to the Page class, thus bypassing Steps 4 to 10.

You can see that abstraction comes at a cost—three entities must work (very hard) in unison to carry out the request: the Internet Information Server, the ASP.NET Runtime, and the CLR. Thankfully, Microsoft has already incurred this cost; you can enjoy the fruits of their labors.

Chapter Summary

ASP.NET is built on top of the .NET Framework, which consists of an execution engine (the CLR), a class framework that forms the building blocks for applications (the Base Class Libraries), and a standard manner in which applications are packaged (assemblies).

ASP.NET employs these aspects of the framework on varying levels. Web Forms are encapsulated through the BCL Page class, which abstracts a web page's lifetime through its Page_Load() and Page_Unload() methods. Web Controls such as textboxes and buttons are also found in the BCL, as are formerly intrinsic ASP objects such as Response and Request.

An ASP.NET application is compiled into an assembly the first time the application is requested. The compiled assembly, which is called a Page class, processes and responds to user requests. The Page class is created only the first time the application is requested, which improves response time thereafter.

Assemblies contain both IL code and metadata, which describes all the types that an assembly exposes. A special section of the metadata, called the Manifest, lists the assembly's dependencies, such as other assemblies it requires in order to run. The infrastructure used to determine assembly dependencies is rigorous and is based on public-key cryptography, whereas side-by-side versioning allows the CLR to house multiple versions of an assembly on one machine. Together these two principles eradicate the DLL Hell problem that currently pervades the Windows Operating System.

ASP.NET's integration with the .NET Framework provides many benefits to developers. Languages are now fully typed and compiled, calls to components are early-bound, and amenities such as object IntelliSense are available. Together, these features greatly simplify application deployment and debugging, while significantly improving performance and reliability.

Chapter 4

—

VISUAL STUDIO.NET AND WEB FORMS

In this chapter we examine two complementary aspects of ASP.NET: the Framework's new Web Form paradigm and the Visual Studio.NET design environment that drives it. As we demonstrated in Chapter 1, it is possible to write applications outside VS.NET by simply writing server-side HTML using a text editor (e.g., Notepad). Nevertheless, ASP.NET is most powerful when coupled with the sophisticated design features of Visual Studio. The first topic in this chapter explores VS.NET.

Web Forms and Web Controls are an integral part of the Framework's intuitive design process. In the second topic in this chapter, we will examine the underpinnings behind these two important technologies to see how ASP.NET performs its magic. As we will see, ASP.NET is based on an HTTP mechanism called POSTBACK.

Topic: Visual Studio.NET

In this topic we examine two important aspects of VS.NET—automation and design. Every time you create a web project in Microsoft's new development environment, the tool implicitly performs a number of important administrative steps behind the scenes. Although these details are transparent when developing in VS.NET, they become important if you decide to develop outside the environment or want to deploy an application to a Web Server.

In the last section in this topic we examine some of the VS.NET design features that you can apply to web applications.

VS.NET—the Files Behind a Project

An ASP.NET application must reside in an IIS virtual directory. In addition to mapping a URL to a physical directory on the hard drive, a virtual directory is the basis for resource sharing in the Framework. All of the files within a virtual directory share resources such as `Application` and `Session` variables, common code made available through global application files, and more. It follows, therefore, that if two ASP.NET scripts (script1.aspx and script2.aspx) are placed in different virtual directories, they will not be able to share such resources.

Create a new web project in VS.NET named MyApplication. During the process, VS.NET allows you to specify the location of the project (Figure 4.1).

Figure 4.1   Web project location

The machine where the application is created (the `Location` parameter in Figure 4.1) will differ depending on your configuration settings. If the Web Server resides on your machine (common during the development stage), then the location will be `localhost`, as in Figure 4.1. If the Web Server resides on a different machine (if you are developing against a production server, for example), then the Location parameter will be the remote machine name (or possibly an IP address). As in traditional ASP, the development environment uses FrontPage Server extensions to communicate with the Web Server.

By default, a web application project created in VS.NET contains a number of files, all of which are listed in the Solution Explorer (Figure 4.2).

The files in Figure 4.2, which we will explain in a moment, constitute the web application. When VS.NET created the project, it created an IIS virtual directory with the same name as the application. Thus, on the Web Server (on either the local or remote machine), there is an IIS virtual directory named MyApplication. Most often, this directory will map to the logical directory `c:\inetpub\wwwroot\MyApplication` on the machine (where `c:\` is the drive where the OS is installed). Within this virtual directory VS.NET creates the following files:

Figure 4.2   Default project files

AssemblyInfo.vb
Recall from the Shared Assembly topic in Chapter 3 that we modified the AssemblyVersion attribute within this file to build our class-library assembly. You will rarely modify this file when you develop a web project, as its contents are generally used for informational purposes not applicable in the context of a web application.

MyApplication.vsdisco
This file is used internally by Visual Studio and utilizes Microsoft's proprietary discovery technology. For more information on discovery, see *CodeNotes for .NET* or ⁰ᶜᴺ→AS040001.

Styles.css
This file allows you to apply Cascading Style Sheets (CSS) effects to web pages in the project. This subject is discussed in the following Design section.

Web.config
As we will see in Chapter 7, this file houses the project's configuration settings. The settings in this file determine such options as application tracing, session storage, and security. Load this file in VS.NET's code editor (by double-clicking it in the Solution Explorer) and you will see that it is in XML format. As we will also see in Chapter 7, storing configuration settings by means of XML offers numerous advantages over the setup in traditional ASP, which stored configuration data in the IIS metabase.

Webform1.aspx

Any time you create a new web application project in VS.NET, the environment gives the project a default Web Form named WebForm1.aspx. This behavior is similar to VB6, which gives Desktop Applications a standard form named Form1. In practice, you would likely rename Webform1.aspx to something more appropriate. In the majority of examples in this book we will operate against this default form. You can add additional Web Forms to the application by going to `Project` → `Add Web Form` in VS.NET.

Global.asax

This file is used to declare application-level events and shared objects. Developers familiar with traditional ASP will recognize this file as the extension of the Global.asa file used with ASP scripts. Those familiar with VB6 can think of this file as the conceptual equivalent of a Visual Basic module (.bas file). The Global.asax file houses three main entities:

1. Event declarations: If you peer inside this file you will find events such as `Application_Start()` and `Session_Start()`, which allow you to write code that is called when the web application is initially requested by anyone and when the application is first requested by a particular user. Other events in this file allow you to respond to other events such as application-wide errors and the unloading of the application. The events in this file trigger when *any* page in the application is requested. For example, if you want to perform an operation the first time a user accesses any page in the application, you write logic behind the `Session_Start()` event. We will employ this technique in our session example in Chapter 7.

2. Namespace references: Within the Global.asax file you can implicitly reference namespaces (via the `using` keyword in C# or `Imports` in VB.NET). If you look at the top of Global.asax you will find the following two lines: `Imports System.Web` and `Imports System.Web.SessionState`. The important point is that namespaces that are referenced in this file apply to *all* pages in the application. Thus, if you wanted to utilize the BCL XML classes throughout a VB.NET web application, you would include the line `Imports System.XML` at the top of Global.asax. (Remember from Chapter 3, however, that to use BCL classes you must not only reference the namespace, but also include a reference to the BCL assembly using VS.NET's `Add Reference` menu option.)

3. Server-side Includes and Object-tag Declarations: A server-side

include allows ASP.NET to "paste" code from external files into Global.asax, thus making the external files' contents accessible to all pages in the application. For example, by placing the following line in Global.asax the contents of MyFunction.dat become globally accessible:

```
<!-- #include File = "MyFunction.dat" -->
```

Listing 4.1   A server-side include

Server-side includes are a carryover from traditional ASP. A more powerful option for sharing code in ASP.NET is to use User Controls, discussed in the following Design section.

You can also place object-tag declarations inside Global.asax, which instruct the Framework to create .NET assemblies or COM objects on the fly on an application or user basis. For examples of both server-side includes and object tags, see ☞AS040002.

Bear in mind that an ASP.NET application does not require these files (with the exception of a basic .aspx file). As we will see in later chapters, however, these files (particularly web.config) greatly simplify configuration and deployment.

Global.asax versus Global.asa

It is important to note that Global.asax does not replace the Global.asa file utilized in traditional ASP. This behavior is by design and allows ASP.NET and traditional ASP scripts to coexist within the same virtual directory. For example, you could place a Global.asa file and .asp scripts in the MyApplication virtual directory that existed independent of ASP.NET. The .asp files would use Global.asa, whereas ASP.NET pages (.aspx files) would use Global.asax.

This separation is reflective of an important aspect of Microsoft's new web technology: ASP and ASP.NET scripts do not share resources. Thus, if you place code within the Session_Start() event in Global.asax, it will not trigger when a traditional ASP file is requested. And, as we will see in Chapter 7, ASP and ASP.NET applications cannot share Session or Application information.

Developing Outside VS.NET

As we have illustrated, Visual Studio.NET performs a number of important steps when you create a web project within its environment. If you decide to develop outside the environment (as we did in the first timer example in Chapter 1), then you must manually create an IIS virtual directory and (optionally) create files such as Global.asax and web.config.

Web Page Design in VS.NET

The primary virtue of ASP.NET is that web-based applications can be designed by means of the drag-and-drop paradigm utilized in VB6. As we saw in Chapter 3, this process is driven by the environment's Web Form Designer (WFD), which produces the appropriate server-side HTML and Web Control declarations behind the scenes. In large part, application development in ASP.NET will proceed along these intuitive lines. Nevertheless, there are a number of mature web-related technologies that can be integrated with the Framework's Web Form paradigm.

Client-side Script

With the exception of the validation controls that we will examine in the next chapter, Web Control code executes entirely on the server. However, you may wish for a Web Control (such as a button) to execute some client-side JavaScript before its server-side code runs. This type of behavior can be accomplished by first adding some JavaScript to the Web Form's design file (.aspx).

```
<script language="JavaScript">
   function Test() {
      alert("Client-side Javascript running!");
   }
</script>
```

Listing 4.2   Client-side JavaScript

Note that the `<script>` element in Listing 4.2 does not have a `runat="server"` attribute, which causes ASP.NET to simply forward the script block to the client's browser. To configure a Web Control button to execute this code (before its server-side code executes), you must utilize its `Attributes` collection, which allows you to modify the control's underlying HTML representation.

```
Private Sub Page_Load(...)
  'Put user code to initialize the page here
  Button1.Attributes("onClick") = "Test()"
End Sub
```

Listing 4.3   Configuring a Web Control to execute client-side script

Listing 4.3 uses the button's Attributes collection to add an HTML attribute named onClick with value Test() (the name of the JavaScript function in Listing 4.3) to the button. Thus, when the Web Control gets converted into its HTML representation at runtime, it contains an HTML attribute that points to the client-side JavaScript we wrote in Listing 4.2:

```
<input type="submit" name="Button1" value="WebForm" onClick="Test()" style=...>
```

Listing 4.4   The client-side HTML

Thus, when the button is clicked, it first executes client script in Listing 4.2 (which simply prints out a message). Immediately after, its server-side code executes.

As you can see, although Web Controls are designed to abstract the details of the web, you can explicitly modify the underlying HTML that ASP.NET generates using the Attributes collection. As we will see in the next chapter, the Attributes collection is most often employed with another family of ASP.NET controls called HTML Server controls.

Cascading Style Sheets (CSS)

Cascading Style Sheets are a part of the Dynamic HTML (DHTML) specification and allow you to group one or more design elements under the umbrella of a single entity. In this way, when you wish to apply a design change to the project (a color adjustment, for example), you can apply the change to the single entity, and the modification will *cascade* to its related elements.

VS.NET gives web projects a default CSS file named Styles.css, and allows you to associate Web Forms with this file. Suppose, for example, that you want every Web Form in the project to derive its background color from this CSS file. First, click Styles.css in the Solution Explorer (Figure 4.2). Next, go to the VS.NET's Style menu and choose Build Style. This will invoke the environment's Style Builder, which allows you to set the properties of the Cascading Style Sheet. Set the background color to purple as depicted in Figure 4.3.

Click OK, and you will notice that the contents of Styles.css will change to reflect the new color (i.e., there is a new line in the file that reads: background-color: purple).

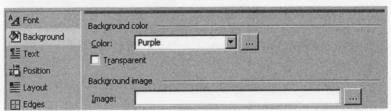

Figure 4.3   VS.NET's style builder

Next, you must associate WebForm1.aspx with the Style Sheet. Click WebForm1.aspx in the Solution Explorer and then go to Format → Document Styles, which will invoke the Document Styles window. Right-click WebForm1.aspx in this window and choose Add Style Link. This will bring up a list of the CSS files within the project. Choose Styles.css and click OK. Run the application by pressing F5, and the Web Form background will appear purple. If you change the background color in Styles.css using the Style Builder, the Web Form will change accordingly. You could apply this relationship to all Web Forms in the project such that they derived their design characteristics (background color, fonts, etc.) from a single CSS file. In so doing, the design parameters of the entire application are located in a single file, which can be easily modified.

This is merely a demonstration of the power of Cascading Style Sheets. For more information on CSS and ASP.NET, see ⌐CN⌐AS040003.

Frames

Frames allow you to divide the client's browser window into independent subwindows, each with their own characteristics and own sets of scrollbars. Each window can also be made resizable, so that users can customize the size of the Frames. With VS.NET, it is possible to utilize Frames such that each subwindow displays a different Web Form in the project. This requires adding a Frameset entity to the web application and configuring it appropriately. We detail this procedure at ⌐CN⌐AS040008. Although Frames can result in very slick designs, they have some definite drawbacks, such as limitations with bookmarks, searching, and printing. For a more involved discussion on Frames see *CodeNotes for Web-Based UI* or ⌐CN⌐AS040004.

User Controls

One of the biggest challenges in web development is the sharing of code between multiple pages. In traditional ASP this was accomplished by means of the server-side include (which is still usable in ASP.NET). A server-side include (discussed in the previous Global.asax explanation) simply "pastes" the contents of an external file into the target file. Often, this technique results in cumbersome and unwieldy code and leads to such problems as name collisions, nested include-file complexity, etc.

A power alternative to server-side includes in ASP.NET are the User Controls. A User Control allows you to group overlapping functionality into one file (with an .ascx extension), which can then be included in those pages that you designate. For example, if there is a company header that must be on every page in the project, you can place it within the auspices of a User Control and simply include the control in the desired forms.

Because a User Control is logically isolated from the rest of the project, problems that arise with server-side includes are eliminated. Furthermore, User Controls offer some capabilities not afforded by server-side includes, such as the ability to be dynamically loaded and expose properties. For more information on User Controls, see oᶜᴺⱽAS040005.

SUMMARY

VS.NET performs many tasks that must be manually carried out whenever you develop web applications outside its environment. In addition to creating an IIS virtual directory for a web application, VS.NET gives the web application two important files that are used for configuration and administration: Global.asax, which houses shared code for the project and application-level events, and web.config, which exposes the project's configuration settings.

Visual Studio also serves as a mature tool for web page design. In addition to the Web Form Designer (WFD) that converts your drag-and-drop actions into code, VS.NET allows you to incorporate popular web technologies into your web-based applications such as Cascading Style Sheets, Frames, and client-side code.

Topic: The Web Form Paradigm

As we have seen thus far, ASP.NET revamps many aspects of web development. Perhaps the most noteworthy innovation is its new Web Form paradigm, which forces developers to rethink the way web-based applications are written. In this topic we examine the new design methodology in ASP.NET by contrasting it with the techniques that you employed in traditional ASP. As we will see in this topic, to facilitate a design paradigm comparable to VB6, the Framework simply utilizes and abstracts many popular web technologies with which you may already be familiar.

CONCEPTS

HTTP

The Internet is data-centric—to obtain information, you usually have to provide it. To perform an Internet search, for example, you must provide the subject of the search. In HTTP, this information is communicated as name-value pairs—the name of the variable being sent (in our case it might be SearchSubject) and the contents of the variable (which might be *CodeNotes*). HTTP defines two procedures for transmitting data over the Internet, namely HTTP GET and HTTP POST. The difference between these two protocols lies in the way these name-value pairs are transported.

An HTTP message consists of two parts, a header and an optional message body. The header consists of information such as the HTTP protocol being used (GET or POST), the URL of the requested resource, etc. The HTTP body contains the actual information being transmitted, which, for a web request, would consist of the page's HTML code.

HTTP GET

In an HTTP GET request, name-value pairs are transmitted as part of the URL request itself. If you were to perform a search for *CodeNotes* on the popular *Google* Internet search site, for example, the address on your browser would look similiar to the following:

```
http://www.google.com/search?q=CodeNotes
```

Listing 4.5   A GET request

Notice the name-value pair in the URL above (sometimes called a QueryString value). "q" represents the name of the variable, which possibly stands for query. The value associated with "q" is our search string, "CodeNotes." HTTP GET requests are formed in the above format by appending name-value pairs to the URL request, a process commonly referred to as URL encoding.

HTTP POST

Similar to GET, HTTP POST sends name-value pairs to a destination on the Internet. The difference is that name-value pairs are not appended to the destination URL, but are instead embedded in the HTTP message body. When you fill out a customer-information form online, such as your name and credit card number, POST is often used instead of GET. By using POST, transmitted data is packaged in the message body and does not appear in the URL, affording a greater amount of security.

As we will see in this topic, the Web Form paradigm is almost exclusivley based on the POST mechanism (although you can still use GET if you wish).

Design in Traditional ASP

The primary purpose of an interactive web application is data exchange. Most often, a user submits information to the Web Server (perhaps the

subject of a search), which is utilized by the application to produce a
client response (the results of the search). The two primary ways of designing web pages in traditional ASP are based on the different HTTP
protocols—GET and POST. Consider the ASP timer application we developed in Chapter 1 (Figure 4.4).

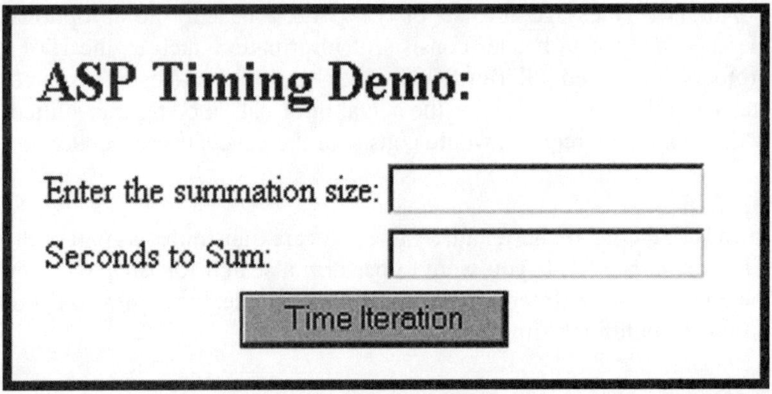

ASP Timing Demo:

Enter the summation size: [   ]

Seconds to Sum: [   ]

[Time Iteration]

Figure 4.4   Timer.ASP

Think of the application in Figure 4.4 as a contract—when given the
summation size by the user, the program reports the duration of the
computation. In order for this exchange to occur, the user's information
(the summation size) must be transmitted to the Web Server.

Timer Using HTTP GET
The first way of designing this application is to use GET to redirect the
user to another web page that actually performs the computation. For
example, when the user clicks the Time Iteration button in Figure 4.4,
we would direct the request to a second web page named Computer.asp:

```
http://localhost/aspTest/Computer.asp?SumSize=100000
```

Listing 4.6   The GET request to Timer.asp

As expected, information in an HTTP GET is transmitted as a part of
the URL itself. Computer.asp would extract this information (SumSize)
using the Request.QueryString() method exposed in ASP. We will not
reproduce the GET code here (you can find it online at ⌐AS040006),
but we can make two general observations about the GET method:

 • GET can be limiting when you need to pass a lot of information
   to the Web Server. If, for example, you need to pass an array of

one thousand numbers, each number must be appended to the URL. Although the HTTP specification does not restrict the length of a URL, many Web Servers and browsers place practical limits on its length.

• GET is also undesirable when sensitive information is being transmitted (a credit card number, for example). Appending confidential data to the URL is unacceptable since it can be easily intercepted and exploited.

Timer Using HTTP POST

The second technique to design the timer application—the one we employed in the first chapter—is to use a POST. Whereas GET simply redirects the user to another page (with information appended to the URL), POST redirects the user to another page but also transmits all the page information (the textbox values in Figure 1.3) along with the request. In other words, a POST request persists information from one page to another, where with a GET, you must manually append any information that you wish to retain onto the URL.

The POSTBACK Mechanism

A common technique in traditional ASP (and, as we will see, in ASP.NET) is to POST to the page itself. That is, when the user clicks the `Time Iteration` button in Figure 4.4, instead of posting to another page such as Computer.asp, we POST to Timer.asp. Recall from Listing 1.2:

```
<FORM NAME="timerForm" ACTION="Timer.asp" METHOD="post">
```

Listing 4.7   The Timer POST action

The concept of a self POST (often referred to as a POSTBACK) may seem complex but it is really quite simple:

1. The first time Timer.asp is requested there is no page information (e.g., textbox values, form values, hidden fields, etc.) that accompany the request.
2. When the user clicks the Time Iteration button, Timer.asp is requested a second time from the Web Server. However, the second request is accompanied with page information, such as the values of the textboxes in Figure 4.1.

When employing the POSTBACK technique in traditional ASP, you must manually write code to differentiate between these two types of requests. In the timer application in Chapter 1, this was accomplished by testing for the presence of a Form variable at the beginning of the script:

```
If Request.Form("num") <> "" then
  // page is being request on a POSTBACK.
  // process user information...
Else
  // page is being request for the first time
  // perform any initialization...
End if
```

Listing 4.8   Determining a POSTBACK

Listing 4.8 (which was extracted from Listing 1.2) determines if the page is being requested on a POSTBACK by testing for the presence of the Form variable num in the incoming request. If the variable is not empty, then we know that the request is a POSTBACK and we can perform the computation; if the variable is empty, then the page is being requested for the first time.

For complex ASP pages that POST to themselves, code can often become convoluted, unwieldy, and difficult to debug. Nevertheless, in traditional ASP, POST is often used to submit a large amount of information to the Web Server. Thankfully, although the POST tradition continues in ASP.NET, its accompanying complexities have been abstracted by the Framework.

Design in ASP.NET–Objects and Events

ASP.NET is almost exclusively based on the object-event model that popularized Visual Basic. As we saw in Chapter 3, every entity in ASP.NET—a button, a textbox, even a web page itself—is really a class in the BCL. An object is simply an instance of a class. Thus, when a Web Form is accessed for the first time, ASP.NET instantiates all the classes that represent the entities within the page.

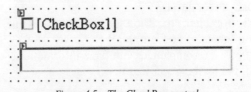

Figure 4.5   The CheckBox control

As we saw in the previous chapters, manipulating the appearance of a Web Form does not require the HTML trickery that it did in classical ASP, but rather involves the manipulation of objects (e.g., to change a control's color use its `BackColor` property). Similarly, to respond to an event such as the click of a button, you don't worry about POST or GETs, but simply write code behind the object's event handler (such as `Button1_Click`). For example, drag a `CheckBox` control onto a Web Form as in Figure 4.5.

Next, double-click the `CheckBox` and insert the highlighted lines in Listing 4.9 into the project.

```
Private Sub CheckBox1_CheckedChanged(...)
  TextBox1.Text = "Status of Checkbox:"& _
    CheckBox1.Checked
End Sub
```

Listing 4.9   Responding to a checkbox click

Before running the application, change `CheckBox1`'s `AutoPostBack` property to `True` using the Property Inspector (we'll examine the role of this property in the following section). Run the application by pressing F5, and every time you click the checkbox the code in Listing 4.4 will execute and alter the textbox's contents. Such simplicity is in stark contrast to traditional ASP, which would require considerably more lines of code for equivalent functionality.

POSTBACK in ASP.NET
Underneath the hood, ASP.NET utilizes the POSTBACK technique we examined in the previous section. That is, when the user performs an action that warrants the execution of server-side code, the Web Form POSTs back to itself to run the code. If you examine the HTML source that ASP.NET produces for a Web Form, you will find the following line that results in the POSTBACK:

```
<form name="Form1" method="post" action="WebForm1.aspx"
id="Form1">
```

Listing 4.10   HTML source for the ASP.NET form

Remember that all the page information is also included with the POSTBACK request. For an ASP.NET Web Form, this information includes:

- The hidden `VIEWSTATE` field we saw in Chapter 1, which maintains the state of the page's Web Controls. We'll examine this field in greater depth in the next chapter.
- The contents of the page's Web Controls, such as `TextBox` and `ListBox` values.

• Other boilerplate information that ASP.NET embeds in the request, such as hidden EVENTTARGET and EVENTARGUMENT fields, which we will examine shortly.

All of this information is utilized by ASP.NET to facilitate its object programming model on the server. For example, as we will see in the next chapter, it is the VIEWSTATE field that allows a Web Control's appearance to be easily manipulated through intuitive properties such as BackColor.

The AutoPostBack Property

By default, only a few Web Controls (such as a button) automatically trigger a page POSTBACK. This behavior is determined through a control's AutoPostBack property, which, when set to True, forces ASP.NET to perform a POSTBACK when the control is modified. Set this property to True for the textbox in Figure 4.5, and then add the code in Listing 4.11 to the project. This code is triggered when the contents of the textbox change.

```
Private Sub TextBox1_TextChanged(...)
   TextBox1.Text = TextBox1.Text.Length
End Sub
```

Listing 4.11   The TextBox_TextChanged() event

Run the application, and enter something into the TextBox (such as "Hello"). Next, tab off the control such that it loses focus, and the page will POSTBACK to the server. The code in Listing 4.11 will execute and the contents of the TextBox will change to report the length of the string you entered (5, in our case).

Those familiar with web development may wonder how ASP.NET determines which control triggered the POSTBACK. For example, in Figure 4.5, both the CheckBox control and the TextBox are capable of posting back to the server (because we changed both AutoPostBack properties to True). How does ASP.NET figure out "who did it"?

If you examine the HTML source that ASP.NET generates for the web page in Figure 4.5, you will find two hidden HTML fields that ASP.NET employs for this purpose—EVENTTARGET and EVENTARGUMENT. Their internal use is beyond the scope of this book; for a more involved examination see ⌥AS040007.

It should be apparent why the POSTBACK architecture is employed by ASP.NET—among other things, it allows the Framework to utilize hidden fields such as VIEWSTATE and EVENTTARGET, which facilitate the intuitive object model that we have illustrated.

POSTBACK and the Page Class

As we established in Chapter 3, a Web Form is programmatically abstracted through the Page class. One of the most useful properties exposed by this class is IsPostBack, which allows you to determine if a Web Form is posting back to itself or is being requested for the first time. Differentiating between these two scenarios is important because oftentimes you will perform an expensive operation upon an initial request, which you want to avoid on a POSTBACK. Consider the sorting application that we developed in Chapter 3.

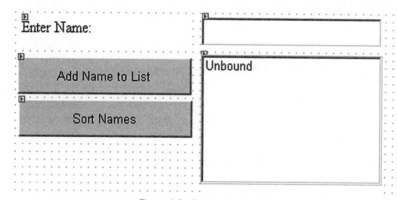

Figure 4.6   Sorting application

When the application is first requested, you may place code within the Page_Load() event to read a database (using ADO or ADO.NET) and populate the listbox. However, you may not want to perform the database query when the Web Form POSTs back to itself (if the user clicked Sort Names, for example). The IsPostBack method permits exactly this type of behavior, as illustrated in Listing 4.12.

```
Private Sub Page_Load(...)
  If Page.IsPostBack Then
    'no database query
  Else
    'populate Listbox from database
  End If
End Sub
```

Listing 4.12   The IsPostBack property

Listing 4.12 is the ASP.NET equivalent of the traditional ASP code in Listing 4.8 (i.e., it detects the presence of a POSTBACK). As a result of this code, the listbox will only be populated when the page is first requested. Thereafter, the database query will not be performed, thus decreasing response time.

Page Properties and Methods

The Page class exposes numerous properties and methods that allow you to control the behavior and appearance of a Web Form. For example, the Trace property toggles the display of the ASP.NET tracing options we will discuss in Chapter 6, whereas the isValid property is used in conjunction with the Validation controls we will examine in Chapter 5. Some other useful entities that are exposed through this class are the intrinsic objects that you used in traditional ASP.

Intrinsic Objects (Response, Request, etc.)
Throughout this book we have used the Response object to write output to the browser:

```
Response.Write("Hello")
```

Listing 4.13   The Response object

Behind the scenes ASP.NET translates this line into:

```
Page.Response.Write("Hello")
```

Listing 4.14   Fully qualified Response object

As can be seen, the intrinsic objects that you used in traditional ASP are accessed through the Page class in the ASP.NET—the Framework simply provides a syntactical shortcut to maintain capability with older ASP scripts. Although they are accessed in the same fashion, the intrinsic objects in ASP.NET have evolved from their ASP counterparts. Some of the methods/properties exposed by these objects have changed, whereas new methods and properties have been added altogether. For example, the Request object now exposes a property named Browser that allows you to easily ascertain the capabilities of the client's browser. Similarly, the Response object exposes a new Filter property, which can be used to filter the outgoing information that ASP.NET sends to a client. For information on these properties, as well as additional new characteristics of intrinsic objects in ASP.NET, see ⌐AS090004.

ASP.NET Development Is Desktop Development

When writing applications in ASP.NET, it helps to think increasingly in terms of traditional desktop development. For example, to toggle the visibility of graphic elements in classical ASP you must pepper the script file with conditional statements similar to Listing 4.2. In ASP.NET, this is accomplished as it is in VB6: by modifying a control's `Visible` property. Behind the scenes, the Framework alters the generated HTML appropriately.

We will see this theme throughout this book. In essence, development in ASP.NET is VB6 desktop development for the web with some additional considerations to account for the architecture of HTTP and other web-related technologies.

SUMMARY

ASP.NET is architecturally based on the HTTP POSTBACK mechanism whereby Web Forms POST to themselves to trigger application events such as the click of a button or the modification of a `TextBox`. The POST architecture is appropriate for ASP.NET because a POST maintains page information such as control values and hidden fields in between server requests. This information is used internally by ASP.NET to facilitate its intuitive object model that you program against.

You can detect if a Web Form is POSTing back to itself using the `Page.isPostBack` property. This property allows you to perform specific operations only when the Web Form is initially requested, allowing you to reduce response time when the page POSTs back thereafter.

Chapter Summary

Visual Studio.NET is Microsoft's new development environment for the .NET Framework. Although the command line compilers that ship with the Framework allow you to write ASP.NET applications outside the environment, the virtues of Microsoft's new web technology are most realized when using this latest version of Visual Studio.

In addition to performing the necessary IIS plumbing when you create a web project within its environment, VS.NET encapsulates all aspects of the application within the confines of a single project: design (.the aspx file), logic (the CodeBehind file), shared code (Global.asax), and configuration (web.config). This not only simplifies management; as we will see in later chapters, it allows you to easily toggle application settings such as tracing and security.

ASP.NET is based on a Web Form paradigm whereby an application consists of a collection of forms, each of which, in turn, houses a collection of Web Controls. This design framework mirrors traditional desktop development in VB6. The Web Form paradigm, coupled with the ease at which VS.NET allows you to employ it, makes rapidly producing ASP.NET web applications a reality.

Chapter 5

—

WEB CONTROLS AND WINDOWS FORMS

Web Controls are one of the primary technologies behind ASP.NET's intuitive design process. Accessed in an object-oriented fashion, they expose properties, methods, and events that you programmatically manipulate. The ASP.NET Runtime renders them as browser-appropriate HTML on the client, in accordance with the characteristics you prescribe.

An ASP.NET application is, to a large extent, a construction of interacting Web Controls. As in VB6, the quality and sophistication of an application hinges significantly upon how well you utilize the graphical entities at your disposal. There are over sixty Web Controls in the Framework, so for complete listings and descriptions you can consult the MSDN. The goal of this chapter will be to examine ASP.NET's Web Control architecture and some of the more interesting controls in the platform.

The .NET Framework allows you to extend its architecture by writing custom Web Controls that other web developers can use. This is a more advanced aspect of ASP.NET and requires knowledge of HTTP and HTML. If you decide to write custom Web Controls, you must familiarize yourself with concepts such as StateBags, rendering, templates, and so on. Information on custom Web Controls can be found at ᴼᶜᴺ⟩AS050001. In addition, a large assortment of Web Controls have been developed by both Microsoft and other vendors, which go beyond the capabilities of the standard set that ships with ASP.NET. For information on prewritten Web Controls such as these, see ᴼᶜᴺ⟩AS050016.

Web Controls run entirely on the server. The last topic in this chapter considers entities that run on the client: ActiveX controls and Windows Forms, the .NET Framework's alternative to ActiveX controls. Like an ActiveX control, a Windows Form control is an executable entity that runs within the browser. Unlike ActiveX controls, Windows Form controls are managed by the CLR and eliminate many of the deployment and security headaches of their predecessors.

CORE CONCEPTS

Control Confusion

The terminology associated with Web Controls can be confusing. You will often hear the terms *Web Control, Server Control,* and *Web Form control* used interchangeably. Because Web Controls are first processed on the server by the ASP.NET Runtime, they are sometimes referred to as Server Controls. What is confusing (and sometimes obscured by the documentation) is that Web Controls actually encompass two different sets of controls:

1. Web Form controls—Up to this point, all of the controls we have been using are Web Form controls. These controls emulate the rich object model of controls found in VB6 and expose properties and events such as Width, BackColor, and Button1_Click. The important point with respect to these controls is that, often, they don't have direct mappings to HTML elements. For example, there is no intrinsic HTML calendar element. Thus, the Calendar Web Form control must be reproduced on the client as a combination of HTML tables and JavaScript. Most of the controls you will use in ASP.NET will be of the Web Form type.
2. HTML Server controls—Like Web Forms controls, HTML Server controls are run on the server before they are rendered on the client. The difference is that these controls map directly to simple HTML elements and are manipulated in accordance with the conventions of HTML. This means that:
   • HTML Server controls are not as rich as their Web Form counterparts.
   • Using HTML Server controls requires some familiarity with HTML.

The differences between these two types of controls are best illustrated by example.

A third family of Web Controls, called Mobile controls, allows you to write ASP.NET applications that target mobile devices. More information on Mobile controls can be found at ⚓AS050002.

EXAMPLE–TWO TYPES OF CONTROLS

To contrast the differences between the two control types, we will write a simple web application that changes the appearance of two textboxes. Create a new web application in VS.NET named ChangeColor, using VB.NET as the base language.

Visual Studio.NET places Web Form controls and HTML Server controls on different panes in its toolbox. Usually, the Web Forms tab is expanded; however, you can use HTML Server controls by clicking the HTML tab in Figure 5.1.

Figure 5.1   VS.NET's toolbox

Using the Web Forms toolbox, drag two buttons and a textbox onto the page. Next, expand the HTML pane and place an HTML Text Field onto the page. Change the control captions to reflect the application depicted in Figure 5.2.

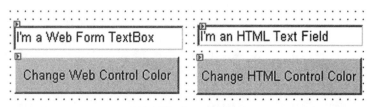

Figure 5.2   Control example

You will notice several differences between the Web Form Textbox and the HTML Text Field. First, the HTML control cannot be resized vertically as can the Web Form control. This constraint exists because of the intrinsic limitations of HTML, namely that text fields cannot be multiline (remember that HTML controls map directly to HTML elements and are thus subject to their limitations). Second, to change the Text Field's caption, you do not modify its Text property (it has no Text property), but instead modify its Value property (because in HTML, captions are specified using Value). Third, if you attempt to click the HTML control so as to attach event code to it, VS.NET will inform you that:

```
To write server-based code for this element, it must be
converted to an HTML server control. Right-click the
element and choose Run As Server Control.
```

Listing 5.1   Converting an HTML control

In fact, the text field you dragged onto the page is not even a Server control, but a regular client-side HTML element. In order to convert it into a server-side control, you must do as VS.NET suggests, and right-click the element and select Run as Server Control. If you perform this conversion and then examine the underlying code in the .aspx file (by clicking the HTML tab in Figure 1.6), you will find the following two lines:

```
<asp:TextBox id="TextBox1" runat="server"...>
  I'm a Web Form Control</asp:TextBox>
<INPUT id="Text1" type="text" name="Text1"
  value="I'm an HTML Control" runat="server">
```

Listing 5.2   The control code

As we learned in the timer example in Chapter 1, Web Form controls are denoted via the asp prefix. The HTML Server control, however, is signified by means of a regular HTML <INPUT> tag. For those unfamiliar with HTML, <INPUT> tags specify elements that accept user input, such as buttons, textboxes, password fields, etc. Were it not for the highlighted runat="server" attribute, the second line of code would be identical to regular client-side HTML. In other words, an HTML Server control is declared as if it were a standard HTML entity, with an additional attribute that informs ASP.NET to first process it on the server. As we will see in a moment, this tag allows you manipulate the control from server-side code (the CodeBehind file).

Changing Control Properties
At the beginning of this example we sought to write an application that would change the appearance of the textboxes. From the VS.NET design

environment, click one of the application's buttons, which will bring up the project's CodeBehind file. Recall from our discussion of the Base Class Libraries (Chapter 3) that Web Controls really map to classes found in the BCL. Thus, the CodeBehind file contains the following declarations:

```
Protected WithEvents TextBox1 As _
  System.Web.UI.WebControls.TextBox
Protected WithEvents Text1 As _
  System.Web.UI.HtmlControls.HtmlInputText
```

Listing 5.3   Control definitions

As discussed in Chapter 3, Web Controls in the design file (the .aspx file) map to CodeBehind classes found in the System.Web.UI .WebControls namespace. Similarly, HTML Server controls, such as the text field, map to classes found in System.Web.UI.HtmlControls.

You can programmatically manipulate either of these classes in the CodeBehind file to affect their appearance in the client. The important point is that whereas Web Form controls expose intuitive properties such as BackColor and Text, HTML Server controls expose properties akin to those found in regular HTML. The difference is illustrated in the following code, which changes the background color of each textbox to dark blue when the application's buttons are clicked.

```
Private Sub Button1_Click(...) Handles Button1.Click
    'Change the color of the Web Form Textbox,
    'Very straighforward:
    TextBox1.BackColor = Color.DarkBlue
End Sub

Private Sub Button2_Click(...) Handles Button2.Click
    'Change the color of the HTML Text Field.
    'Not so intuitive
    Text1.Attributes.Add("style", _
      "background-color=#000080")
End Sub
```

Listing 5.4   Changing control backgrounds

Both button event handlers in Listing 5.4 change the colors of their respective textboxes. As you can see, however, the Web Form code is much more intuitive. Web Form controls expose a property called BackColor, which, as expected, is used to change the control's background color. To manipulate an HTML Server control, on the other hand, you must use the `Attributes` collection it exposes. In HTML, the characteristics of an element are specified by means of attributes within the `<input>` tag:

```
<input name="Text1" type="text" value="Control caption"
style="background-color..."/>
```

Listing 5.5   Changing HTML backgrounds

For example, the `value` attribute is used to specify a control's caption, whereas the `style` attribute is used to specify its appearance on the screen (location, color, etc.). Thus, to change the `Text` field's color, we have to add a `style` element to its `Attributes` collection. This collection maps directly to the generated HTML client code, thus changing the control's color in the browser.

SUMMARY

The inescapable conclusion of this example is that, in order to use HTML Server controls, you must be well versed in the details of HTML—something that ASP.NET promised to abolish. Furthermore, it seems redundant and counterproductive to have two sets of controls that accomplish essentially the same thing.

As we will see, each family of controls has its respective advantages. In general, you will almost always want to use Web Form controls because of the abstraction they offer and the rich event models they expose. HTML Server controls are useful in migration scenarios such as converting a web page developed in Microsoft FrontPage to ASP.NET. Additionally, these controls offer some capabilities not found with Web Forms (see the HTML Server control topic in this chapter for details).

Topic: A Survey of Web Form Controls

Space constraints do not permit us to list the capabilities and nuances of every control in the ASP.NET Framework. In large part, your understanding of these controls will come through experience. For full details on each control, you can consult the MSDN. However, to give you an idea of the diversity and power of ASP.NET, this topic is dedicated to a brief discussion of some of the more important controls that you are likely to utilize. Some of these controls will be illustrated in subsequent examples in this book.

CONCEPTS

Basic Controls

The following controls should be self-explanatory, as they map directly to common HTML elements: HyperLink, LinkButton, Image, Panel, Label, Button, TextBox, CheckBox, RadioButton, ImageButton, Table, TableRow, TableCell.

Remember that although these entities have direct HTML equivalents, they are Web Controls that abstract HTML specifics through intuitive properties. For example, you can set a textbox's TextMode property to Password, such that the user's keystrokes appear as asterisks when they type. Behind the scenes, the Web Control creates an HTML <input> element with an attribute of type="password".

Data Controls

Both the DataGrid and DataList controls are used in conjunction with the ADO.NET classes. Basically, these controls allow you to display and format data retrieved from a database. An important property exposed by these controls is DataSource, which specifies the underlying data store used to populate the control. The DataGrid control in particular, allows you to display the results of database queries in a sophisticated manner. For more information on these controls, see ⌐^{CN}AS050015.

List Controls

As suggested by their names, the following controls allow the selection of an element within a list: CheckBoxList, DropDownList, ListBox, RadioButtonList. An important property exposed by these controls is AutoPostBack, which determines whether the application POSTs back to the server automatically whenever an item in the list is selected. By default, this property is set to False. If you set it to True, then ASP.NET will generate client-side JavaScript that POSTs back to the server as soon as an item in the list has been selected.

AutoPostBack is useful when the selection of an item might change the rest of the page. For example, a DropDownList may expose a number of options that determine the way a page renders (e.g., Frames or no Frames). Using this property, you could update the page immediately when the user made his or her selection.

Like data controls, list controls can also derive their contents from a DataSource property.

Validation Controls

The following controls are dedicated to validating user input: RequiredFieldValidator, CompareValidator, RangeValidator,

RegularExpressionValidator, CustomValidator. As we will see in the
Validation topic later in this chapter, these controls are capable of validating user input on the client (through JavaScript) if the browser supports it, or on the server if the browser is less capable.

Miscellaneous Controls
The following controls don't map directly to HTML or other common
components, but may be very useful.

AdRotator—This control is similar to the AdRotator component
that was packaged with ASP. As in ASP, this control can be used
to rotate banners (images) on the top of your page (usually for
advertising purposes). This latest incarnation of AdRotator contains a couple of extras, such as the ability to filter content
through its KeyWordFilter property and the ability to configure itself based on an XML configuration file (using the
AdvertisementFile property).

Calendar—This powerful control allows the user to select a date
from a graphical calendar. If you add this control to a web project and then examine the underlying client-side code that
ASP.NET generates, you'll see that the Framework produces a
lot of HTML and JavaScript to re-create the calendar in the
browser. The Calendar control exposes various properties that
determine how it is rendered. For example, the ShowNextPrev
Month property determines whether the user can scroll to other
months.

≤	December 2001					≥
Sun	Mon	Tue	Wed	Thu	Fri	Sat
25	26	27	28	29	30	1
2	3	4	5	6	7	8
9	10	11	12	13	14	15
16	17	18	19	20	21	22
23	24	25	26	27	28	29
30	31	1	2	3	4	5

Figure 5.3   The Calendar control

An example using the Calendar control can be found at o^{CN}⇥AS050003.

XML—Increasingly, web developers are turning to XML as a means of representing data. The XML component allows you to embed an XML document directly into an ASP.NET page. This is, in itself, a powerful capability, but the XML component goes further. An important XML technology called XSLT (eXtensible Stylesheet Language Transformations) allows you to translate XML into HTML. In addition to accepting an XML file through its DocumentSource property, the XML component also exposes a property called TransformSource. This optional property points to an XSLT file, which prescribes how the XML document translates into HTML such that it can be displayed in the browser. This is an extremely useful component, which can result in very sophisticated ASP.NET pages. An example of this component working with XML and XSLT files can be found at o^{CN}⇥AS050004.

Extending Web Controls

Remember that all the controls discussed in this topic are really classes found in the System.Web.UI.WebControls namespace. Thus it is possible to create your own specialized versions of these controls by writing classes that extend the base classes in the BCL. By doing so, you can override the default behavior of a control where desired and inherit the functionality with which you are satisfied. For example, if you are unsatisfied with the way the Calendar control renders on a particular browser (e.g., Netscape 6), you can write your own custom Calendar that provides its own implementation for Netscape, but falls back to the default behavior for other browsers.

SUMMARY

As you experiment with the different Web Controls, you will see that some are almost identical to basic HTML, whereas others provide significant value in terms of the amount of boilerplate functionality that is automatically coded for you. Web Controls, combined with the drag-and-drop-form generation, make ASP.NET a powerful platform for rapid application development. You don't have to spend the time on routine code (such as validating a textbox) because ASP.NET will take care of it for you. Simply adjust a few settings and the necessary HTML and JavaScript will automatically appear.

Topic: Web Control Architecture (EnableViewState)

The primary function of a Web Control is abstraction. As we saw in this chapter's first example, rather than changing a Web Control's background color using HTML attributes, we used its BackColor property. Because all Web Controls derive from the base class System.Web.UI.WebControls .WebControl, they expose a common set of properties and methods. As you dive into the world of Web Controls, you will discover that these properties can significantly influence appearance, behavior, and performance.

For example, the AccessKey property allows a user to quickly place focus on a control via a keyboard shortcut (e.g., ALT-X), whereas the CssClass property is used to associate the control with a Cascading Style Sheets (CSS) class in order to affect its appearance. The full list of Web Control properties (and samples illustrating them) can be found in the MSDN—most of them are very easy to use. In this topic we consider the most important Web Control property from a performance and architectural perspective: EnableViewState.

CONCEPTS

The VIEWSTATE Field

Consider the application we developed in the Base Class Library topic in Chapter 3.

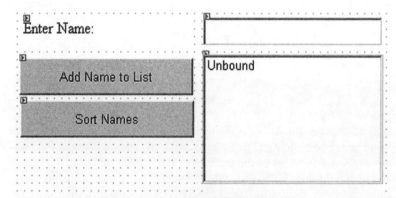

Figure 5.4   Sorting example from Chapter 3

The primary control in this example was the ListBox, which allowed us to add elements to it. Run the application, add a couple of names to the ListBox, and then examine the client-side code that was generated by going to View→Source in your browser. As expected, the ListBox control manifests itself as regular HTML on the client:

```
<select name="ListBox1" id="ListBox1" ...">
  <option value="Jessica">Jessica</option>
  <option value="Deborah">Deborah</option>
  <option value="Sajid">Sajid</option>
</select>
```

Listing 5.6   The ListBox's underlying HTML

Next, examine the server-side code that sorts the ListBox when the user clicks the Sort Names button:

```
Dim aList As New ArrayList()
Dim k As Integer

'Read the items of the ListBox into the array:
For k = 0 To ListBox1.Items.Count() - 1
  aList.Add(ListBox1.Items(k).ToString)
Next

'Sort the array and repopulate the Listbox:
aList.Sort()
ListBox1.Items.Clear()

For k = 0 To aList.Count() - 1
  ListBox1.Items.Add(aList.Item(k))
Next
```

Listing 5.7   Code to sort the ListBox

Consider this example carefully, and you may realize that there appear to be two conflicting representations of the ListBox. On the client, the ListBox is plain HTML, as represented by the <select> and <option> tags. On the server, it is a regular object and exposes properties such as Count(), Add(), and Remove(). This dual identity is, of course, one of the primary virtues of ASP.NET. But how exactly does the Framework transition between these two very different worlds? In other words, how does ASP.NET take the contents of the HTML in Listing 5.6 (the names you entered) and make them programmatically accessible to the code in Listing 5.7?

The path that the developers at Microsoft chose to take was to encode a control's state (its appearance, contents, etc.) into a hidden HTML field called VIEWSTATE. If you examine the client source again, you will find a line similar to the following:

```
<input type="hidden" name="__VIEWSTATE"
value="dDwtMTE5MTYyOTA1NjtOPDtsPGk8MT47PjtsPHQ8O2w8aTwxP
js+O2w8dDxOPDtwPGw8aTwwPjtpPDE+O2k8Mj47PjtsPHA8SmVzc2ljY
TtKZXNzaWNhPjtwPER1Ym9yYWg7RGVib3JhaD47cDxTYWppZDtTYWppZ
D47Pj47Pjs7Pjs+Pjs+PjtsPExpc3RCb3gxOz4+"/>
```

Listing 5.8   The hidden VIEWSTATE field

This hidden field stores the state of *all* the controls on the page. Thus, in addition to storing the display characteristics of the ListBox, TextBox, and Button controls, it also contains encoded representations of the names you entered (in our case, Jessica, Deborah, and Sajid). When you click the Sort Names button, the ASP.NET Runtime parses this hidden field and extracts the ListBox's contents so that they can be sorted. As one might expect, the size of the hidden field is proportional to the amount of information it must store; the more names you add to the ListBox, the greater the size of the VIEWSTATE.

Notes on Viewstate

Although ASP.NET's use of the VIEWSTATE field may seem like an internal implementation detail of the Framework, it can tangibly influence the performance of your applications. In this example, every time the server must update the page, the contents of the listbox are sent to the client twice; first, as regular HTML (Listing 5.6), and then as encoded values in the VIEWSTATE field (Listing 5.8). If an application has many controls that contain a lot of information, this hidden field can grow to sizable proportions. Because this field is transmitted as part of ASP.NET's response to a client, it can adversely affect transmission time.

Remember that the purpose of the VIEWSTATE is to make the properties of a Web Control accessible when the user POSTs back to the server. In other words, it is only required when a control must maintain state (i.e., remember its values) in between client requests. Such functionality is not always required. For example, the ListBox in Figure 5.4 might be part of a read-only report. Since the user cannot modify the ListBox and send it back to the server, there is no need to keep its information in the VIEWSTATE field.

In such situations, you can make a control "stateless" by setting its EnableViewState property to False (using the Property Inspector). As a result, ASP.NET will not store the control's contents in the VIEWSTATE field. Apply this property change to the ListBox in Figure 5.4, and two aspects of the application will change:

1. The size of the VIEWSTATE will be considerably smaller.
2. Even though the underlying code hasn't changed, the ListBox will only maintain *one* name. Setting EnableViewState to False turns it into a "stateless" object—it has no memory of previous events. Every time you click Add Name to List (and thus POST back to the server), the ListBox starts with an empty slate.

Although it is inappropriate for this application, you can disable VIEWSTATE for those controls that do not have to maintain state, and thus reduce the amount of information transmitted between the client and server. Setting this property to False also changes the manner in which the control is declared in the design (.aspx) file:

```
<asp:ListBox id="ListBox1" EnableViewState="False" ...>
</asp:ListBox>
```

Listing 5.9   Disabling viewstate

Alternatively, you can disable VIEWSTATE for the entire page by placing the EnableViewState="False" attribute in the Page directive we examined in Chapter 3. All the controls in the Page will then be stateless.

Templates

Before we leave the topic of Web Controls, one aspect of the architecture you should be aware of are control templates. Templates allow developers to override certain aspects of a control's visual appearance. For example, you can customize how a column appears in a DataGrid control by providing it with a template that describes the column's graphical interface. Conversely, if you author your own Web Controls, you might have a control accept a template such that users can extend visual aspects of the control. For more information on templates, see ᵒ꜀ᴺ⁾AS050005.

HOW AND WHY

How Do I Determine the Size of the VIEWSTATE Field?

There are two ways to determine the size of the VIEWSTATE field. Programmatically, you can obtain its value using ASP.NET's Request object:

```
size = Request("__VIEWSTATE").Length
```

Listing 5.10   Finding the size of the VIEWSTATE field

The other option is to use the Tracing techniques we will discuss in Chapter 6.

How Do I Store My Own Information in the Viewstate Field?

The `Page` class we examined in Chapter 4 exposes a property called `ViewState`, which allows you to store your own information in the hidden `VIEWSTATE` field. This capability will be discussed when we consider the concept of Session in Chapter 7.

SUMMARY

ASP.NET maintains the state of Web Controls through a client-side HTML field named `VIEWSTATE`. This hidden field is transmitted as part of ASP.NET's response to the client. Thus, the contents of a Web Control are transmitted to the client twice: as regular HTML, and as part of the `VIEWSTATE` field.

You can reduce the amount of information that is persisted to a client by setting a control's `EnableViewState` property to `False`. As a result, the control's contents will not be included in the `VIEWSTATE` field. The disadvantage of this setting is that the control will be stateless—it won't retain its contents between client requests.

Topic: Validation Controls

Validating user input has always been a prime concern for developers, and the web is no exception. Enterprise applications often confirm a user's credentials (age, e-mail address, password, etc.) before granting him or her access to certain resources. The code for such operations can reside in one of two places: on the browser, in the form of client-side JavaScript or VBScript; or on the server, in whatever language/technology the application is written in (ASP.NET/ASP, JSP, CGI, etc.).

ASP.NET's Validation controls give you the best of both worlds—they can generate either client-side or server-side code depending upon the browser's capabilities. Furthermore, these controls don't require you to write any code. Instead, they abstract common validation tasks, such as determining whether a control's value falls within a given range. You can configure these tasks using simple property settings and let ASP.NET take care of the specific code.

CONCEPTS

Control Types

There are six Validation controls that ship with the .NET Framework. These controls regulate other Web Controls in your application. For example, you could use one of the following Validation controls on a TextBox to ensure that the TextBox contents meet certain requirements (e.g., that the value is a phone number).

1. RequiredFieldValidator: Checks that a control contains a value when the user submits a form.
2. CompareValidator: Validates the contents of a control based on a comparison with some given value. A CompareValidator is very useful for comparing sets of data. For example, you can use a CompareValidator to ensure that a user enters a password the same way twice.
3. RangeValidator: Ensures that the control's value falls within a prescribed range.
4. RegularExpressionValidator: Validates the control's value against a given regular expression, such as a pattern for a phone number.
5. CustomValidator: Passes a control's value to a specified server-side validation function. A CustomValidator lets you implement complex logic that can't be achieved through a combination of other validators.
6. ValidationSummary: Contains the error information for all of the Validation controls on a page. Use this control when you want all of the errors to be accumulated in a single place rather than spread across the page.

Note that you can attach multiple Validation objects to one control. For example, you could apply both a RequiredFieldValdiator and RangeValidator to a TextBox to ensure that: (1) it contained some value and (2) the value was within a given range.

Control Properties

The following properties are common to each of the controls, except for ValidationSummary:

- controlToValidate—specifies which control a Validation control is validating.
- errorMessage—specifies the error message that is displayed when the contents of the control being checked are invalid.

- Display—used to specify the manner in which error messages are displayed (more on this in the upcoming example).

EXAMPLE

In this example we will use the CompareValidator control to perform a frequent operation in the web arena: validating a user's password. Although straightforward, this example will give you a basis for using more involved Validation controls, such as the RegularExpression Validator. After going through this example, you can consult the more complex validation example at ⁰ᶜᴺᵧ AS050006.

Create a new web application project in VS.NET (use VB.NET as the language) and drag Web Controls onto the page such that you have an application like the one in Figure 5.5 (change the control captions appropriately).

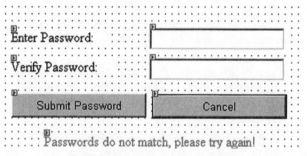

Figure 5.5   CompareValidator example

The one control that might be new to you is the CompareValidator. When you drag this control onto a page it looks like a regular Label, except that its text is red by default. Change the CompareValidator ErrorMessage property so that, like Figure 5.5, it reads, "Passwords do not match, please try again!"

As can be seen from Figure 5.5, we wish to verify that the user has entered the same password. To this end, set the Operator property of the CompareValidator to Equals. You can employ different validation logic by setting the Operator property to values such as NotEqual, GreaterThan, LessThan, etc.

Next, you must associate the CompareValidator with the control it will validate. CompareValidator exposes two properties to this effect:

1. ControlToValidate—the control to validate. Use the Property Inspector and set this to the second textbox (TextBox2).

2. ControlToCompare—the control to which to compare the target control. Set this property to the first textbox (TextBox1).

The function of the Validation control is very simple: When TextBox2 loses focus, CompareValidator compares its value with TextBox1. If they are not equal, then CompareValidator effectively becomes a label containing the text of the error message. As a result of the error message, the user can presumably correct the mistake (there is a little more to a Validation control, as we'll see).

Change the TextMode property of the two TextBox controls to password, run the application, and enter different values into each password field. The moment you scroll off the second textbox (such that it loses focus), the ControlToValidate error message will appear. In addition, if you try to click the Submit button in order to send invalid data to the server, nothing happens (the button is disabled). We will examine this behavior in a moment; but if you examine the client-side code for the application (View → Source using IE's menus), you will find that ASP.NET has automatically generated client-side JavaScript for us. Accordingly, all validation is performed in the browser—a round-trip to the server isn't necessary.

The CausesValidation Property

The preceding behavior (the disabling of both buttons due to an incorrect password) seems logical. After all, we don't want to waste time with a server round-trip each time the user has entered invalid data. Consider the Cancel button in Figure 5.5, however. It doesn't make sense that this button should also be disabled, as it presumably cancels the operation and sends the user to another page.

All Web Control buttons expose a property called CausesValidation, which allows you to determine whether the button validates the page when it is clicked. By default, this property is set to True. Thus, clicking either button when the page is invalid (i.e., if TextBox1 does not equal TextBox2) does not result in a POST to the server; rather, the button triggers the page's client-side JavaScript, which determines that invalid data is present and cancels the server request. When you set CausesValidation to False, however, the control does not trigger validation (it simply ignores all the Validation controls on the page). This setting would be appropriate for the Cancel button in Figure 5.5, as its underlying logic probably isn't concerned with the Validation controls on the page (it would probably just redirect the user to another page).

UpLevel and DownLevel Browsers

ASP.NET only generates client-side validation code if it detects that the user has an UpLevel browser. Recall from Chapter 1 that, as of this writing, UpLevel distinction is only given to Internet Explorer versions 4 and higher.

If you examine the application using a DownLevel browser (Netscape 4.0, for example), you will notice considerably different behavior. Specifically, all validation will be done on the server. Thus, if you give the application two different passwords, the error message won't be displayed until you explicitly click the Submit button. Furthermore, in the case of DownLevel validation, there is a little extra coding to do.

ServerSide Validation

Consider the event code that might be attached to the Submit button in Figure 5.5. Because the user is submitting his or her password, you would presumably check this information against a datastore (e.g., a database). In any case, if the application is running on an UpLevel browser, the server-side code is assured that the data is valid (the POST to the server wouldn't have occurred otherwise). In the case of a Down-Level browser, you must explicitly check that the page's data is valid by using its isValid property. Thus, the event code for the Submit button might look something like the following:

```
Private Sub Button3_Click(..,) Handles Button3.Click
  If Page.IsValid Then
    // passwords are equal, check database etc...
  End If
End Sub
```

Listing 5.11   Server-side validation code

In Listing 5.11 the button's event code will execute only if the page is valid (i.e., if the passwords are equal). If the page is not valid, then the event code will do nothing, and the user will receive the CompareValidator error message (when ASP.NET POSTs the page back to the client).

When using Validation controls it is a good idea to write server-side code that *always* checks if the page is valid. At first glance, this practice may seem unsuitable (and redundant) for UpLevel browsers. Because UpLevel browsers perform validation on the client, you may ask yourself:

1. Why it is necessary to check if the page is valid on the server, since the check was already performed on the client?

2. How can the server-side code in Listing 5.11 even determine whether the page is valid, given that validation was performed on the client?

The following facet of ASP.NET's validation architecture quickly dispels the confusion: Validation checks are always performed on the server, even if they have already been performed on the client.

Thus, the only behavioral difference between UpLevel and Down-Level browsers is that UpLevel browsers perform additional checks on the client, potentially saving time by avoiding a round-trip. Irrespective of the browser type, ASP.NET still performs server-side checks. The benefits of this apparent redundancy are twofold:

1. You can program on the server uniformly. That is, the server-side code in Listing 5.11 will work in any browser scenario, be it UpLevel or DownLevel.
2. Extra security benefits—because the client-side JavaScript generated by ASP.NET resides in the user's browser, he or she can modify it to get around your validation rules. Since ASP.NET also performs these checks on the server, however, such efforts are thwarted.

Client-side Code on Non-IE Browsers

You could argue that ASP.NET's categorization of UpLevel and Down-Level browsers is unfair, and possibly limiting. After all, browsers such as Netscape and Opera are capable of executing client-side JavaScript, albeit slightly different variations from Microsoft's implementation.

Unfortunately, as of this writing, this is an inherent limitation of ASP.NET. Even if you force the Framework to deliver client-side script to non-IE browsers (we'll see how in this topic's How and Why section), they won't be able to interpret it correctly, since the script is targeted specifically for IE. You have two options to get client-side validation script running on such browsers, both of which require manual coding:

1. Write a custom Web Control that delivers compatible script to browsers such as Netscape and Opera. For example, you could write a control called MyValidator, which extends the CompareValidator control used above. You would then override certain methods in the class to generate client-side code in the case of a DownLevel browser. Custom Web Controls are discussed online at ⌖AS050001.
2. Replace ASP.NET's validation script library with your own implementation. By default, the Framework keeps all the client-

side JavaScript for Validation controls in the following file (where versionNum is the particular version of the .NET Framework you have installed): localhost\aspnet_client\ system_web\versionNum\WebUIValidation.js.

Because ASP.NET autogenerates this file, you shouldn't modify it. However, you can point ASP.NET to your own script library by adding the following line to the project's web.config file:

```
<webControls clientScriptsLocation="/aspTest/"/>
```

Listing 5.12   Linking to external JavaScript code

As a result of this line, ASP.NET will load the client-side validation file (WebUIValidation.js) from the aspTest virtual directory we created in Chapter 2 rather than the default validation file.

The Display Property

Another interesting property exposed by Validation controls is Display, which determines whether ASP.NET reserves space for the control when it is not visible. If this property is set to Static, the Validation control will take up space in the page's layout even if it is invisible. If the property is set to Dynamic, then the control only takes up space when it is visible (as when turned on by Validation code).

When the Display attribute is set to None, the control does not display an error message. Instead, you use the ValidationSummary control to display a summary of errors for all of the Validation controls on the web page in a single location. The online example at °CN⟩AS050007 illustrates the ValidationSummary control.

Other Validation Controls

Remember that this example has illustrated but one of the Validation controls in ASP.NET. Two Validation controls that you should consider are RegularExpressionValidator and CustomValidator.

As its name suggests, the RegularExpressionValidator allows the use of regular expressions in order to match a control's contents against a prescribed format. For example, the following regular expression could validate e-mail addresses: .*@.*\..*. If you are unfamiliar with regular expressions, the online example at °CN⟩AS050014 gives a brief overview along with an example. Basically, a regular expression is a statement that allows a string to be checked against a specific pattern. Using regular expressions, you could ensure that a TextBox contained a postal code, phone number, etc.

For those operations that fall outside the capabilities of ASP.NET's prebuilt controls, you can turn to the CustomValidator. The Custom-Validator allows you to write specialized validation code and is demonstrated in the example at ◦^{CN}↦AS050008.

HOW AND WHY

How Do I Force ASP.NET to Perform All Validation on the Server?

This may seem like an odd question, but there are situations where you might want to always perform validation on the server (and not perform any client-side checks). One such situation is during the debugging of applications. Because VS.NET uses Internet Explorer (an UpLevel browser) when you debug within its environment, you cannot (by default) test applications under DownLevel conditions. Thus, you may wish to force ASP.NET to forgo altogether the generation of client-side script (simulating DownLevel browsers). There are two ways to accomplish this.

First, you can set a Page's clientTarget property to DownLevel (using the Property Inspector). Doing so changes the .aspx file's Page directive as follows:

```
<%@ Page clientTarget="DownLevel" ..
```

Listing 5.13   Forcing DownLevel behavior

As a result, all browsers will be treated as DownLevel, and validation will only occur on the server. Similarly, if you set the clientTarget property to UpLevel, all browsers will receive client-side validation code even if they are not capable of interpreting it. This option is useful if you override ASP.NET's validation library with your own browser-neutral implementation.

The primary shortcoming of forcing server-side validation in this fashion is that it disables the other amenities associated with UpLevel browsers (e.g., SmartNavigation, sophisticated control layout, etc.). For this reason, the following programmatic method of disabling client-side validation is preferable:

```
Private Sub Page_Load(...)
'Turn off client-side scripting for each validation
'control.  Theoretically, the code should perform
'error-checking.
'See AS050009 for a more robust implementation.
  Dim i As IValidator
  For Each i In Page.Validators
```

```
    Dim con As BaseValidator = CType(i, BaseValidator)
    con.EnableClientScript = False
  Next
End Sub
```

Listing 5.14   Programmatically disabling client-side validation

Listing 5.14 may look complex, but it is really quite simple. Remember from Chapter 3 that the Page class abstracts an ASP.NET Web Form. One of the properties it exposes is Validators, which is a collection of all the Validation controls on the page. By iterating through this collection using VB's For Each statement, we can programmatically turn off client-side scripting for each control in the page (using the EnableClientScript property).

The one complication in Listing 5.14 is the casting of each control in the collection into the BaseValidator class from which all Validation controls derive. Casting, for those who are unfamiliar with the concept, is the conversion of a class into one of its derived types. Because Listing 5.14 is placed within the Page's Load event, when the page is rendered its Validation controls will not generate client-side script.

Why Do I Get the Following Server Error When I Attempt to Run My Application?

Page.IsValid cannot be called before validation has taken place. It should be queried in the event handler for a control with Causes-Validation=True or after a call to Page.Validate.

This error results if you try to query the status of a page using isValid() before ASP.NET has validated the page. Usually, this error is the byproduct of one of two scenarios:

1. You called Page.isValid in the Page's Load() event.
2. You called Page.isValid in the event handler of a control whose CausesValidation property was set to False.

In either case, you can eliminate this error by explicitly forcing validation on the page before calling isValid:

```
Page.Validate() 'Force ASP.NET to validate the page
if Page.isValid then ...
```

Listing 5.15   Forcing validation

SUMMARY

Validating data on the web has always been a problematic issue involving numerous trade-offs, repetitive code, and custom "hacks" to avoid browser issues. ASP.NET's Validation controls cut through these issues by providing a simple set of components that can be combined to implement almost any set of rules imaginable. The beauty of these controls is that the ASP.NET Framework automatically determines whether validation should be client-side or server-side based on the browser's abilities. For UpLevel browsers (Internet Explorer version 4 or greater), ASP.NET generates client-side script to avoid unnecessary trips to the server. For DownLevel browsers, validation occurs on the server.

Topic: HTML Server Controls

As illustrated in the previous topics, Web Form controls provide a rich and flexible architecture for designing ASP.NET pages. Although these entities are the "controls of choice" in the ASP.NET Framework, your other option is to use HTML Server controls.

HTML Server controls are most useful when you are migrating existing applications to ASP.NET. For example, you can import the pages generated by such tools as FrontPage and Dreamweaver into VS.NET's design environment, and then "upgrade" the HTML entities to Server controls such that they are programmatically accessible from code.

Additionally, some HTML Server controls afford functionality not found with Web Forms. For example, the HTMLInputFile control allows users to upload files easily to a Web Server—functionality that ASP developers have long desired. An example illustrating this control can be found at ⌀CN⌀AS050010.

Remember that unlike using Web Forms controls, utilizing HTML Server controls requires knowledge of HTML. These controls do not abstract HTML elements, but instead evolve them to make them accessible to server-side code.

CONCEPTS

Migration from FrontPage
A large number of web applications today are written using graphical editors such as Microsoft FrontPage. A practical use for HTML Server controls is the migration of a page developed in one of these tools to

ASP.NET. Consider the web page in Figure 5.6, which was developed using FrontPage's "Guest Book" template (this file is available online at ⟨CN⟩AS050011).

We'd like to know what you think about our web site. Please leave your comments in this public guest book so we can share your thoughts with other visitors.

Add Your Comments

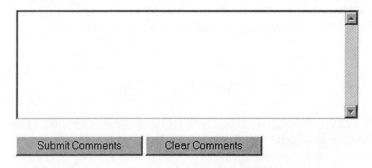

After you submit your comments, you will need to reload this page with your browser in order to see your additions to the log.

Figure 5.6   FrontPage.html—A web page developed in FrontPage

The primary shortcoming with tools such as FrontPage is that, unlike VS.NET, they don't allow you to attach event code to a page's elements. Thankfully, migrating this page to ASP.NET is fairly straightforward given the Framework's HTML Server control technology.

First, rename the file to give it an aspx extension (in this example, rename FrontPage.html to FrontPage.aspx). Next, create a new web application in VS.NET named FrontPageMigrate. As always, VS.NET will give your project an initial web page named WebForm1.aspx. Delete this file using the Solutions Explorer (right-click WebForm1.aspx and select Delete), and then add FrontPage.aspx to your project by going to Project → Add Existing File. VS.NET will inform you that there is no class file (CodeBehind file) associated with FrontPage.aspx and will ask if you wish to create one. Click Yes, and the file will be added to your web project. Make this file the project's startup page by right-clicking it and selecting Set as Start Page. Click FrontPage.aspx in the Solution Explorer and VS.NET will load the file in its page designer. As depicted in Figure 5.6, the web page consists of two buttons, and an HTML Text Area element.

Remember that because this form was authored in FrontPage, its controls are plain HTML entities. If you double-click one of the buttons, VS.NET will inform you that you must upgrade it to an HTML Server control. Perform this upgrade by right-clicking all the page's controls and choosing Run As Server Control. Click the button again, and VS.NET will load the CodeBehind file. As in the example at the beginning of this chapter, the CodeBehind file declares classes that map directly to the controls you just upgraded:

```
Protected WithEvents TEXTAREA1 As _
    System.Web.UI.HtmlControls.HtmlTextArea
Protected WithEvents Reset1 As _
    System.Web.UI.HtmlControls.HtmlInputButton
Protected WithEvents Submit1 As _
    System.Web.UI.HtmlControls.HtmlInputButton
```

Listing 5.16 Upgraded class declarations

You can now attach event code to the buttons and manipulate the controls programmatically. Furthermore, you can also add Web Form Controls (Validation, Calendar, etc.) to the page itself. Before you run the application, however, there is a little housekeeping that you must perform.

If you examine the .aspx file's underlying code, you will discover that it is peppered with <!–webbot> tags (also notice that VS.NET inserted a <%Page> directive at the top of the file). These tags denote FrontPage WebBot components, which are lesser versions of ASP.NET Web Controls (they execute on the server and require FrontPage Server extensions). Since these components don't make sense in the context of ASP.NET, remove all the webbot tags, and then change the line: <form action="--WEBBOT-SELF--" method="POST"> to: <form runat= "server" method="post">.

The <form> element is the HTML entity used to send information to the user. By changing this line you are stipulating that the form should first be processed on the server, before it is rendered on the client. As a rule, Web Controls must reside in a <form> element marked with the runat="server" attribute. Forms created directly inside VS.NET are given the runat="server" attribute by default. Because we imported this page from FrontPage, however, we must make this change ourselves.

Keep in mind that WebBots are specific to FrontPage. If you import pages from other tools such as Macromedia, Inc.'s Dreamweaver or Adobe Systems, Inc.'s GoLive, you will have to account for similar idiosyncrasies, generally by removing the unnecessary attributes.

You have now successfully migrated this page to ASP.NET, and you can run it by pressing F5 from within VS.NET.

SUMMARY

As this example illustrates, HTML Server controls can be used to migrate existing HTML pages to ASP.NET. Simply give the HTML file an aspx extension, add it to your ASP.NET application, accept VS.NET's offer to create a CodeBehind file for you, and then upgrade the page's HTML elements to HTML Server controls. You can then manipulate the page's controls in typical ASP.NET fashion—by accessing them through server-side code in an object-oriented manner.

Topic: ActiveX Controls and Windows Forms

At the end of the day a Web Control is simply an abstraction for HTML that is rendered on the client. While this abstraction is certainly an important virtue of ASP.NET, it also means that Web Controls are subject to the inherent limitations of HTTP. For example, a Web Control cannot maintain continual contact with a server so as to obtain "real-time" information because the HTML to which it is ultimately converted is "dormant" on the client's browser (HTML can only respond to user events—it cannot execute on its own).

Sophisticated enterprise applications must often transcend such limitations. For instance, applications that provide stock prices are a common requirement in the financial industry. As you can imagine, such applications are extremely volatile—the information they supply must be as up-to-date as possible.

To facilitate such functionality there must be some executable code that constantly runs within the browser. Most often, this code takes on the form of a Java applet that is executed by the browser's VM. In the Microsoft realm you have two alternatives: "pre-.NET" ActiveX controls and Windows Forms controls. Ironically (as of this writing), the VS.NET designer has intrinsic support for older ActiveX controls, but not for newer Windows Forms. This topic examines how to use both of these entities in ASP.NET.

Before proceeding, realize that using these technologies in your applications entails the following restrictions:

- Applications will only work on IE (ActiveX controls can possibly work on versions of Netscape if you use a software add-on called a plug-in).
- Applications that use ActiveX controls raise certain security concerns, which complicates deployment.
- Applications that use newer Windows Forms controls will only work on versions of IE 5.5 or higher and must have the .NET Framework running on the client machine.

Because of these restrictions, these technologies are most often used in Intranet environments where the client's browser and platform can be standardized.

CONCEPTS

ActiveX Controls

ActiveX controls are COM-based entities authored in either Visual C++, Visual Basic, or, in some cases, Visual J++. Because ActiveX controls are unmanaged (i.e., they execute outside the CLR), they can be dangerous as their code cannot be verified before it is run. For this reason, there is a formidable security infrastructure surrounding their use in web applications. Without going into too much detail, ActiveX controls are usually "signed" by an authorized distributor who ensures that they are not malicious. Usually, signed ActiveX controls are executed by the browser without warning, whereas unsigned ActiveX controls elicit a cautionary message to the user (these options can be overridden in Internet Explorer).

Additionally, an ActiveX control must be registered before it can be used. As discussed in the Shared Assembly topic in Chapter 3, this process populates the registry with type and version information. When an ActiveX-enabled web page is requested, the browser dynamically downloads, registers, and runs the control. Although this is a seemingly straightforward process, experienced web developers will attest to the many problems that plague ActiveX-web interoperability (problems with failed registration, component downloads, and so on). It is beyond the scope of this book to investigate such details (ActiveX is not .NET technology); merely recognize that if you employ ActiveX controls in ASP.NET, you will be subject to such concerns.

EXAMPLE

Using ActiveX controls in Visual Studio.NET is straightforward. This example requires the CodeNotes ActiveX control, which you can download at AS050012. This control, written in Visual Basic 6, is a timer that displays the number of seconds since the control was first launched.

After following the online instructions to register the control, create a new web project in VS.NET named ActiveXApp. Go to the Toolbox, click the General tab, right-click the toolbar, and select Customize ToolBox. As shown in Figure 5.7, select the CodeNotes ActiveX control.

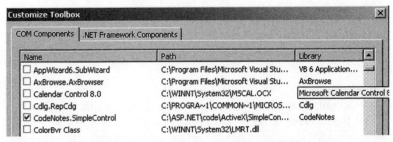

Figure 5.7 Adding an ActiveX control to VS.NET

Click OK, and the CodeNotes control will appear in the General toolbox. Drag it onto the Web Form and, like a Web Control, VS.NET will render the control on the page.

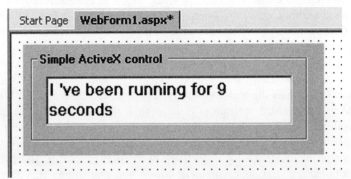

Figure 5.8 An ActiveX control in an ASP.NET application

Run the application by pressing F5, and the control will continually report how long it has been executing. Note that you may receive a warning message from IE before the application loads, informing you that the control is possibly dangerous. This message results because the control is unsigned. (If the control does not render, see the How and Why section at the end of this chapter for the possible reason.)

Although the control in Figure 5.8 is trivial, it is important to realize that ActiveX controls permit functionality that is impossible to accomplish with regular HTML. For example, our control could establish a connection with the server and constantly update itself with information. Many ActiveX controls used on the web offer sophisticated graphing tools, such as the ability to display three-dimensional bar and pie charts.

If you examine the underlying HTML for the Web Form (the .aspx file), you'll find a line similar to the following:

```
<OBJECT height="111" width="314" classid="clsid:2DFFEC12-911F-
4A6B-B3AD-1D6687094910">
```

Listing 5.17   The ActiveX object link

This line represents the ActiveX control embedded on the page. Developers who have worked with ActiveX controls before will recognize both the <OBJECT> tag and classid attribute in the previous line. A classid is a unique number used in COM to identify components. When the browser sees the classid above, it consults the system registry and determines that the control in question is our CodeNotes control.

If you venture into the world of ActiveX, you must concern yourself with the issues previously mentioned. Again, such details are beyond the scope of this book, but if you try to view the application from another machine you will see one such issue: the control does not render at all.

For ActiveX web applications to work on other machines, you must specify a CodeBase attribute in the previous <OBJECT> line. This attribute specifies where the control can be located on the Internet, such that it can be downloaded and registered on the client. Quite often, this file takes on the form of a compressed Microsoft Cabinet (.CAB) file:

```
<OBJECT CLASSID="clsid:..."
CODEBASE="http://MyWebserver/MyControl.cab">
```

Lisiting 5.18   A downloadable ActiveX control

When the browser encounters this line, it goes to the specified URL, downloads and uncompresses the file on the fly, and then registers and runs the control. Information on Cabinet files, automatic registration, and ActiveX controls in general can be found in the MSDN or at ⟨CN⟩AS050013.

Windows Forms

Because of the aforementioned problems with ActiveX controls, the .NET Framework offers a simplified alternative. In Chapter 3, we discovered that Web Controls are really BCL classes found in the `System.Web.UI.WebControls` namespace. Similarly, if you write standard Desktop Applications in .NET, intrinsic VB6 controls such as textboxes and buttons can be found in the `System.Windows.Forms` namespace.

So, just as there is a `TextBox` Web Form class that represents textboxes in ASP.NET, there is a `TextBox` Windows Form class that is used when you draw a textbox in a .NET Desktop Application (you can see this by creating a VB Windows Application in VS.NET and examining the underlying code). And just as you can author your own custom Web Control, you can write your own Windows Form control in VS.NET. This Windows Form control takes the place of the ActiveX control in our previous example—it is a unit of code that can execute within Internet Explorer. This technology is sometimes referred to as Internet Explorer hosting.

EXAMPLE

In this example we will write (and then use) a Windows Form control similar to the ActiveX control in the previous example. Start by creating a new VB project called FirstControl in VS.NET. Under project templates choose `Windows Control Library`. As its name suggests, a Windows Control Library is a DLL assembly that exposes a number of Windows controls. Click `OK`, and VS.NET will create your project, which contains a form representing the viewable area of the control.

Drag a textbox and timer onto the form such that it resembles Figure 5.9 and set the textbox's `MultiLine` property to True. VB developers should note that invisible controls such as timers are now placed in a separate pane underneath the form, as opposed to directly on the form as in VB6.

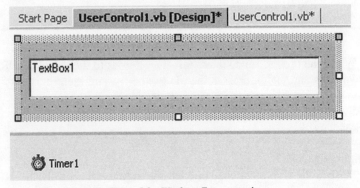

Figure 5.9   Windows Form control

As Figure 5.9 depicts, our control consists of two other controls: a `Timer` and a `TextBox`. All we have to do is give the control some logic. Like VB6, a `Timer` control executes a block of code repeatedly. Change its Interval property to 1000, and its Enabled property to True. As a result, when the control is loaded the timer will execute its event code every second. Next, double-click the `Timer` and the highlighted code in Listing 5.19 to the control.

```
Public Class MyControl
    Inherits System.Windows.Forms.UserControl

    Dim Before As Double

    Private Sub MyControl_Load(ByVal..
        Before = Microsoft.VisualBasic.Timer
    End Sub

    Private Sub Timer1_Tick(ByVal..
        TextBox1.Text = "I've been running for " &_
       CStr(CLng(Microsoft.VisualBasic.Timer - Before)) & _
       " seconds"
    End Sub

End Class
```

Listing 5.19   Windows control logic

Listing 5.19 does the same thing as the ActiveX control in the previous example—every second, the control updates its textbox to reflect how long it has been running. To use this control in ASP.NET, click the form and change its name from `UserControl1` to `myControl`. Compile the project by going to Build → Build Solution, and then create a new VB web application project named `TimerControl`.

Using Windows Controls in ASP.NET

As of this writing, Visual Studio.NET does not natively support using Windows controls in ASP.NET. However, you can simulate design-time support using the technique outlined here. First, copy the control library you just created (`FirstControl.DLL`) into the virtual directory you created in Chapter 2 (`aspTest`). Next, ensure that the Web Form's `targetSchema` property (Figure 1.9) is set to Internet Explorer 5.0. Finally, add the following lines to the Web Form's design file (Webform1.aspx).

```
<!-- Delete the line breaks -->
<OBJECT id="FirstControl" style="Z-INDEX: 102; LEFT:
16px; WIDTH: 311px; POSITION: absolute; TOP: 28px;
HEIGHT: 54px"
classid="http://localhost/aspTest/First
Control.dll#FirstControl.MyControl" VIEWASTEXT>
</OBJECT>
```

Listing 5.20   Using a Windows control

As in the ActiveX example, the `<Object>` tag informs ASP.NET that the page contains an external object. Unlike the ActiveX tag, however, the classid is not a cryptic number, but the URL where the control is located. The classid for Windows Form controls is written as follows: `Classid="URL/Assembly.DLL#namespace.ClassName"`. When the browser comes across the `<Object>` tag, it downloads `First Control.DLL` from the `aspTest` virtual directory, and then loads `MyControl` found in the `FirstControl` namespace.

Flip back to the Web Form's design in VS.NET, and you will not see the control but simply an empty outline.

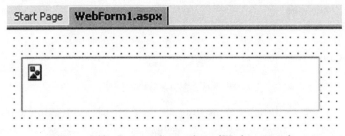

Figure 5.10   Empty outline in place of Windows control

You can manipulate this outline in order to determine where on the page the control resides. Before you can run the application and see the control, you must modify the virtual directory settings.

Virtual Directory Settings

An essential requirement when embedding Windows Forms controls inside Internet Explorer is that the virtual directory containing the control must have its IIS `Execute Permission` option set to `Scripts only`. This option can be found by right-clicking the `Virtual Directory` in the Internet Services Manager (Figure 1.1), selecting `Properties`, and looking under the `Virtual Directory` tab.

After configuring the aspTest virtual directory according to this rule, run the application and, like its ActiveX twin, the Windows Forms control will consistently report how long it has been running. Although these two examples are functionally similar, there are some notable differences between them.

Security

Unlike the ActiveX example, the browser won't raise a warning when you attempt to access the web application. Because Windows Forms controls are managed, they are subject to the CLR's Code Access Security (CAS) policy, which we examine in depth at ☜AS010010. Basically, CAS allows the CLR to prescribe certain rules for code depending upon the origin of the code. Hence, there is no need for the browser to warn about potentially dangerous controls, as the CLR will stop the code if the latter steps outside the boundaries of the former.

Iterative Downloading

Recall from Chapter 3 that the manifest of an assembly lists the dependencies of the assembly itself. A nice feature of Windows controls hosted inside IE is that the CLR will automatically determine the other assemblies on which the control depends and will download them as their functionality is required. Thus, if FirstControl uses another assembly, Control2, the CLR will download Control2 only when it is required by FirstControl. This allows you to partition a collection of controls into numerous assemblies and have them downloaded on a need-by-need basis, as opposed to overwhelming the client with a large download all at once.

Client Deployment

Remember that to use this technique the client machine must have the .NET Framework installed. In this respect, Windows Forms controls are even more restrictive than older ActiveX technology, which only required the client to have Internet Explorer. Given this restriction, you may wonder if Windows Forms controls are at all practical.

One area where this technique might be used is the deployment of browser-based applications in an Intranet scenario. Because a Windows control is like a form, it can encapsulate an entire Desktop Application. Instead of a complex deployment scheme, clients would simply point their browsers to a specified URL. At runtime, the CLR determines if a new version of the control should be downloaded to the user's machine, or if the old version is up to date. In this way, the only application that needs to be kept current is the control on the server—the CLR automatically downloads it to clients as required.

HOW AND WHY

Why Does the ActiveX Control Not Render on My Browser?
It is likely that you have Internet Explorer configured to ignore unsigned ActiveX controls. Change these options by going to Tools → Options → Security → Custom Level, and then set "Download unsigned ActiveX controls" to Prompt, and "Initialize and script ActiveX controls not marked as safe" to Enabled. Remember that our example will only run a computer on which the CodeNotes control has been registered.

SUMMARY

Unlike Web Controls, both ActiveX and Windows Forms controls are downloaded and executed on a client's machine. Using either of these technologies restricts the target browser to IE and, with the latter technology, the client must also have the .NET Framework installed.

A Windows Forms control is a managed component that executes entirely within the user's browser. As such, Windows Forms controls are not hindered by the limitations of HTML and can take advantage of native OS functions such as screen painting (e.g., controls that render complex graphics), File I/O (e.g., controls that download/upload to servers), and communication mechanisms (e.g., controls that establish contact with a server so as to provide real-time information). The CLR's Code Access Security (CAS) infrastructure eliminates many of the security and deployment concerns that existed with ActiveX controls, the COM-based predecessor to Windows Forms controls. ActiveX controls can also be used natively from VS.NET.

Chapter Summary

In this chapter we have illustrated the graphical entities that you can use to construct ASP.NET applications. These components fall into one of two categories: Web Controls, which are entirely server-based and generate HTML appropriate for the client, and ActiveX and Windows Form controls, which are downloaded and execute within the client's browser.

Web Controls represent a quantum leap forward in rapid application design for the web. This rich collection of Web Controls in ASP.NET provides support for validation, displaying data and regular HTML elements, rotating advertisement images, and even complex operations involving translation technologies such as XSLT. Web Controls are particularly sophisticated in that they generate browser-friendly HTML to render themselves on the client. When the browser supports it, they take advantage of features such as SmartNavigation. When it does not, they fall back on regular HTML.

As powerful as Web Controls are, they are subject to the normal limitations of the HTTP. They cannot continually execute in the user's browser or perform sophisticated operations such as real-time information feeds. In Intranet scenarios, where client machines have both IE and .NET Framework installed, Windows Form controls offer considerable power and flexibility.

Windows Form controls provide the power of ActiveX controls without any of the deployment or security nuisances. Because Windows Forms controls are subject to the CLR's Code Access Security infrastructure, users do not receive annoying warning messages as they did with ActiveX. Windows Form controls can take advantage of iterative downloading, whereby the CLR dynamically downloads additional components as they are required.

Chapter 6

—

DEBUGGING, TRACING, and CACHING

As we have seen throughout this book, Visual Studio.NET is the backbone of ASP.NET development. The environment's Web Form Designer (WFD) not only allows you to design web-based applications in a Visual Basic–like manner; it also abstracts web idiosyncrasies such as HTML and HTTP requests. As we will see in this chapter, the virtues of VS.NET go beyond simple rapid web-based application development. Specifically, VS.NET addresses a problem that has plagued traditional ASP development for years—debugging.

Unlike Visual InterDev (the development environment for traditional ASP), VS.NET offers sophisticated debugging options that one would expect from a mature Integrated Development Environment (IDE). Features such as breakpoints, instant watches, and code stepping are all tools that you can use when debugging ASP.NET applications. These features, coupled with ASP.NET's native tracing capabilities (the first topic in this chapter), make debugging web applications significantly easier than doing the same in traditional ASP.

The last topic in this chapter examines caching, an important technique for increasing application performance. The principle of caching is based on static data and request frequency: some (unchanging) information is requested so often that it makes sense for the Runtime to store it in rendered form as opposed to constantly generating it on the fly. For example, as we learned in Chapter 5, Web Controls generate browser-appropriate HTML depending upon a client's capabilities. There are thus numerous client-side "representations" of a web page specific to a particular browser. Instead of constantly converting a page to Netscape-compatible HTML, ASP.NET can cache its Netscape representation and forgo subsequent regeneration, thereby decreasing response time. ASP.NET's cache engine can also be accessed by classes in the BCL, allowing developers to cache their own custom data.

Topic: Tracing

Tracing is the ability to determine a program's path of execution. This capability is invaluable when one is trying to figure out why an application is not executing correctly. Using tracing, a developer can iteratively narrow down the problematic section of an application, right down to a specific line of code.

CONCEPTS

Tracing in ASP

In traditional ASP, tracing was usually accomplished using `Response` `.Write` statements. By peppering a script file with `Response.Writes`, the application's execution path could be determined by way of its output on the browser. Consider the ASP code in Listing 6.1, which uses this technique in a straightforward manner:

```
<%
  Response.Write("Before calling Foo")
  Foo()
  Response.Write("...called Foo successfully")
%>
```

Listing 6.1   trace.asp

If you run the application and it outputs *"Before calling Foo . . . called Foo successfully"*, you are assured that `Foo()` executed without error (i.e., the second `Response.Write` statement executed, meaning that `Foo()` must also have executed). Of course, `Foo()` could represent any operation whose validity you wanted to test: the opening of a database by means of ADO, a function you've written yourself, or the method of a COM object. In addition to testing functional validity, `Reponse.Write` is often used to output the value of interesting variables (e.g., the connection string for a database, the value of the counter variable of a loop, etc.).

Although this technique can still be used in ASP.NET (since intrinsic objects such as Response are still accessible in the Framework), it is undesirable for a number of reasons. First, debugging statements must be removed when the application is deployed. Although this is straightforward in Listing 6.1, longer and more complex scripts pose more of a challenge. Forgetting to remove debug statements can be not only embarrassing, but it can corrupt the application's output as well.

Second, when using Response.Write, there is no easy way to toggle whether debug statements are displayed. In other words, after deploying the application, an administrator cannot seamlessly revert back to debug mode if required.

ASP.NET addresses these limitations through its new tracing features, which are best illustrated by example.

EXAMPLE–TRACING IN ASP.NET

Tracing in ASP.NET is very similar to using the Response.Writes you used in ASP, with two exceptions:

1. You no longer use Response.Write, but instead use Trace.Write (or Trace.Warn).
2. You can toggle whether output statements are displayed using the Page directive's Trace attribute. Alternatively, you can enable tracing using a special option in the project's web.config file.

Create a new web application project in VS.NET named TraceDemo. Add a button to the application, and then add the following code to the project's Page_Load()event:

```
Private Sub Page_Load(...)
  Trace.Write("myMessage", "In Page_Load")
End Sub
```

Listing 6.2   Trace.Write in ASP.NET

Listing 6.2 simply writes out a statement informing us that the Page is loading. Note that unlike Response.Write, Trace.Write accepts two strings (we'll see what they do in a moment).

If you run the application by pressing F5, you will see that, unlike the Response object, Trace.Write does not affect the application's output. The page will display the button but will not show your message. In other words, by default, the application executes as if the `Trace.Write` command weren't there.

Displaying Trace Information

In order to see the trace statement in Listing 6.2, you must turn on tracing explicitly by adding the following attribute to the design (.aspx) file's Page directive:

```
<%@ Page Trace="true" Language="vb" ... "%>
```

Listing 6.3   Turning on tracing

Before running the application with tracing enabled, there is one small peculiarity you must account for. Recall from Chapter 1 (Figure 1.9) that a Page's `targetSchema` property determines how controls are laid out on the Web Form. By default, this property is set to `Internet Explorer 5.0`. As of this writing, there appear to be some problems with this setting when tracing is enabled (we'll explain this occurrence in a moment). Using the Property Inspector, change the Web Form's `target-Schema` property to either `Internet Explorer 3.0` or `Netscape 4.0`.

Rerun the application by pressing F5, and the application's output will change dramatically. As depicted in Figure 6.1, appended to the Page's output is a plethora of debug information, including the trace string we added in Listing 6.2.

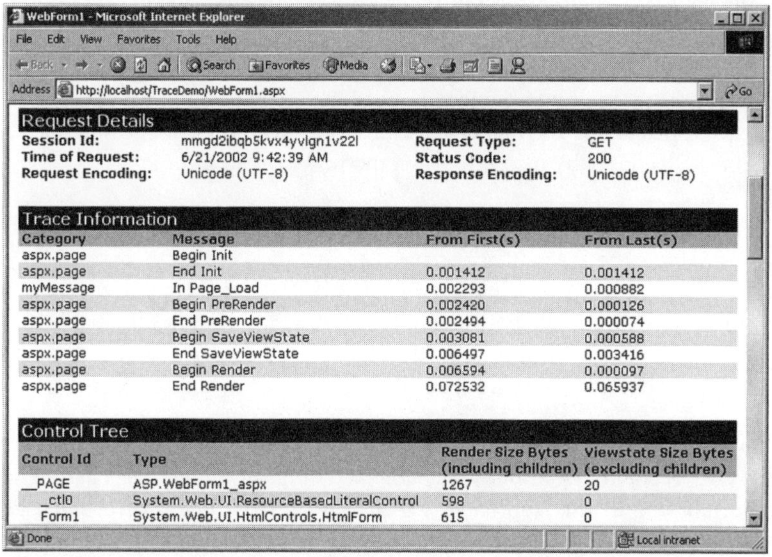

Figure 6.1   Tracing output appears after the application (button not shown)

As depicted in Figure 6.1, debug information is always placed under the application itself (we have scrolled past the button in the figure).

TargetSchema Caveat
If you do not change the Page's targetSchema property from Internet Explorer 5.0, as we just did, then you will receive the obscured output illustrated in Figure 6.2 (the application is placed *on top* of the tracing output, instead of *before it* as in Figure 6.1.)

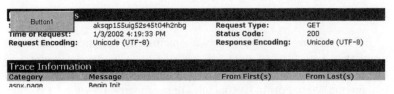

Figure 6.2   Obscured tracing output

Interpreting the Trace Results
Examine the debug information in Figure 6.1 and you will see that in addition to our trace statement, there is a lot of additional information provided by ASP.NET: a millisecond breakdown of the various Page events that were triggered; the size of the VIEWSTATE variable used by the application's Web Controls (see Chapter 5 for details), a list of client-side cookies ASP.NET is using (see Chapter 7 for details), HTTP request details such as browser and OS types, and many other details that might prove useful in debugging scenarios.

As Figure 6.1 illustrates (highlighted line), the two strings in the Trace.Write method are placed under the Category and Message headings, respectively. You can also differentiate your own debug statements from ASP.NET's by using the Warn method instead of Write:

```
Trace.Warn("myMessage", "In Page_Load")
```

Listing 6.4   The Warn method

The only difference between the preceding line and Listing 6.1 is that messages written using the Warn method appear as red text instead of black (the default), making it easier to spot your own comments.

Application-level Tracing
In the preceding example we enabled tracing on a per-page basis. The shortcoming of this approach is that *every* page in the project must be configured individually. If, for example, we added another page to the project (by going to Project → Add Web Form), we would have to en-

able tracing manually for the second page (by setting `Trace="true"` in its Page directive). For this reason, configuring tracing in such a manner is referred to as Page-level tracing.

In practice, you may want to enable tracing on the application level. By turning on application tracing, *every* page in the application outputs the debug information in Figure 6.1. This is accomplished by editing the `<trace>` element in the project's web.config file. Recall from Chapter 4 that the web.config file houses the configuration settings for an entire ASP.NET application. If you examine this file by double-clicking it in VS.NET's Solution Explorer, you will find a line similar to the following:

```
<trace enabled="false" requestLimit="10"
pageOutput="false"
traceMode="SortByTime"
localOnly="true" />
```

Listing 6.5   Web.config trace setting

As you can see, there are five attributes that determine the tracing characteristics of an ASP.NET application:

- `enabled`—turns tracing on or off for every page in the application.
- `requestLimit`—One of the most powerful capabilities of application-level tracing is the ability to dump trace statements to a log file. This attribute determines the number of application tracing requests the log file stores. For example, a setting of 10 prescribes that the last ten traces should be logged. We'll examine this setting in the upcoming example.
- `pageOutput`—determines whether trace output is written to the screen (in addition to being logged to a file). If this attribute is set to `true`, then all pages within the application will also output debug information to the browser (as in Figure 6.1).
- `traceMode`—Look at Figure 6.1 and you will see a section of the trace output entitled `Trace Information`. If this attribute is set to `SortByTime` (the default), then the Page's events (`Begin Init`, `End Init`, etc.) are listed in the order in which they are triggered (chronologically). This attribute can also be set to `SortByCategory`, whereby events are listed alphabetically according to their respective `Category` headings. In this case, our trace comments would appear after ASP.NET's, as our `Category` heading (`myMessage`) follows ASP.NET's (aspx.page).
- `localOnly`—We will examine this attribute in the upcoming ex-

ample, which determines whether the trace log file can be viewed from a remote machine.

EXAMPLE–APPLICATION-LEVEL TRACING

To enable application-level tracing, remove the Trace="true" attribute from the Page directive you inserted, and modify the <trace> element in the project's web.config file so that it reads:

```
<trace enabled="true" requestLimit="10"
pageOutput="false" traceMode="SortByTime"
localOnly="true" />
```

Listing 6.6   Enabling application-level tracing

Run the application and note that trace information is not written to the screen. Instead, ASP.NET writes all statements to a log file behind the scenes. This log file is named Trace.axd and is placed in the project's virtual directory. To examine the log file for TraceDemo, you would navigate to the following URL: http://localhost/TraceDemo/Trace.axd. ASP.NET will then render all the trace information that it has logged, as illustrated in Figure 6.3.

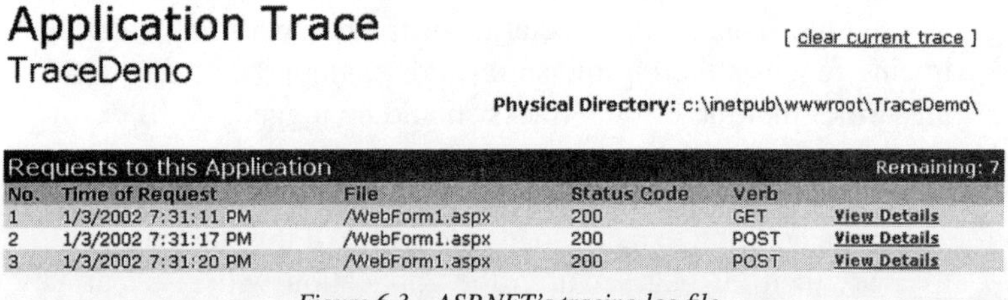

Application Trace
TraceDemo

[clear current trace]

Physical Directory: c:\inetpub\wwwroot\TraceDemo\

No.	Time of Request	File	Status Code	Verb	
		Requests to this Application		Remaining: 7	
1	1/3/2002 7:31:11 PM	/WebForm1.aspx	200	GET	View Details
2	1/3/2002 7:31:17 PM	/WebForm1.aspx	200	POST	View Details
3	1/3/2002 7:31:20 PM	/WebForm1.aspx	200	POST	View Details

Figure 6.3   ASP.NET's tracing log file

Three different trace outputs have been logged in Figure 6.3 (remember that according to our settings, the log file keeps only the last ten requests). You can examine a specific request by clicking on View Details. Clicking on this link brings up the trace information for the request in question, similar to the information depicted in Figure 6.1.

By default, the trace URL is accessible only from the machine on which the Web Server resides. In order to make the trace log accessible to remote machines, you must set the <trace> element's localOnly attribute to false:

```
<trace . . . localOnly="false" />
```

Remember that you can also increase the number of logged trace requests by changing the `requestLimit` attribute to a higher value:

```
<trace enabled="true" requestLimit="100"../>
```

One nice aspect of application-level tracing is that you can trace requests as a web site is live. Using the statistics in Figure 6.1, you could determine which pages users are viewing most often, where a particular page spends the majority of its processing time, etc.

HOW AND WHY

How Do I Turn On Tracing for Every Application?

Although application-level tracing enables tracing for all the pages within an ASP.NET application, you may wish to enable tracing for *all* applications on the machine. As we will see in Chapter 7, global settings for the .NET Framework are stored in the machine.config file: `\%winroot%\` `Microsoft.NET\Framework\versionNum\config\machine.config`.

We will examine the machine.config file in greater depth in the next chapter, but if you open it using Notepad (it is very large), you will see the following line in the `<system.web>` section of the file:

```
<trace enabled="false" localOnly="true"
pageOutput="false" requestLimit="10"..>
```

You might think that changes to this line will affect the tracing characteristics for *all* ASP.NET applications on the machine. Unfortunately, things aren't so simple. In the next chapter we will examine the relationship between the machine.config and web.config files and investigate how to globally enable tracing for all applications.

How Do I Toggle Tracing Programmatically?

In addition to controlling tracing through the directives we have illustrated, you can also toggle tracing programmatically by using the `isEnabled` property of the `Trace` object. A nice technique is to toggle tracing based on a QueryString value in the URL. Add the following code to TraceDemo's `Page_Load()` handler:

```
Private Sub Page_Load(..)
  If Request.QueryString("Trace") <> "" Then
    Trace.IsEnabled = True
  End If
End Sub
```

Listing 6.10   Toggling tracing programmatically

Listing 6.10 toggles tracing based on the presence of a `Trace` Query-String in the URL. Thus, navigating to the following URL results in the application being displayed with trace information: `http://localhost/TraceDemo/WebForm1.aspx?Trace="On"`

Removing `?Trace="On"` from the URL results in the application being rendered normally (i.e., without debug information).

SUMMARY

Tracing is a technique whereby a developer can determine a program's path of execution. In traditional ASP, tracing was accomplished by inserting informative `Response.Write` statements into a script. Although `Response.Write` can still be used in ASP.NET, the Framework offers a more versatile tracing mechanism through the `Trace` object. Like the `Response` object, the `Trace` object allows developers to write debug information to the screen: `Trace.Write("myADOCommand","I am opening a connection")`.

Unlike the `Response` object, the new directives in ASP.NET allow developers to determine when trace statements are outputted with varying levels of granularity:

- Page-level tracing turns on tracing for a particular page. This is accomplished by adding the `Trace="true"` attribute to the Page's `<@%Page` directive.
- Application-level tracing toggles tracing for *every* page within an ASP.NET application. This is accomplished by modifying the `<trace>` element in the project's `web.config` file. This option has the added benefit of being able to record trace information to a log file, while the site is "live."

Topic: Debugging in VS.NET

As demonstrated in the previous topic, ASP.NET's tracing capabilities are a significant improvement over the debugging options available in traditional ASP. Even more powerful, however, are the debugging features of Visual Studio.NET. In this topic, we illustrate features such as code stepping and instant watches, which greatly simplify debugging ASP.NET applications.

One thorny aspect of debugging traditional ASP applications pertained to COM components. Because COM components are written in either Visual Basic or Visual C++, you must debug them outside ASP's development environment (Visual InterDev). As we will see in this example, the .NET Framework's replacement for COM components, assemblies, can be debugged directly inside the same environment as the web applications that leverage them (VS.NET).

CONCEPTS

Debugging in VS.NET

This example uses the `WhereAmI` application we wrote in the Assembly topic in Chapter 3. To recap, recall that this example consisted of the following two entities:

- A class library assembly named `myAssembly` written in C#, which exposed a class called `processInfo`. This class, in turn, exposed a method called `WhatProcess()`, which reported the process the assembly was executing within.
- A VB.NET web application project named `WhereAmI`, which used `myAssembly` to output its host process to a textbox:

```
Private Sub Button1_Click(...) Handles Button1.Click
  Dim oProc As New myAssembly.ProcessInfo()
  TextBox1.Text = oProc.WhatProcess()
End Sub
```

Listing 6.11   WhereAmI application

Reload the `WhereAmI` project in VS.NET (it might also be a good idea to review the example in Chapter 3), and then set a breakpoint in the application by right-clicking on the second line in Listing 6.11; select `Insert BreakPoint`. After performing this operation VS.NET will highlight the line within its environment, as shown in Figure 6.4.

```
Private Sub Button1_Click(ByVal sender As System.Object
    Dim oProc As New myAssembly.ProcessInfo()
    TextBox1.Text = oProc.WhatProcess(False)
End Sub
```

Figure 6.4   Inserting a breakpoint in VS.NET

For those unfamiliar with the concept, placing a breakpoint on a particular line of code causes VS.NET to return to the IDE before the line of code is executed. Once inside the IDE, you can step through subsequent lines of code individually, inspect variable values, and so on. In other words, VS.NET now provides web developers with the same debugging amenities that have been available for years when writing Desktop Applications and component libraries.

Run the application by pressing F5, click on the application's button, and, as described above, VS.NET will return to its code window. At this point application execution is "paused," and you can use VS.NET's debugging options to ascertain the values of variables, step through code, etc. For example, to examine the characteristics of the application's

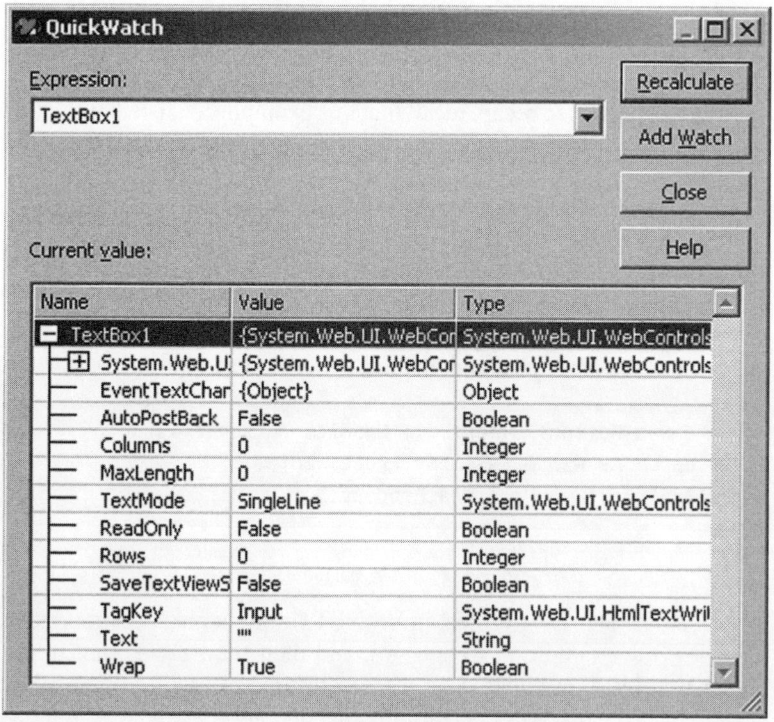

Figure 6.5   QuickWatching in VS.NET

textbox, press ALT-CTRL-Q to invoke VS.NET's QuickWatch window and enter "TextBox1" under Expression. Press enter and VS.NET will populate the screen with the information shown in Figure 6.5.

As Figure 6.5 illustrates, QuickWatch lists the values of the textbox's properties (AutoPostBack, Text, etc.). This technique is considerably more powerful and easier than determining the values of a variable using ASP's Response.Write method. In addition, you can QuickWatch other variables simply by entering their names in the Expression box. Enter oProc, for example, and QuickWatch will list information about the oProc variable (its type, value, etc). As you can see, QuickWatch is a powerful feature that can be used to "peek" into an application's state in the middle of its execution.

Cross-language Debugging and Code Stepping

As its name suggests, code stepping allows you to step through individual lines of code. Once VS.NET has returned to its code window (as the result of an inserted breakpoint), you can step through the next line of code by pressing F11 in the environment. VS.NET executes the line and then returns to its code window, where you can examine what the line of code did (which variables it changed, which files it opened, etc).

Look under VS.NET's Debug menu and you will see that pressing F11 steps "into" code, whereas pressing F10 steps "over" it. We'll explain the difference between these two options in a moment, but for now step "into" the highlighted line of code in Figure 6.4. This line calls myAssembly's WhatProcess() method in order to determine the web application's host process. What happens as you step into this method call may surprise you.

When you press F11 on this line, VS.NET steps into the source code for the WhatProcess() method. This may not seem noteworthy, until you realize that WhatProcess() is an "external" method housed in myAssembly.DLL. Similarly, its underlying code is not a part of the WhereAmI project, but is located in the myAssembly class-library project we created in Chapter 3.

Behind the scenes, the environment loads the source for the myAssembly component the web application is utilizing. Moreover, you have not only stepped across programmatic entities (i.e., web application to class-library assembly), you have also stepped across languages, as the web application is written in VB.NET and myAssembly is written in C#. As you can see, the universality of VS.NET simplifies debugging considerably.

Stepping Over versus Stepping Into

Unlike stepping "into" code, stepping "over" code does not step through the source for any methods or functions that the particular line of code is calling. For example, if you stepped over the highlighted line in Figure 6.4 (by pressing F10), then VS.NET would call WhatProcess() immediately without loading its underlying code. In other words, stepping over code treats function and method calls as if they were single statements.

If you press F11 repeatedly such that VS.NET traverses Figure 6.4, the environment will eventually return to the browser, as the button's event code will have fully executed (remember that we placed a breakpoint within the button's event handler).

Think of code stepping as the controlled execution of an application. This is an excellent technique to determine the execution path a program is taking, and allows you to scrutinize code on a line-by-line basis. For years, desktop and component developers have enjoyed this luxury, and it is now available to the world of web development, thanks to VS.NET.

Debug and Release Builds

You may wonder how VS.NET loaded the source code for myAssembly automatically, given that it resides in a different directory than the current project (how did VS.NET know where the myAssembly source was located?). The answer to this question involves the two ways in which a component can be built in the .NET Framework: Debug and Release.

By default, components such as myAssembly are built in debug mode, which places additional information inside the assembly file itself (myAssembly.DLL). This information, in turn, denotes the location of the component's source code. VS.NET consults this information as you step into code to load the component's source dynamically, as required.

Bear in mind that building components with the debug option results in larger and slower-executing files and should only be used during the testing phase. When deploying assemblies and applications, always build them with the release option (which you can set by going to Build → Configuration Manager in VS.NET). Note that if you try to step into a component compiled in release mode, VS.NET will not be able to dynamically load source code and will simply step "over" calls to the assembly.

The <Compilation> Element

If you look in the project's web.config file, you will find an additional option that must also be set to allow ASP.NET applications to be debugged:

```
<compilation defaultLanguage="vb" debug="true" />
```

Listing 6.12   The compilation setting

The `<compilation>` element determines the manner in which ASP.NET compiles the application's CodeBehind file. When the `debug` attribute is set to `true` (which it is by default), then ASP.NET builds the project in debug mode so that you can use the debugging options we just examined. This option results in slower-running applications, and so the `debug` attribute should be set to `false` as applications are deployed.

VS.NET also provides several debug windows within its environment as you step through code. These windows, depicted in Figure 6.6, are usually located at the bottom right of the environment.

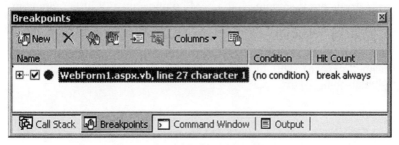

Figure 6.6   VS.NET's debug windows

VS.NET offers four screens that can be used for debugging purposes: Call Stack, Breakpoints, Command Windows, and Output. As can be seen in Figure 6.6, the Breakpoint screen lists all the breakpoints you have set. The Call Stack screen lists all the functions and methods that have been called recently, and the Output screen lists information produced by the IDE itself, such as the assemblies that it had to load to run the project, compiler warnings, etc. The final window, Command, which should be familiar to VB6 developers, allows you to execute individual program statements against the application. For example, using the Command window you could change a variable's value and then continue program execution against this modification. For more information on these windows, see ᴄɴ⤵AS060001.

In addition to debugging with VS.NET, you can also debug ASP.NET applications using the debugger that ships with the .NET Framework (`DbgCLR.EXE`). Although less versatile, this debugger can be used if you do not possess a copy of VS.NET. For information on this debugger, see ᴄɴ⤵AS060002. Finally, ASP.NET offers some advanced features, such as software counters that allow you to profile applications to determine

how they perform under various scenarios. For more information, see
⚬^{CN}AS060003.

HOW AND WHY

Can I Step into a COM Component?
As we will see in Chapter 9, COM components can be used directly
from ASP.NET in a far more intuitive manner than using ASP's Create
Object() mechanism. Because a COM component is conceptually
equivalent to a class-library assembly (i.e., it is an external component
callable from an application), you might wonder whether you can step
into COM components as easily as we did with assemblies in this example.

Unfortunately, stepping into COM components is a little more complex. The difficulty arises because COM components are native entities
that execute outside the CLR. In order to step into a COM component you must "attach" VS.NET to the ASP.NET Runtime process
(aspnet_wp.exe). This more involved approach is illustrated online at
⚬^{CN}AS060004.

SUMMARY

With Visual Studio.NET, developers can debug web applications using
the same powerful techniques that are applied to Desktop Application
development. Features such as code stepping and variable watching
allow developers to determine an application's execution path and inner
workings so that problems can be quickly diagnosed and eliminated.

VS.NET also makes it easier to debug components that an ASP.NET
application uses. If you step into a line of code that calls an external assembly, VS.NET loads the assembly's source dynamically, allowing you
to step through it as well. This practice is possible even if the web application and assembly have been written in different languages, a technique referred to as cross-language debugging.

Topic: Caching

Caching is the ability to store frequently accessed data in memory in
order to reduce response time. Certain operations, such as database
queries, are very expensive and time-consuming to perform. Rather than

carry out these operations every time they are requested, it makes sense to store their resulting data in memory for future requests. Employing caching in an application can significantly increase its scalability and performance.

Caching is a valuable technique that predates the Web. Processors (such as the Intel Pentium) use caching to increase the rate at which they carry out instructions. Hard drives use similar techniques to improve the rate at which data is retrieved. In the examples for this topic, we will see how caching can improve the performance of web-based applications in ASP.NET.

CONCEPTS

Page-level Caching

With page-level caching, a page's output is stored and served directly upon subsequent requests. By caching pages, ASP.NET does not have to regenerate dynamic content on every request, which can significantly re-duce load time. With this type of caching, you specify an expiration policy that determines how long a given page is maintained in the cache. For example, you can prescribe that a given page should be kept in the cache for thirty minutes, at which point it is discarded and regenerated. The first example in this topic illustrates page-level caching.

Page-fragment Caching

Fragment caching allows developers to cache segments of a page. Quite often, a certain portion of a page *must* be dynamically generated on every request (a real-time stock quote, for example). By using fragment caching, developers can separate those portions of a page that are static and can be cached from those that require dynamic generation upon every request.

Fragment caching is a more involved process that requires using user controls (.ascx files) mentioned in Chapter 4. Recall that a user control is a collection of design elements (Web Controls, HTML elements) that can be dragged onto an ASP.NET Web Form. In other words, a user con-trol treats a collection of design elements as one unit. A Web Form, in turn, can consist of multiple user controls. Using fragment caching, de-velopers can cache user controls with different parameters, and there-fore cache different segments of a web page as they see fit. For more information on fragment caching, see ᴄᴺᐅ AS060005.

Programmatic Caching

ASP.NET exposes classes in the BCL that allow developers to cache their own data programmatically. For example, you may wish to cache the results of a database query that is shared by multiple pages. The Cache API gives developers direct access to ASP.NET's cache engine, which can be used to design custom caching solutions where page-level and fragment caching are inadequate. The second example in this topic illustrates ASP.NET's Cache API.

EXAMPLE–PAGE–LEVEL CACHING

In the early days of the Internet, web pages were static. A client would request a Hyper Text Markup Language (HTML) file from a server, and the server would simply deliver the file to the client. In a sense, the entire system was nothing more than a glorified file-transfer mechanism. ASP.NET pages, on the other hand, are dynamic entities. Consider the straightforward program in Listing 6.13.

```
<%
   Response.Write("The Current time is: ")
   Response.Write(DateTime.Now.TimeOfDay.ToString)
%>
```

Listing 6.13   Cache.aspx

Run this application in Internet Explorer (place the file in the aspTest virtual directory we created in Chapter 2), and, as expected, it will report the current time:

```
The current time is: 18:50:38.3397936
```

What you are seeing in the browser is ASP.NET's client-side response for Cache.aspx. As detailed in the final topic in Chapter 3, the ASP.NET Runtime processes Cache.aspx in order produce the browser-compatible HTML that you are looking at it. You can think of this HTML as the static client-side representation of Listing 6.13 (the HTML delivered to the browser is considered static because it doesn't change once received by the browser). Listing 6.13, however, has an infinite number of static client-side representations, as determined by the time of day. Every time you request the application, a new static client-side version is sent to the browser.

Enabling Page-level Caching
Page-level caching in ASP.NET is simply the ability to store a web page's client-side representation in memory so that it doesn't have to be

regenerated upon every request. To enable page-level caching you must use the Framework's OutputCache directive and specify the period of time you wish to maintain the cached page (in seconds). Recall that a directive (such as the Page directive) is prefixed with the '<@%' characters and is placed at the top of the page's design file (.aspx).

```
<%@ OutputCache Duration="10" VaryByParam="none" %>
```

Listing 6.14   The OutputCache directive

By adding Listing 6.14 to the top of Listing 6.13, you are prescribing that the static representation of the Page should be kept in ASP.NET's cache for ten seconds, and used for subsequent requests until it is invalidated (ignore the VaryByParam attribute for now).

Run the application, and you will observe the effects of this addition: the time reported by the application will remain constant for all requests performed within a ten-second window. After ten seconds, ASP.NET will store a new static representation of the application in the cache, with an updated time.

At this point, caching may not seem particularly useful. After all, the purpose of Listing 6.13 is to report the current time, but because we are caching the application in ten-second intervals, the value it returns is usually inaccurate. To fully appreciate caching we must consider a more involved example. Nevertheless, we can make three observations thus far:

1. After a page has been cached, the server does not have to perform *any* processing because the client-side response is already stored in memory. Although the speed gain in this example is negligible, caching can improve performance significantly for complex scripts.

2. The Duration attribute of the OutputCache directive determines how long ASP.NET keeps the page in the cache. As we will see momentarily, additional attributes can determine other aspects of the caching process (such as whether ASP.NET caches numerous copies of the application depending upon user input, etc.).

3. By default, caching applies to *all* clients. In the previous example, if you change the Duration attribute to 1000 and then attempt to access the application from multiple browser instances (even on different machines), the application will report a constant time (i.e., ASP.NET uses the same cache for all clients).

EXAMPLE–CACHING BASED ON USER INPUT

Caching is only useful if the data that ASP.NET is storing remains valid when it is delivered. This was not the case in the previous example, as the program's response was based on the current time (in general, time-based applications are not good candidates for caching). In this example we consider a more pragmatic application in order to illustrate a powerful aspect of caching—the ability to cache different copies of an application based upon user input.

Caching based on user input is highly desirable because user input alone frequently determines ASP.NET's response to the client. Consider an application that adds two numbers. In this case, ASP.NET's client response (the answer) depends exclusively on what the user entered. The response can be cached and reused if another user makes an identical request, thus eliminating a second computation. Another application that falls into this category is the timer application we developed in Chapter 1, using traditional ASP in Listing 1.2). Recall that this application times how long it takes to sum a set of numbers. Listing 6.15 contains a modified version of the timer application, such that it executes under ASP.NET (in Chapter 9 we will investigate how to convert an ASP application to ASP.NET).

```
<HTML><HEAD><TITLE>ASP Timer Test</TITLE></HEAD>
<BODY> <H2>ASP Timing Demo:</H2>
<%
    dim TimeStamp
    dim i, output, total, count
    If Request.Form("num") <> "" then
        count = Request.Form("num")
        TimeStamp = timer
        for i = 1 to count
            total = total + i
        next
        TimeStamp = CStr(timer - TimeStamp)
        Response.Write("Performed computation at: ")
        Response.Write(DateTime.Now.TimeOfDay.ToString)
    End If
%>

<FORM NAME="timerForm" ACTION="Cache2.aspx"
  METHOD="post">
<TABLE>
  <TR>
```

```
    <TD>Enter the summation size:</TD>
    <TD><INPUT TYPE="text" name="num"
        value="<%= Request.Form("num")%>"></TD>
  </TR>
  <TR>
    <TD>Sum Value:</TD><TD><INPUT TYPE="text"
        value="<%=total%>"></TD>
  </TR>
  <TR>
    <TD COLSPAN="2"><CENTER><INPUT TYPE="Submit"
        VALUE="Perfom Summation"></CENTER></TD>
  </TR>
</TABLE>
</FORM></BODY></HTML>
```

Listing 6.15   The ASP.NET timer application (Cache2.aspx)

Listing 6.15 differs from the ASP timer application in Chapter 1 in three respects (all highlighted in the source). First, the file has been renamed Cache2.aspx to reflect its migration to ASP.NET. Second, instead of reporting how long it takes to perform the summation, the program returns the value of the summation itself. For example, if you run the program and enter in a summation value of 100, the program will return a value of 5050. Third, the program also prints out the time of day at which it completed the computation. Also, note that the user's input (the summation size) is stored in the form's num variable.

The VaryByParam Attribute

Listing 6.15 is an excellent candidate for caching because its output is based solely on user input. For example, once the program has performed the summation for 100, ASP.NET can cache the resulting response (which returns an answer of 5050) and reuse it for any other summation request of 100. To enable this type of caching, we must use the second attribute in the OutputCache directive, VaryByParam:

```
<%@ OutputCache Duration="3600" VaryByParam="num" %>
```

Listing 6.16   The VaryByParam attribute

By placing this line at the top of Listing 6.15, we are instructing ASP.NET to cache multiple copies of the page based on the form's num variable. Run the application, and enter a sum value of 1 million. After a few seconds the program will return an answer of 500000500000, along with the time the computation was completed (e.g,10:05:22). Enter in another value (say, 1000) to perform another computation.

Now, enter in a value of 1 million again, so as to perform the first computation you requested, and you will observe two interesting results.

First, the program produces the answer instantaneously (as opposed to taking a few seconds, as it did during the first request). Second, the program reports that it performed the computation at 10:05:22 (or whatever time it reported for the first request). In other words, the summation was not recalculated because the answer was already in ASP.NET's cache. When the request is made the second time, ASP.NET consults its cache to determine whether it contains a client-side response for Listing 6.15, where the num variable is 1 million. If the response is in the cache, then it is returned to the client immediately. If the response is not in the cache, then ASP.NET must first process it on the server. Also note that because the Duration attribute is set to 3600, all pages are cached for one hour, at which point they are invalidated.

Caching—The Trade-off

You can see how caching can dramatically reduce response time—once a summation is computed, it can be reused for subsequent requests. You could apply this technique for more practical operations such as caching based on Login IDs and passwords. Like all performance enhancements, however, caching comes at a price. In the previous example, every time a user requests a unique computation, the response is stored in ASP.NET's cache (for an hour). If many users are performing many computations, caching can quickly saturate the amount of memory on the server. When employing caching, carefully consider which operations are worthy of the memory required to cache results. In Chapter 9, we will investigate ways to reduce the sum computation to a fraction of a second, such that caching (and thus additional resources on the server) is not required.

Other OutputCache Attributes

The OutputCache directive exposes additional attributes that determine other characteristics of the caching mechanism. For example, the Location attribute prescribes where cached pages are actually stored (on the server, on the client's browser, etc.), whereas the VaryByHeader attribute can be used to cache based on raw HTTP headers (browser type, host computer, etc.). For more information on these attributes, see ᴄᴺ AS060006.

The Cache API

Closely related to the concept of caching is the notion of expiration. Items in a cache are only "good" for a period of time, at which point they are removed. ASP.NET exposes an object called Cache, which allows you to store your own custom data in the cache. This data could be anything: the results of a database query, an XML document, an array of numbers, etc.

The Cache object is best understood against the Application object you used in traditional ASP. Recall that Application is used to store global data available to *all* clients (in contrast to the Session object, which stores data on a per-client basis). The Cache object functions identically to the Application object with one important twist: items stored using Cache have expiration and dependency policies that determine when they are no longer valid.

Expiration policies are time-based, which allows you to specify that an object should be removed from the cache after ten minutes, for example. Dependency policies allow you to remove an item from the cache if a directory or file changes, and are best illustrated by example.

EXAMPLE–THE CACHE API

In this example we will cache a stock price that is retrieved from a text file. We will establish a dependency between the stock price and the file, such that if the file is modified the stock price is removed from the cache. This situation often arises in the enterprise setting: a web application pulls data from a file that is continually updated by some external mechanism. In traditional ASP, you had to write your own code to detect that a file has been updated (perhaps a COM object that continually polled the file). With ASP.NET's caching infrastructure, manual code such as this is no longer required.

Create a new web application project in VS.NET named CacheFile, add two labels to the Web Form (rename them Message and StockPrice), and then add the following code to the project:

```
Private Sub Page_Load(...)
  'Is the stock price in the cache?
  If IsNothing(Cache("ACMEStock")) Then
    'Load the stock price from the file
    Message.Text = "Price not in cache," & _
      "loading from file"
    LoadStockPrice()
  Else
    'Stock Price is already in Cache:
    Message.Text = "Price is in Cache"
```

```
  End If

  'Print out stock price:
  StockPrice.Text = "ACME stock price is:"&_
    Cache("ACMEStock")
End Sub

Private Sub LoadStockPrice()
  Dim fName As String = "StockPrice.txt"
  Dim price As String

  'Convert the file to an absolute name (required):
  fName = Server.MapPath(fName)

  'Open file and load stock price. Note that FileIO
  'functions are a little different from
  'VBScript or VB.NET. See AS060007 for details
  FileOpen(1, fName, OpenMode.Input)
  Input(1, price)
  FileClose(1)

  'Insert the stock price into the cache with a
  'dependency on the file.
  Dim depend As New CacheDependency(fName)
  Cache.Insert("ACMEStock", CDbl(price), depend)
End Sub
```

Listing 6.17   Using the Cache object

As illustrated in Listing 6.17, the Cache object functions similarly to the Session and Application objects, allowing you to store and retrieve values from its collection. Listing 6.17 first checks to see whether an item named ACMEStock is in the cache. If it isn't, the program calls the LoadStockPrice() method. This method retrieves the stock price from a file named StockPrice.txt, which is located in the virtual root of the application.

The most interesting part of Listing 6.17 is the code that actually places the stock price within the cache. This is accomplished using the Cache object's Insert() method, which accepts a value (the stock price), a key name (ACMEStock), and a CacheDependency object. A CacheDependency object specifies the dependency policy for the item being inserted.

The CacheDependency Object

Observe that prior to the insertion we have declared a CacheDependency object named depend, based on the file name (StockPrice.txt) that contains the stock price. By passing this variable into the Insert() method we establish a dependency between the inserted item and the file. As soon as the file is modified the item is removed from the cache, which causes Listing 6.17 to read the updated file to the next time it is requested.

CacheDependencies are valuable tools for linking a cached item to an external occurrence such as the modification of a file. A Cache Dependency object can also be configured to trigger if any files in a particular directory change.

Running the Example

In order to run the example you must first create a file named StockPrice.txt in the project's virtual directory. This virtual directory maps to the physical directory C:\Inetpub\wwwroot\CacheFile (where C:\ is the directory where the OS is installed). Using the text editor of your choice, create a file in this directory named StockPrice.txt that contains one number (the stock price): 11.53.

Run the application by pressing F5, and because the cache is empty, the application will return:

```
Price not in cache, loading from file
ACME stock price is: 11.53
```

Listing 6.18   Noncached output

Click the browser's refresh button, and the application will now output:

```
Price is in Cache
ACME stock price is: 11.53
```

Listing 6.19   Cached output

As you can see, upon the second request the stock price is pulled from the cache instead of being read from the file. Remember that caching applies to *all* clients (like the Application object). If you access the application from another browser instance, you will receive the second (cached) output.

Also remember that caching is based on the concept of expiration. In Listing 6.17, expiration is triggered by changing the file that contains the stock price. If you change the price in StockFile.txt (to 20.02), and click refresh in the browser, the application will output:

```
Price not in cache, loading from file
ACME stock price is: 20.02
```

Listing 6.20   Refreshing based on dependency

Behind the scenes, ASP.NET automatically detects that the file has been modified, and removes the stock price from the cache, forcing Listing 6.17 to read the modified file. In addition to basing expiration on file modifications, you can establish dependencies between numerous items in the cache (such that if one item expires, another item also expires). You can also expire based on time. For example, we could modify Listing 6.17 to expire the stock price when the file was modified *or* after sixty minutes had passed. See ᴄᴺAS060008 for details.

HOW AND WHY

How Do I Configure Page-level Caching Programmatically?
In addition to using the OutputCache directive to configure page-level caching, you can enable it programmatically using the HttpCachePolicy class exposed by the Response object. This class offers some options not exposed by the OutputCache directive, such as the ability to expire an item based on the absolute time of day. For details on using this programmatic option, see ᴄᴺAS060009.

How Do I Create a Page-level Cache Based on Multiple Form Values?
In the first example in this topic we cached based on one form value—num. You may wish to cache pages based on a combination of values, such as UserID and Password. This is accomplished by separating the form values using semicolons in the VaryByParam attribute:

```
<%@ OutputCache Duration="3600"
VaryByParam="UserId;Password" %>
```

Listing 6.21   Caching based on multiple parameters

You can also use an asterisk with the VaryByParam attribute to specify that *every* combination of user input values should be cached:

```
<%@ OutputCache Duration="3600" VaryByParam="*" %>
```

Listing 6.22   Caching based on every parameter

For more information on these options, see ᴄᴺAS060010.

How Do I Get Notification That an Item Has Been Removed from the Cache?

In the previous example the stock price is removed from the cache when the underlying file (StockPrice.txt) was modified. Situations may arise where you want explicit notification that an item is being removed from the cache the moment expiration occurs (perhaps you make the decision to reinsert it). This type of notification requires utilizing delegates, the new type of callback mechanism in the .NET Framework. For information on using delegates to facilitate this type of functionality, see ⟨CN⟩AS060011.

SUMMARY

Caching is a powerful technique that can dramatically reduce how long it takes ASP.NET applications to respond to user requests. Page-level caching caches the individual pages of an application and is enabled by means of the OutputPage directive. One powerful aspect of this type of caching is the ability to cache multiple copies of a web page based on user input, which avoids unnecessary work on the server. Each time a page is requested, ASP.NET caches the client-side response it generates so that subsequent identical requests can be delivered directly to the user without any processing. User-input-based caching is accomplished using the VaryByParam attribute.

Developers can also cache custom application data by using the Cache object. Like the Application object, Cache can be used to store data that is accessible to all clients. Unlike the Application object, items in the cache expire based on time or dependencies such as file modifications.

Chapter Summary

ASP.NET and Visual Studio.NET both give web developers powerful options to debug web-based applications. ASP.NET's built-in tracing capabilities replace the unwieldy Response.Write mechanism that was the bane of debugging in traditional ASP.

With ASP.NET tracing, developers can toggle whether debug statements are displayed on the page level or application level. Tracing also permits developers to log debug statements to a file while a site is being viewed live. VS.NET also offers a variety of sophisticated debugging options such as breakpoints, code stepping, and variable watching, which should be familiar to anyone who has developed traditional Desktop Applications.

ASP.NET's powerful caching engine allows developers to fine-tune applications in order to decrease response time. Page-level caching allows an entire page to be cached according to certain options such as user input, whereas fragment caching allows the various segments of a page to be cached. Using the Cache object, developers can cache their own data to implement custom solutions.

Chapter 7

—

CONFIGURATION AND DEPLOYMENT

In this chapter we investigate how to configure and deploy ASP.NET applications. Along the way we will highlight some important administrative aspects of the Framework.

ASP.NET exposes many configuration settings that give developers considerable control in determining how applications execute. For example, as we discovered in Chapter 3, the ASP.NET Runtime executes within a special process named aspnet_wp.exe. A dedicated runtime process is considerably more robust than traditional ASP, which shares its process with IIS (by default). As we will see in the first topic in this chapter, it is possible to restart the ASP.NET Runtime at regular intervals in order to circumvent problems that plague Windows processes as they execute over long periods of time (e.g., memory leaks, access violations, etc.).

Another powerful configuration option exposed by ASP.NET is the ability to store Session data in various locations. Session, which is explained in detail in the second topic of this chapter, is used by an application to maintain state across client requests. In traditional ASP, Session was stored inside the ASP Runtime. As we will see, ASP.NET offers robust alternatives, such as the ability to store Session data inside a dedicated "service" process or an SQL Server database.

The final topic in this chapter lists the steps required to deploy an ASP.NET application to a Web Server.

CORE CONCEPTS

The IIS Metabase

At the beginning of Chapter 3 (the CLR topic), we used IIS to change an ASP.NET application's Protection setting. As we saw in that chapter, this setting had *no effect* on the application's host process (even though it did affect the traditional ASP application we configured before).

From a configuration standpoint, few IIS settings (security being the primary exception) apply to ASP.NET. This behavior is largely motivated by IIS's configuration datastore—the IIS metabase. Whenever you modify settings using the Internet Services Manager, as we did in Chapter 3, the underlying settings are written to the Web Server's metabase. (In case you are wondering, the metabase is located in the following file: %winroot%\system32\inetsrv\Metabase.bin.)

There are two primary shortcomings with the metabase. First, it is stored in a proprietary format on your machine, which makes it difficult (if not impossible) to modify outside IIS. Second, because the location of the metabase is obscured by the OS, it is difficult to replicate in Web Farm scenarios (see the following concept). (Incidentally, these restrictions have been eliminated in the latest version of IIS (6.0), which stores the metabase as XML and exposes a number of metabase administrative options.)

As we will see in this chapter, ASP.NET configuration settings are stored as easily readable XML files. This makes ASP.NET applications easy to deploy on Web Servers and simple to replicate in Web Farm scenarios. ASP.NET offers another significant improvement over IIS configuration. As we will see in this chapter's first topic, a Web Server restart is not required in order for new configuration changes to take effect.

Web Farms

A Web Farm is a group of computers that service requests to the same website. For sites with heavy traffic, Web Farming is a practical way to improve performance. For example, an e-commerce site may have ten computers (all installed with Web Servers) that respond to user requests. More computers mean additional computational bandwidth and faster response time.

Web Farms pose numerous challenges. For example, if a web application must be reconfigured, the change must be applied to all machines in the farm. Reconfiguration is a task that is difficult to automate in traditional ASP, given the metabase's proprietary format. Sharing Session data is another problem. Many Web Farms are configured such that requests are directed to alternating machines. For example, the first request to www.webfarm.com may propagate to Machine #1 and the second may be given to Machine #3. In order for applications to function correctly, Machines 1 and 3 (and all other machines in the farm) must be able to share Session information.

Web Farming in traditional ASP was a difficult chore that was often accompanied with proprietary software such as low-level COM objects, or dedicated products such as Microsoft's Application Center 2000. ASP.NET simplifies the task considerably. Replication is easier, thanks to easily deployable XML configuration files; and as we will see in the second topic in this chapter, Session data can be stored inside an SQL Server database or a dedicated process, which all machines in the farm can share.

Web Gardening

Web Gardening is a lesser version of Web Farming. Whereas a Web Farm uses multiple machines to service the same website, a Web Garden uses multiple processors on one machine, all servicing the same site. For example, on a quad-processor system it is possible to configure a copy of ASP.NET Runtime to execute on each processor, such that four instances run on the one machine. As we will see in the first topic, you can also configure the runtime to execute only on specified processors (processors 2 and 4, for example).

Topic: ASP.NET Configuration

As with traditional ASP, ASP.NET encapsulates its entities within a web application. A web application is an abstract term for all the resources within the confines of an IIS virtual directory. A web application may consist of one or more ASP.NET pages, Class-Library Assemblies, configuration files, graphics, and more. Recall from Chapter 4 that when you create a new web application project in VS.NET, the development environment implicitly creates an IIS virtual directory for you behind the scenes.

CONCEPTS

Web.Config and Machine.Config

There are two configuration files that determine the running characteristics of an ASP.NET application: the machine-wide configuration file (machine.config) and the application's configuration file (web.config). In fact, there is no stipulation that an application must have a web.config file (all projects created in VS.NET are given one implicitly). For example, the ASP.NET timer applications that we created in Chapter 1 did not have web.config files associated with them.

Whereas a web.config file is located in the project's virtual root, the machine.config file can be found in the following directory: `\%winroot%\ Microsoft.NET\Framework\versionNum\config`.

It is important to understand the relationship between these two files. When a web application executes, the ASP.NET Runtime first consults web.config. Next, it examines machine.config. If it encounters conflicting configuration parameters, then the settings in web.config are enforced. In other words, the information in the web.config file takes precedence. If an application does not have a web.config file, then ASP.NET uses the default settings inside machine.config.

Enabling Tracing for All Applications

To illustrate the interplay between machine.config and web.config, let's revisit a question from the Tracing topic in the previous chapter: how to toggle tracing for all applications on the machine. Consider what would happen if you modified the `<trace>` element in machine.config such that it read:

```
<trace enabled="true" localOnly="true"
pageOutput="false" requestLimit="10"..>
```

Listing 7.1   The application-level tracing directive

Although ASP.NET would read the preceding line, which enables tracing (temporarily), it first consults the project's web.config file, which, by default, contains:

```
<trace enabled="false" localOnly="true"
pageOutput="false" requestLimit="10"..>
```

Listing 7.2   The web.config tracing directive

This line negates the setting in machine.config and ultimately results in tracing being turned off. In order for the settings in machine.config to take effect, you must remove the `<trace>` element from the project's web.config file. In other words, in order to toggle settings globally in machine.config, applications cannot have conflicting settings in their own configuration files.

A Tour of Machine.config

Open the machine.config file using your favorite text editor (try using VS.NET itself, as the environment provides XML syntax coloring). Remember that this file houses settings for the *entire* .NET Framework; those specific to ASP.NET can be found in the `<system.web>` section of the file.

It is beyond the scope of this book to examine every ASP.NET configuration setting within this file. We will describe some of the important settings, and relegate detailed explanations of them to the online article at ⊶AS070001. In addition, the inline comments inside machine.config explain ASP.NET's configuration settings, as does the MSDN.

<authentication>, <authorization>, <identity>, and <securityPolicy>
These elements are associated with ASP.NET security and prescribe the mechanisms that the Framework employs to relegate access to applications. We will examine these settings in the next chapter (on Security).

<httpModule> and <httpHandlers>
Recall from Chapter 1 that httpHandlers are ASP.NET's replacement for ISAPI components. Like ISAPI components, httpHandlers are entities that can interpret raw HTTP requests and process them (httpModules differ slightly in that they *filter* requests and pass them to other entities). When you write an httpModule or httpHandler you must use one of these configuration elements to register it with ASP.NET.

Look closely in the machine.config file and you will see that ASP.NET itself uses httpHandlers to process certain files. For example, within the `<httpHandler>` element you will find the following line:

```
<add verb="*" path="*.aspx"
type="System.Web.UI.PageHandlerFactory"/>
```

Listing 7.3   Handling ASP requests

This line instructs the Framework to forward all requests to .aspx files to the `PageHandlerFactory` class, which is the class that actually processes ASP.NET pages. Another handler declared in this file is `System.Web.HttpForbiddenHandler`, a class we'll examine in the chapter on security.

Because httpHandlers give you direct access to the raw HTTP that is sent to a client, they are also useful in scenarios where you want to create a graphic on the fly for a web page. This technique is accomplished by using an `httpHandler` in conjunction with the GDI+ (Graphic Device Interface) classes exposed by the BCL. For more information, see ⊶AS070002.

<Pages>
As we have seen throughout this book, a page's behavior depends largely upon the attributes placed within its Page directive. The `Pages`

element allows you to set global page settings. For example, in Chapter 5 we learned that the EnableViewState attribute toggles whether a page maintains state during server round-trips (utilizing the hidden VIEWSTATE field). Using the <Pages> configuration element, you could turn off VIEWSTATE for all ASP.NET applications on the machine. This setting could, of course, be overridden by a project's web.config file, or by the Page itself.

<customErrors>

This element allows you to determine how ASP.NET handles HTTP errors. You can prescribe, for example, that HTTP 404 (File not found) errors should be redirected to a specially designated web page. For an example, see ⌐CN AS070003.

<trace> and <sessionState>

These elements determine the tracing and session-storage characteristics of an application, respectively. We saw the <trace> element in the previous chapter, which controls whether Trace.Write statements are written to the screen. The second topic in this chapter will examine <sessionState>, which exposes the numerous ways in which Session data can be stored in ASP.NET.

<globalization>

Preparing a website for use in multiple languages is a challenge that developers must frequently address. This element allows you to configure aspects of an application that may differ when it is deployed to various countries, languages, etc. Settings in this element control how dates are displayed, which character sets are to be used, etc.

<compilation>

We saw this element in the previous chapter's Debugging topic, which determines ASP.NET's compilation parameters. In addition to specifying which compilers ASP.NET uses for a given operation, this element is also used to toggle whether or not pages are built in debug or release mode (see the previous chapter for details).

<appSettings> and <processModel>

We will examine these elements in the upcoming examples in this topic, which allow you to embed custom information inside configuration files and configure various aspects of the ASP.NET Runtime, respectively.

What About IIS?

Some of the configuration elements we have listed might seem confusing and redundant to experienced ASP developers. Consider the <customErrors> element, which, according to the description above, is used to redirect HTTP errors to a special web page. Developers familiar with IIS will note that the Web Server itself also exposes this capability.

Remember from our discussion in Chapter 1 that before the ASP.NET Runtime even sees requests, they are first processed by IIS. IIS then looks at its application mappings (Figure 1.2) to forward the request to the appropriate Runtime. Thus, the settings in machine.config apply only to those requests that are received by ASP.NET, which, based on Figure 1.2, includes files with extensions such as .aspx, .asmx, .axd, etc.

Therefore, the <customErrors> element is only relevant to requests received by ASP.NET. For example, when the user requests http://localhost/BadFile.aspx, the request is handled by ASP.NET according to the parameters specified by the <customErrors> element. Conversely, when the user requests http://localhost/BadFile.asp, ASP.NET does not even see the request and the error is handled by IIS.

Because IIS directs an .aspx file request to the ASP.NET Runtime (aspnet_wp.exe), another configuration setting that may puzzle you is the <httpHandler> element, which maps .aspx requests to the PageHandlerFactory class. Although these settings may seem to contradict each other, both are actually used upon an incoming .aspx request in the following fashion:

1. The request is first processed in the unmanaged/native realm of IIS, which directs the request to the ASP.NET Runtime (aspnet_wp.exe).
2. The request is then processed by the managed ASP.NET Runtime, which uses the <httpHandler> element to propagate the request to the PageHandlerFactory class.

Therefore, if you were to write your own httpHandler to process requests to files with the extension .foo, you would have to configure both IIS and the ASP.NET Runtime to direct requests to the handler. See AS070004 for an example of such a handler and how to configure it.

Recycling ASP.NET Runtime Process

The <processModel> configuration element can be used to control certain aspects of the ASP.NET Runtime. One of the most useful settings in this element is the ability to recycle (or restart) the runtime process according to certain criteria.

As the runtime executes over a period of time (hours, days, etc.), memory leaks, access violations, and other unwieldy elements can adversely affect its performance. Restarting the runtime at regular intervals can improve its response time, just as rebooting your system after a couple days can sharpen its overall performance. In addition, recycling the Runtime process can avoid catastrophic failures, such as the crash of a Web Server due to memory saturation on the system.

The <processMode> element exposes many configurable attributes, which are depicted in Listing 7.4.

```
<processModel enable="true"
    timeout="Infinite"
    idleTimeout="Infinite"
    shutdownTimeout="0:00:05"
    requestLimit="Infinite"
    requestQueueLimit="5000"
    restartQueueLimit="10"
    memoryLimit="60"
    webGarden="false"
    cpuMask="0xffffffff"
    userName="machine"
    password="AutoGenerate"
    logLevel="Errors"
    clientConnectedCheck="0:00:05"
    comAuthenticationLevel="Connect"
    comImpersonationLevel="Impersonate"
    responseRestartDeadlockInterval="00:09:00"
    responseDeadlockInterval="00:03:00"
    maxWorkerThreads="25"
    maxIoThreads="25"
/>
```

Listing 7.4   The <processModel> configuration element

We will not examine all the attributes in Listing 7.4, but for a full description, see ᶜᴺ⁾AS070005. What interests us most are those attributes that determine how and when the Runtime process is recycled: timeout, requestLimit, and memoryLimit.

Each of these three attributes recycles the Runtime according to different requirements. timeout simply restarts the process after a given number of minutes (it is set to Infinite by default). requestLimit, on the other hand, restarts the process after ASP.NET has serviced a specific number of requests (e.g., 5000). Finally, memoryLimit recycles the Runtime when it has used a certain portion of the system's total memory (60 percent, by default).

You can also combine these settings. For example, you may prescribe that the Runtime should restart itself if it has serviced ten thousand requests or has consumed 90 percent of total system memory (whichever comes first):

```
<processModel enable="true"
    requestLimit="10000"
    memoryLimit="90"
/>
```

Listing 7.5   Modifying the restart settings

Recycling the Runtime process is not without its side effects. For example, what do you do if the process restarts and you have allocated resources such as database connections and COM objects? One technique is to perform the appropriate "cleanup" steps inside the global.asax file's `Application_End()` routine, which is called when the process shuts down. In the next topic, we will see that certain ASP.NET options allow Session information to persist even when the Runtime is recycled.

Caveats

Before dispensing with the topic of process recycling, there are a couple points worth noting. First, unlike other configuration settings in ASP.NET, the IIS must be restarted in order for the changes in the `<processModel>` element to take effect. Second, these settings only apply if the ASP.NET Runtime is executing under IIS 5.0 or 5.1 (the versions that ship with Windows 2000 and XP, respectively). If you are running ASP.NET under IIS 6.0 (which ships with the Windows .NET Server OS), then the settings in Listing 7.4 will have no affect on the Runtime because IIS 6.0 has its own process-recycling model. See ᴄᴺ⮑AS070006 for details.

Web Gardening

Listing 7.4 exposes two attributes specific to Web Gardening. The first attribute, `WebGarden`, can be set to `True` to allow ASP.NET to utilize multiple processors on the machine. The second attribute, `cpuMask`, is used to specify which processors ASP.NET takes advantage of. This attribute accepts a bit mask that identifies available processors. For details on these attributes and some issues that arise in Web Gardening scenarios, see ᴄᴺ⮑AS070007.

EXAMPLE–ADDING CUSTOM INFORMATION
TO CONFIGURATION FILES

In this example we illustrate two important aspects of configuration under ASP.NET:

1. ASP.NET's configuration infrastructure is extensible, which allows you to add custom data to the machine.config and web.config files and extract them at runtime.
2. Changes to configuration files are detected immediately by ASP.NET and are implemented on subsequent requests; resetting the Web Server is not required.

Create a new project in VS.NET named ConfigDemo. As always, VS.NET gives the application a web.config file that houses configuration settings specific to the project. In order to add your own information to this file, you must place it within the <appSettings> element, as depicted in Listing 7.6.

```
<?xml version="1.0" encoding="utf-8" ?>
<configuration>
 <appSettings>
    <add key="someName" value="John"/>
 </appSettings>
 <system.web>
<!-- Rest of file omitted -->
```

Listing 7.6   Adding custom data to web.config

Custom configuration information in ASP.NET is specified by means of key-value pairs. In Listing 7.6 we have added an element called someName with the value John. It is very important that you place custom data between the <configuration> and <system.web> elements, as illustrated in Listing 7.6.

Now that this information has been added to the web.config file, we can extract it programmatically by using a special class in the BCL called ConfigurationSettings. Add the code in Listing 7.7 to the project's Page_Load() event, and the application will print out "John" when you run it.

```
Private Sub Page_Load(...)
  Dim name As String
  name = ConfigurationSettings.AppSettings("someName")
```

```
Response.Write(name)
End Sub
```

Listing 7.7   Extracting configuration information programmatically

As illustrated in Listing 7.7, user-embedded information is obtained using the class's AppSettings() method. Simply provide this method with the key name (someName), and it will return the corresponding value (John). Before we close the application, let's try one more operation that demonstrates an important virtue of ASP.NET.

Modifying Configuration Files Online

Using a text editor such as Notepad, load the project's web.config file, change the key's value from John to Stacy, and then save it (remember that you are doing this while the application is open in the browser). Wait a few seconds, and then click the browser's refresh button. Instead of printing out "John," the application should now print out "Stacy." Behind the scenes, ASP.NET automatically detects that web.config was modified and applies the change the next time the application is requested. This behavior is in stark contrast to ASP, which requires an IIS restart in order for such changes to take effect.

Any information that is storable via key-value pairs can be embedded into web.config: database connection strings, TCP/IP addresses, etc. In addition, if you want such information to be available to *all* web applications, then you can add an <appSection> element to the global-wide machine.config file.

Configuration Handlers

The information we added in Listing 7.7 is nice, but there may be times when you want to store data for which key-value pairs are unsuitable. For true versatility you can write your own Configuration Handler. If you examine the machine.config file again and look under the <configSections> element, you will find the following line:

```
<section name="appSettings"
    type="System.Configuration.NameValueFileSectionHandler,
System..."/>
```

Listing 7.8   ConfigHandler definition

A Configuration Handler is a special .NET class that is capable of interpreting XML configuration information. The <configSections> section of machine.config informs the .NET Framework as to which classes handle which configuration elements. Look at the preceding declaration, and you can see that the <appSettings> element maps to the NameValueFileSectionHandler class found in the System.Configuration namespace. Thus, whenever the .NET Framework comes across the <appSettings> element, it uses this class to process its associated information.

You can implement sophisticated configuration mechanisms by writing your own Configuration Handler. An example handler is illustrated online at ⚬ᴺ⤳AS070008.

HOW AND WHY

How Do I Obtain Information About Process Restarts Programmatically?

You can programmatically obtain information about the ASP.NET Runtime process by using the ProcessModeInfo class found in the System.Web namespace. For an example illustrating this class, see ⚬ᴺ⤳AS070009.

SUMMARY

Configuration settings in the ASP.NET Framework are stored as XML and are located in the machine.config and web.config files. Machine .config houses configuration information for the entire .NET Framework, and changes to this file affect all ASP.NET applications on the machine. The settings in web.config, on the other hand, apply only to the specific application contained within the same IIS virtual directory as the file.

ASP.NET applies configuration settings in a hierarchical fashion, first consulting the application-specific web.config file and then the global-wide machine.config file. When the two files have conflicting settings, those in web.config prevail. Both of these files expose numerous settings that determine the running characteristics of an application. One of the most powerful settings is exposed through the <processModel> element, which is used to recycle the ASP.NET Runtime at various intervals in order to make it more durable.

Changes to configuration files are detected automatically by ASP.NET and are implemented the next time an application is requested. This behavior is superior to that of traditional ASP, which requires the Web Server to be restarted in order for configuration changes to take effect.

Topic: Session Information

HTTP, the underlying transport of the web, is a memory-less protocol. Every time a client requests an application, HTTP has no idea of the caller's identity—it simply forwards the request to the Web Server. To allow for a level of continuity in a web-based application, you must utilize the technologies discussed in this topic, which allow ASP.NET applications to retain state in between client requests.

Maintaining state in traditional ASP was accomplished by means of the Session and Application objects. Whereas the Session object was used to store data unique to a particular client (such as a password), the Application object was used to store data accessible to *all* clients (such as a variable to store site hits). As we will see, both of these objects are used in exactly the same fashion in ASP.NET. What ASP.NET changes, however, are the options developers have with respect to where state information is stored. If you are unfamiliar with the concept of Session and the various underlying technologies that come into play, the analogy below will paint a clear picture of why state-related technologies are such an important facet of web development.

CONCEPTS

Analogy—the Banker with No Memory

Imagine the difficulties in having a conversation with a memory-less banker. You walk into the bank and converse with the banker to arrange a future transaction, only to arrive thereafter to discover that the banker has no knowledge of you, your business, or what the two of you discussed. To avoid future incidents and loss of business, the two of you devise a system. He gives you a ticket with an ID number, takes notes during your meeting, and locks his notes in a specially marked vault. On subsequent visits you present him with your ticket, which he uses to retrieve his notes so that you can continue your dialogue. He applies this system not only to business dealings with you, but to every one of his customers, who receive tickets with unique IDs that denote corresponding vaults. In this way, his amnesia is no longer a hindrance to his job, and operations can proceed smoothly.

The banker's predicament (and solution) is analogous to the situation that exists on the web. In order for the Web Server (the banker) to differentiate incoming requests (his customers), it must give the requesting browser a unique piece of information (a ticket) that is presented on subsequent visits. The Web Server uses this ticket to retrieve Session information (the banker's notes) from a durable storage area (the vault). As an ASP.NET developer you are the banker, and the Framework gives you a number of options to configure the types of ticket you give customers, the accessibility of your notes (which customers, if any, can see them), and protection in the event that your notes are stolen (i.e., the strength of the vault).

Cookies (the Ticket)

In traditional ASP (and many other web technologies), the ticket in the previous analogy is a cookie—a small piece of information that is retained in the client's browser and presented to the server on subsequent requests. By default, ASP.NET also uses cookies. The primary drawback with cookies is that corporations frequently disable them for security reasons. You will also hear that legacy browsers don't support them, which is true, but only for outdated browsers written several years ago. Even the earliest 32-bit versions of Netscape and IE had cookie support. As we will see in this topic, ASP.NET can be configured such that it doesn't use cookies (the "cookieless" option).

Visibility of State Data (Who Can See Your Notes)

State data in ASP.NET can be stored with varying levels of visibility. The first two levels continue from traditional ASP, and the third is a feature of ASP.NET's new Web Form paradigm.

1. Application—Application data is visible to *all* clients. Therefore, it makes sense to use the `Application` object to store information that should be globally accessible. Because the `Application` object can be used by multiple clients simultaneously, you must use the `Lock()` and `UnLock()` methods to access it:

```
Application.Lock
Application("ACMEStockPrice") = 44.10
Application.UnLock
```

Listing 7.9   Application data

The `Lock` and `UnLock` methods provide a degree of transaction control over Application-level data. In other words, if you use `Lock` and `UnLock`, you won't accidentally corrupt your own data.

An alternative to the `Application` object is the `Cache` object discussed in the previous chapter. Recall that information stored using `Cache` is also accessible to all clients. The difference is that unlike Application-stored data, cached data can be associated with time and dependency events that trigger the expiration of information inside the cache.

2. Session—Session is the most utilized type of state data and is particular to a specific browser instance. Using the `Session` object, you would store information particular to a user, such as his password, items he wished to purchase, etc.:

```
Session("UserID") = "Shannon Fernandez"
```

Listing 7.10   Using Session data

3. Page—As we saw in Chapter 5, ASP.NET maintains the characteristics of a Web Control (its color, its contents, etc.) by using a hidden HTML variable called `VIEWSTATE`. In fact, this variable maintains state for all the controls on a web page, as well as for the web page itself. As we will see, it is possible to store your own information inside the `VIEWSTATE` field using a class appropriately named `ViewState`. Remember, however, that `VIEWSTATE` is specific to a page; if the user navigates to another page, you will lose whatever custom data has been stored through this mechanism.

The upcoming examples in this topic examine these three options. As we will see, ASP.NET gives developers a tremendous amount of flexibility as to where and how state information is stored.

Where Session Information Is Stored (the Location of the Vault)

In traditional ASP, Session information was stored in the same process as the ASP Runtime. As we saw in Chapter 3 (Listing 3.4), this process is usually the host process of IIS—INETINFO.EXE. There are two major problems with storing Session information in this location. First, if the Web Server (IIS) crashes, you lose all the information you have stored. Second, storing Session in such a manner presents challenges for Web Farm scenarios, where multiple machines must share Session data. Each computer in the farm has its own process and, therefore, its own memory area for Session data.

ASP.NET is considerably more versatile than its predecessor, and allows you to store Session information in one of three locations:

1. Inside the ASP.NET Runtime process (aspnet_wp.exe). This is the default option and is the best choice from a performance perspective but suffers from the same problem as ASP Session storage: if the Web Server crashes you will lose all information.

2. Inside a dedicated Windows Service. A Windows Service is a

durable process that usually starts when the computer boots and can survive logins and logouts (in fact, IIS itself runs as a Windows Service). This technique is slower than the first option, because the ASP.NET Runtime must retrieve Session information from the external Service, rather than from its own process. However, this option is more durable, as Session information persists even if the Web Server crashes (or is restarted).

3. Inside an SQL Server database. This option is the most durable of the three. Although the second option protects against Web Server crashes, Session information is still lost if the entire machine crashes. Because this third option logs Session to a database (as opposed to the computer's memory), it will survive even a machine reboot. From a performance perspective, this option is by far the slowest.

Note that these options only apply to Session data; they do not apply to Application or Page data. Application data is always stored as part of the Framework's Runtime process, whereas Page data is persisted to the user's browser in the VIEWSTATE field and consumes no memory on the server whatsoever. In the last example in this topic we will examine ways to protect Application-stored data against a server reboot. Options two and three are also noteworthy because they can be used to share Session information in Web Farm situations across multiple machines.

In the following examples we explore the various state storage options in ASP.NET.

EXAMPLE–STORING DATA IN VIEWSTATE

In Chapter 5 we discovered that ASP.NET maintains the state of a Web Form by using a hidden and encrypted HTML field called VIEWSTATE. In our analogy, this would equate to the banker giving a customer a scrambled copy of his notes, which the customer would present to him along with his or her ticket during the next visit. The most obvious benefit of maintaining information in this fashion is that is doesn't consume any resources on the server (i.e., take up space in the bank's vault). The corresponding drawback is that this information must be transmitted to and from the client.

ASP.NET exposes a class named ViewState, which allows developers to store their own information in this hidden field. Create a new project in VS.NET with a Button and TextBox, and then add the following code to the button's event handler:

```
Private Sub Button1_Click(..)
  ViewState("SomeName") = ViewState("SomeName") & _
    "John"
  TextBox1.Text = ViewState("SomeName")
End Sub
```

Listing 7.11   Storing information inside ViewState

As Listing 7.11 illustrates, the ViewState object is accessed in a similar manner to the Session and Application objects. Each time the button is clicked, John is appended to the ViewState variable SomeName, which, in turn, is persisted to the TextBox. As the size of the variable grows (John, JohnJohn, JohnJohnJohn, etc.), so does the size of the hidden field:

```
value="dDwONDgzMjkxOTk7Oz4=" />
value="dDwONDgzMjkxOTk7dDxwPGw8U29tZU5hbWU7PjtsPEpvaG47P
j47Oz47Pg=="
value="dDwONDgzMjkxOTk7dDxwPGw8U29tZU5hbWU7PjtsPEpvaG5Kb
2huOz4+Ozs+Oz4="
```

Listing 7.12   Output of the ViewState variable

As you can see, the contents of VIEWSTATE are encrypted (it would be very difficult for a user to decipher the hidden field above in order to determine that it stored John). Also remember that this technique doesn't use any resources on the Web Server.

ViewState—Disadvantages

There are two disadvantages with storing state information using the ViewState class. First, it increases the amount of data transferred between client and server. If you store a lot of information in the VIEWSTATE (such as an array of numbers), the size of the hidden field can grow to extremely large proportions, thus increasing transmission time.

Second, and more important, the contents of the VIEWSTATE are specific to a particular page. As soon as the user navigates to another page, any information you've stored in the VIEWSTATE is lost. For example, if you run the application in Listing 7.11, click the button twice such that the TextBox reads JohnJohn, navigate to another page, and then return to the application (by reentering in the URL—not by pressing the browser's back button), the TextBox will be empty (i.e., the contents of the someName are lost).

LoadPageStateFromPersistenceMedium() and
SavePageStateToPersistenceMedium()

The described behavior of the VIEWSTATE field—the fact that its information is lost the moment the user navigates to another page—can have
subtle yet damaging consequences. Recall that VIEWSTATE is used internally by ASP.NET to maintain the state of Web Controls. Consider the
sorting application we developed in Chapter 3:

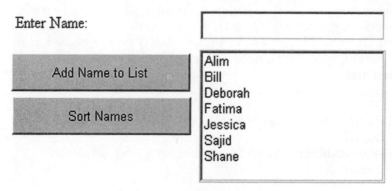

Figure 7.1   Sorting application

A number of names has been added to the ListBox in Figure 7.1. The
moment we navigate to another page, however, we lose its contents that
we have painstakingly entered. Ideally, we would want the page to retain
its contents if we returned to it at a later point.

As it stands, the architecture behind ASP.NET does not permit this
type of behavior. Because VIEWSTATE is stored in the client's browser, it
is lost when the user navigates to another page.

However, Microsoft has exposed two methods in the Page class
that you can override to address this shortcoming: LoadPageStateFrom
PersistenceMedium() and SavePageStateToPersistenceMedium(). By
implementing these methods you could store the page's VIEWSTATE to an
area (such as a Session variable) that would persist even if the user left
and then returned to the page. This more complex approach is illustrated
online at 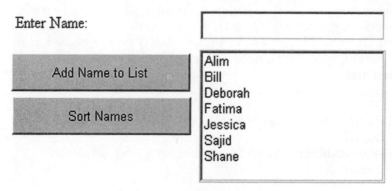AS070010.

EXAMPLE–STORING SESSION IN DIFFERENT LOCATIONS

Whereas VIEWSTATE information is stored inside the client's browser,
Session data, which is accessed through the Session object, is stored on
the Web Server. As such, Session data persists as the user browses

through multiple pages. Session in ASP.NET is configured by the <sessionState> element, which you'll find in both the web.config and machine.config files that we examined in the first topic in this chapter.

```
<sessionState
  mode="InProc"
  stateConnectionString="tcpip=127.0.0.1:42424"
  sqlConnectionString=
    "data source=localhost;user id=sa;password="
  cookieless="false"
  timeout="20"
/>
```

Listing 7.13 Session configuration

The most important attribute in Listing 7.13 is mode, which can be set to InProc, StateServer, or SQLServer, in order to determine where Session data is stored. These three settings, which will be illustrated by this example, correspond to the three Session storage options we listed at the beginning of this topic.

The timeout setting in Listing 7.13 determines the period of time during which ASP.NET maintains an individual Session (in minutes). Recall that Session data is specific to a browser instance. If the user remains idle for a period of time equal to the timeout attribute (twenty minutes by default), then ASP.NET will invalidate their Session information and remove it from wherever it is being stored. Listing 7.13 also depicts the cookieless attribute, which will be examined in the next example.

Storing Session Data In-process

By default, ASP.NET stores Session information inside its Runtime process. The shortcoming of this setting is that Session data does not survive a Web Server restart. To illustrate this problem, create a new project in VS.NET named SessionDemo, and then add the following code to the project's global.asax file.

```
Sub Session_Start(...)
  'Fires when the session is started
  Response.Write("Session started<p>")
  Session("StartTime") =
    DateTime.Now.TimeOfDay.ToString()
End Sub
```

Listing 7.14 Storing Session in Session_Start

As explained in Chapter 4, global.asax is ASP.NET's equivalent of the global.asa file that you used in ASP—it houses code that is accessible to all pages within the application. In addition, this file houses methods such as Application_Start and Session_Start that are triggered when the ASP.NET application starts and when an individual session starts, respectively. Thus, the code in Listing 7.14 stores the time at which the client accessed the application into the Session variable StartTime.

Next, add the following code to the project's Page_Load() event, which prints out the contents of the StartTime variable.

```
Private Sub Page_Load(...)
  'Put user code to initialize the page here
  Response.Write("Session stored at: ")
  Response.Write(Session("StartTime"))
End Sub
```

Listing 7.15   SessionDemo application

Run the application by pressing F5, and the browser will output something similar to the following:

```
Session started
Session stored at: 15:26:55.7489696
```

Listing 7.16   SessionDemo output

Press the browser's refresh button, and the first line in the output will disappear because Listing 7.14 executes only on new client instances. The point of this exercise is that when Session information is stored in process, it does not survive a Web Server shutdown. If you type iisreset at a Command Prompt to restart IIS, and then try to access the application again, the time it reports will change. In other words, ASP.NET did not persist the StartTime variable when the Web Server was restarted.

Storing Session Inside the Windows Service
It is possible to store Session information apart from the ASP.NET Runtime inside a Windows Service named aspnet_state. To enable this option you must first modify the project's web.config file as follows:

```
<sessionState
  mode="StateServer"
  stateConnectionString="tcpip=127.0.0.1:42424"
/>
```

Listing 7.17   Storing Session out of process

Next, you must start the ASP Windows Service, which will store Session data. There are two ways to accomplish this. First, you can go to the Command Prompt and type `net start aspnet_state`. Second, you can go to Start → Programs → Administrative Tools → Computer Management, click `Service Applications` and then `Services`, which will bring up a screen similar to Figure 7.2.

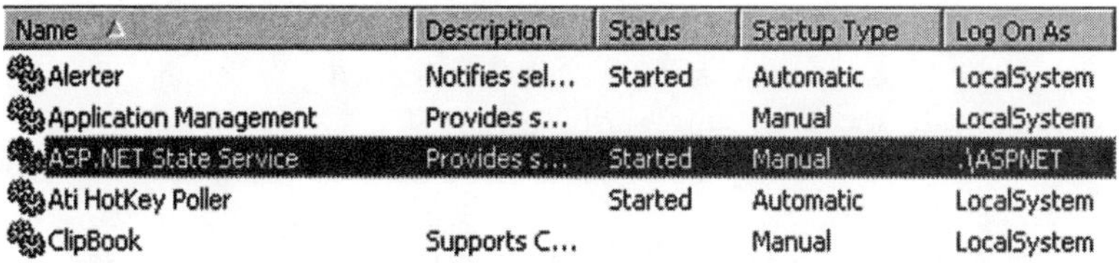

Name	Description	Status	Startup Type	Log On As
Alerter	Notifies sel...	Started	Automatic	LocalSystem
Application Management	Provides s...		Manual	LocalSystem
ASP.NET State Service	Provides s...	Started	Manual	.\ASPNET
Ati HotKey Poller		Started	Automatic	LocalSystem
ClipBook	Supports C...		Manual	LocalSystem

Figure 7.2   Starting the ASP Session service

Right-click `ASP.NET State Service` and select `Start`. As illustrated in Figure 7.2, this service must be started manually (look under the `Startup Type` heading). If you plan to use this Session storage option, then you can configure the service to start automatically when the OS boots, by right-clicking `ASP.NET State Service`, selecting `Properties`, and then changing `Startup Type` from `Manual` to `Automatic`.

As a result of these settings, Session information will be stored inside the Windows Service (aspnet_state.exe), as opposed to the ASP.NET Runtime itself. Thus, Session will persist even on a Web Server restart. Run the application again by pressing `F5`, and as expected, the application will report the time the Session started by printing out the `StartTime` variable. Restart IIS by typing `iisreset` at the Command Prompt, click the browser's `refresh` button, and you will observe the effects of storing Session out of process: the reported time will remain the same, indicating that Session information persisted through the restart.

The *stateConnectionString* Attribute

Look at Listing 7.17 and you will see an additional attribute called `stateConnectionString`. This attribute specifies the TCP/IP address where the ASP.NET Service is located. Those familiar with TCP/IP will recognize that the address in Listing 7.17 (127.0.0.1) is a special TCP/IP value, which informs ASP.NET that the Service is located on the current machine. With this setting it is possible to direct ASP.NET to a Windows Service on another machine, a capability that is useful in Web Farm scenarios. For example, all machines in the farm could specify the same address and thus store (and share) Session on a dedicated computer. More information on this attribute can be found at ⚓AS070011.

Storing Session in SQL Server

Your last option when storing Session information in ASP.NET is to store it in a Microsoft SQL Server database (version 7 or greater required). Employing this option is straightforward, but requires more Administrative steps than the first two options. We outline the process briefly here; for full treatment on the subject, see ^{CN}AS070012.

In order to store ASP.NET Session information inside SQL Server you must:

1. Have SQL Server version 7 or 2000 installed.
2. Execute the following script using SQL's Query Analyzer, which creates the database that ASP.NET uses to store Session:

```
\%winroot%\Microsoft.NET\Framework\versionNum\InstallSql
State.sql
```

3. Modify the web.config file appropriately (where the connection String attribute denotes the connection string that should be used to open the database):

```
<sessionState
  mode="SQLServer"
  sqlConnectionString=
    "data source=127.0.0.1;user id=sa;password="
/>
```

Listing 7.18   Connecting to SQL Server

Storing Session inside SQL Server is the most durable option, as information persists even if the machine crashes. This is the slowest option of the three, however, because Session data must be accessed from disk rather than directly from memory, a process thousands of times slower. Note that as with the Windows Service option, you can point ASP.NET to a Session store on a different machine, which is also appropriate in Web Farm settings.

References to COM Objects

A common technique in traditional ASP is to use Session variables to store references to COM objects so that they can be used at a later time:

```
Set Session("MyObject") =
  CreateObject("WhatProc.WhatProc")
```

Listing 7.19   Storing a COM object reference

If you intend on employing this technique in ASP.NET, then you *must* store all Session information in process (the default option). Attempting to store it in either the Windows Service or SQL Server results in an error similar to the following:

```
The type System.__ComObject in Assembly mscorlib...is
not marked as serializable.
```

In addition, if you wish to store Session references to regular .NET classes, then they must be Serializable. For an explanation of these restrictions and Serializable classes, see ⌒CN⟩AS070013.

EXAMPLE–COOKIE CONFIGURATION IN ASP.NET

Our demonstrations up to this point have concentrated on where Session information is stored (the location of the vault). In this example we concern ourselves with how ASP.NET identifies incoming clients (the ticket). Recall that by default, ASP.NET utilizes cookies—a small amount of information that is embedded into the clients' browsers and used on subsequent requests. You can disable ASP.NET's use of cookies by modifying the project's web.config, in order to enable its cookieless option:

```
<sessionState
   mode="InProc"
   cookieless="true"
   ... rest of config
/>
```

Listing 7.20   ASP.NET's cookieless feature

Modify SessionDemo's web.config file according to Listing 7.20, run the application by pressing F5, and it will function as it did in the previous example—the application will report the time the Session started. Take a close look at the URL, however, and you will notice something strikingly different:

```
http://localhost/SessionD/(cadssl45tpxh4sbdhauu30ri)/Web
Form1.aspx
```

As you can see, ASP.NET embeds the SessionID (the ticket) into the URL itself, a process sometimes referred to as cookie munging. You may wonder what occurs if users bookmark this cryptic URL so that they can return to it at a later time. Remember that if the user is idle, Session information will persist for a period of time equal to the timeout attribute. If the user returns to the page after this prescribed amount of time, the SessionID in URL will be invalid, at which point ASP.NET will create a new Session for the user.

In addition to disabling cookies in ASP.NET, you can also embed your own cookie information into the client's browser by using the Framework's HttpCookie class. In our analogy, this would be equivalent to writing information on the customer's ticket, which we would then scrutinize upon the next visit. For details on employing the HttpCookie class, see ⟨CN⟩AS070014.

The Application Object

Unlike Session information, data that is stored through the Application object is visible to *all* clients. Unfortunately, Application-stored data is *always* stored inside the ASP.NET Runtime process. Accordingly, if the Web Server crashes, you will lose whatever information was stored using this object. If you are storing sensitive data, a worthwhile alternative is to store information inside a database using ADO or ADO.NET.

One occurrence that you can explicitly account for is the recycling of the ASP.NET Runtime. Recall from the first topic in this chapter that the Runtime process can be recycled at various intervals by means of the <processModel> configuration element. When the process recycles, the Application_End() method (located in global.asax) is triggered. Within this method you could transfer Application-stored information to a database, such that it persisted during the restart.

Shared Variables

An alternative to using the Application object to store globalwide data is to use Shared class variables in VB.NET (static variables in C#, Java, and C++). Recall from the end of Chapter 3 that an ASP.NET application is compiled into a Page class behind the scenes. As their names suggest, shared/static variables are shared among multiple instances of a class and are hence accessible to multiple clients of an application. For an example that uses shared/static variables in ASP.NET, see ⟨CN⟩AS070015.

HOW AND WHY

How Do I Share Session Data Between ASP and ASP.NET?

As we learned in Chapter 3, the ASP and ASP.NET Runtimes execute within different processes (inetinfo.exe and aspnet_wp.exe, respectively).

As a result, traditional ASP scripts (.asp) and ASP.NET applications (.aspx) cannot share Session information. For example, if an ASP.NET application stores a value of 30.03 in a Session variable called ACMEStock, an ASP application cannot retrieve this value through Session("ACME Stock"). In order to share information between classical ASP and ASP.NET, you must use alternate techniques such as sharing a database or COM component. For more information on this issue, see ⟟AS070016.

SUMMARY

To retain information between client requests, applications must maintain state using the technologies discussed in this chapter. There are three ways to store state data in ASP.NET:

1. On a per-page basis using the ViewState class. This class can be used to embed custom information into the hidden VIEWSTATE field that ASP.NET generates as part of its response to clients. However, any information that is stored using this class is lost if the user navigates to another page.
2. On a per-user basis using the Session object. By default, Session information in ASP.NET is stored inside its Runtime process. Options in the <sessionState> configuration element, however, allow developers to store Session in more durable locations: a Windows Service or SQL Server Database. Session information stored in either of these two locations persists even if the Web Server crashes and is applicable in Web Farm scenarios where numerous machines must share Session.
3. On an application basis using the Application object. Application-stored data is accessible to all users of an application and should be accessed using the Application object's Lock() and UnLock() methods. Another way to store global-wide data is to use shared/static class variables.

Topic: Deploying to a Web Server

In this topic we consider the steps required to deploy an application to a Web Server. Although the exact procedure will vary from application to application, there are some general guidelines and practices that we can highlight. One aspect of deployment that we will illustrate is the ability to update a component without having to shut down the Web Server beforehand—a notorious problem that plagued traditional ASP/COM development.

CONCEPTS

Deploying .NET Framework
In most cases, a production Web Server will not have a copy of Visual Studio.NET installed. However, to run ASP.NET applications they will require an installed copy of the .NET Framework (CLR, BCL, etc.). Remember that the .NET Framework is installed as part of the .NET Windows Component Update (see Chapter 2).

Building a Web Application
As we saw in Chapter 4, when you create a web application project in VS.NET the development tool performs the following administrative steps behind the scenes:

1. It creates an IIS virtual directory with the same name as your application.
2. It creates a subdirectory named bin within this virtual directory, which houses the application's assemblies.
3. It creates a number of hidden subdirectories within the virtual directory (_vti_txt, _vti_cnf, etc.), which are required by the FrontPage Server extension technology utilized by VS.NET.

To deploy an application to a Web Server, you must perform Steps 1 and 2 manually on the target machine, and then copy the project's files to their corresponding directories (Step 3, the creation of hidden directories such as _vti_txt, is *not* required). We'll illustrate this procedure by example in a moment, but some additional considerations are:

- Ensure that both the web application and any class-library assemblies it uses are built using the Release option. Recall from our discussion on debugging in Chapter 6 that applications are normally built in Debug mode, which results in larger and slower code.
- If you are utilizing shared assemblies (Chapter 3), then they must be registered in the Web Server's Global Assembly Cache via the GACUTIL utility.
- If you are utilizing COM components through the COM Interop

technology discussed in Chapter 9, then you must register these components on the Web Server (using regsvr32.exe). In addition, if these components utilize COM+ services, they must be "configured" on the Web Server (configuration means importing the component into the COM+ subsystem; ignore this step if you are not using COM+).

- If you are leveraging COM+ natively from .NET using the System.EnterpriseServices classes examined in oᶜᴺ₎AS090012, then you must register applicable class-library assemblies with COM+, using the RegSvcs.exe utility.
- Use the IIS/ASP.NET settings we will detail in Chapter 8 to configure security appropriately.
- Don't forget to turn off those options that are inappropriate for production deployment—tracing, debug comments, etc.

EXAMPLE–DEPLOYING THE WHEREAMI APPLICATION

In this example we illustrate how to deploy the WhereAmI application we developed in Chapter 3 to a Web Server. Recall that this application used a private assembly named myAssembly to print out its host process. As this example illustrates, it is possible to update assemblies even while the web application is running. This is in contrast to COM components used in traditional ASP, which can only be updated by shutting down the Web Server.

To fully appreciate this example it is recommended (though not required) that you have a second machine with only the .NET Framework installed (not VS.NET). In the absence of a separate machine, use the development box you have been utilizing up to this point. Note that the Enterprise version of VS.NET can perform a lot of the installation steps we outline here by means of a Microsoft Installation (.MSI) file that it produces. For details see oᶜᴺ₎AS090007.

When we created the WhereAmI application in Chapter 3, VS.NET created an IIS virtual directory also named WhereAmI. Usually, this virtual directory maps to the logical directory C:\Inetpub\wwwroot\ WhereAmI on the machine (where C:\ is the OS directory). This directory contains:

1. Files that constitute the application, such as Global.asax, WebForm1.aspx, and Web.config. The directory also houses the application's CodeBehind source files, such as WebForm1.aspx.vb.
2. A bin directory that contains a CodeBehind assembly (WhereAmI.DLL), which is a compiled amalgamation of the proj-

ect's CodeBehind source files. This directory also houses any private assemblies that the application uses (myAssembly.DLL in our case).

In order to deploy this application, create a virtual directory on the Web Server using the instructions in Chapter 2. The virtual directory can be named anything (it doesn't have to take on the same name as the project)—for this example name it aspPort. Recall from Chapter 2 that to create a virtual directory you must map it as a logical directory on the hard drive. Use c:\aspPort for this example, and then give this directory a subdirectory named bin.

Deploying the application is simply a matter of performing the following two operations:

1. Copy project files from C:\Inetpub\wwwroot\WhereAmI to c:\aspPort. When you are performing this step it is generally a good idea to omit CodeBehind source files (such as WebForm1 .aspx.vb), as they are not required for deployment.
2. Copy assembly files from C:\Inetpub\wwwroot\WhereAmI\bin to c:\aspPort\bin.
3. After completing these two operations, the application can be accessed from the Web Server by navigating to http: //localhost/aspPort/WebForm1.aspx (if you are accessing the Web Server from another machine, then replace localhost with the appropriate address).

Updating Assemblies

In ASP.NET you can update assemblies without having to shut down IIS (note that this does *not* apply to COM components). Run the WhereAmI application and click its button, and it will use myAssembly to print out its host process: %winroot%\Microsoft.NET\Framework \vX.xxx\ASPNET_WP.EXE

While the browser is open, load the myAssembly project that we created in Chapter 3, and replace the code for WhatProcess() with the following trivial implementation:

```
namespace myAssembly
{
  public class ProcessInfo
  {
    public string WhatProcess()
    {
```

```
      return "I don't know";
   }
 }
}
```

Listing 7.21   myAssembly—reports what process we're running in

Compile the project, and then copy the new assembly file (myAssembly.DLL) to the C:\aspPort\bin directory. Click the browser's refresh button, and the application will now display "I don't know" (if you don't see the new output, consult the How and Why section of this topic).

Behind the scenes, the ASP.NET Runtime detects the new assembly automatically and uses it upon the next request (similar to the manner in which it automatically detected changed configuration files in the first topic of this chapter).

The Src Attribute
Recall from Chapter 3 that the CodeBehind attribute specifies the name of a Page's CodeBehind file:

```
<%@ Page Language="vb" CodeBehind="WebForm1.aspx.vb"
Inherits="Client1.WebForm1"%>
```

Listing 7.22   The CodeBehind link

Similarly, the Inherits attribute denotes the CodeBehind class of the page. When ASP.NET comes across this attribute, it immediately looks in the project's bin directory for an assembly that contains such a class. When it finds a match, it uses this "CodeBehind" assembly to create a second Page assembly that ultimately serves client requests (see the end of Chapter 3 for details).

In the previous example the CodeBehind assembly was called WhereAmI.DLL and we copied it to the c:\aspPort\bin directory. The assembly was produced by VS.NET when you compiled the project; copying it to the Web Server is a necessity—if you remove it from the bin directory then ASP.NET will generate an error.

In certain situations you may want the Web Server to compile the CodeBehind assembly on the fly as incoming requests are received. In other words, you may wish for ASP.NET to generate the CodeBehind assembly at runtime, as opposed to copying it a priori.

One advantage of this approach is that it ensures that assemblies are compatible with the version of the Framework installed on the Web Server. As .NET matures, numerous versions of the Framework will likely be released. It might be the case that a project is developed using version 1.0.3617 of the Framework, and then deployed onto a server with version 1.0.3215. This leads to the dangerous predicament of the Web Server trying to interpret an assembly that was created with a newer version of the Framework.

In order to produce CodeBehind assemblies on the fly you must use a special attribute named Src, which specifies the names of the Code-Behind source file. This attribute must be applied to every page in the application, as well as to the project's global.asax file. It also requires some minor modifications to the application's source. We detail this procedure online at ⟨CN⟩AS070017.

HOW AND WHY

Why Doesn't the Application Display the New Output Even Though I Copied the New Version of myAssembly.DLL?
Recall that we wrote the myAssembly class library in Chapter 3. At a later point in that chapter, we also registered this assembly in the Global Assembly Cache in order to illustrate the shared assembly concept. When an assembly is shared, ASP.NET always loads it from the GAC instead of the project's bin directory. To see the application's new output, remove myAssembly from the GAC by going to %winroot%\ assembly directory using the Windows Explorer (Figure 3.9), right-clicking myAssembly, and selecting *Delete*.

SUMMARY

To deploy an application to a Web Server you must copy the project's files to an IIS virtual directory that you've created on the target machine. In addition, you must copy the project's assembly files (.DLLs) to the bin subdirectory within the virtual directory. After accounting for other special requirements, such as registering shared assemblies in the GAC and registering COM components, the application can be accessed from the Web Server.

Class-Library Assemblies that an application is utilizing can be updated simply by copying them to the application's bin directory (while the application is running). The next time the application is requested, ASP.NET will use the new components automatically. This deployment scheme is an improvement over COM components used in ASP, which were locked down by the Web Server and thus required an IIS restart to be updated.

Chapter Summary

ASP.NET offers noteworthy administration improvements over ASP. Web application information is now stored in XML format, where it can be parsed and easily manipulated. This is in contrast to ASP, which stored configuration information in IIS's proprietary metabase and made it difficult to retrieve.

ASP.NET offers a host of configuration options not available in ASP. Its Runtime process can be recycled at regular intervals in order to improve reliability; Session information can be stored in durable locations such as an SQL Server database, which simplifies Web Farm deployment; and the Framework can be configured to run on multiple processors on a single machine. Changes to configuration settings are detected on the fly by the runtime and are used on subsequent requests.

Chapter 8

—

SECURITY

Enterprise web-based applications must frequently process and deliver sensitive information. Unfortunately, accessible applications are also exploitable ones. It is therefore vital that developers control who can access such applications and what they can or cannot do with them once access has been granted. In this chapter, we survey the technologies that allow you to secure web applications in ASP.NET.

Security in ASP.NET is based on two principles: authentication, which establishes a user's identity based on some supplied credentials (e.g., UserID and password); and authorization, which determines which aspects of an application a user can access once his or her identity has been established through authentication. Phrased alternatively (and in the order in which they occur):

1. Authentication either permits or revokes access by verifying credentials such as a password.
2. Authorization uses the identity obtained in Step 1 to determine which application resources and options the user can access.

As this chapter will illustrate, ASP.NET exposes numerous options both to authenticate and to authorize incoming requests.

As we have stressed throughout this book, requests to the ASP.NET Runtime are first received and processed by Internet Information Server (IIS). Therefore, the IIS technologies used to secure traditional ASP applications (Secure Socket Layers, IP Security, etc.) apply equally well in

ASP.NET. A notable portion of this chapter is devoted to exploring IIS's security options.

Another security-related topic in .NET is the CLR's Code Access Security (CAS) infrastructure, which does not relegate access to web applications, but instead enforces security on all .NET entities (web applications, Desktop Application, class-library assemblies, etc.). One powerful aspect of CAS is the ability of the CLR to assign an application certain rights depending upon the origin of the code for the application. For example, code that originates from the Internet might not be allowed to read the registry, whereas code executed from the user's hard drive would be given full permissions. A full discussion of CAS can be found at ☞AS010010.

CORE CONCEPTS

Domains and Active Directory
In the language of the Windows Operating System, a domain is a family of computers that can share resources and be treated collectively as a unit. For example, as a member of the CODENOTES domain, a computer would gain access to resources such as a Microsoft Exchange server (for e-mail), shared printers on the domain, etc. In addition to encapsulating a collection of computers, a domain keeps track of which users can access its resources. Whereas the Administrator user is normally given unlimited access, a user such as TheNovice might be granted substantially fewer capabilities.

On Windows 2000 and XP, all domain-related information, such as computer names and user IDs, are maintained in a central database called Active Directory. On Windows NT4 this information is stored in an entity named the Security Accounts Manager (SAM) database (which is actually located in the system registry). Another difference between NT4 and newer versions of the OS is the protocol that it utilizes to validate users of the domain (i.e., to log in the user). Whereas NT4 uses the NT Lan Manager (NTLM), Windows 2000 and XP use a robust protocol named Kerberos (which was originally developed at MIT). Both of these protocols can be employed in ASP.NET to determine whether a user should be granted access to an application. In other words, with ASP.NET you can determine admittance based on a user's membership in a domain, an option we'll explore in the first topic.

Group/Role
On the Windows Operating System it is possible to treat a collection of users as one entity by putting them into a group (also known as a role).

When a user is placed within a group, it inherits all the privileges associated with the group. In fact, the Windows OS ships with a number of built-in groups such as Administrators, Power Users, and Guests, which it uses for security purposes. For example, by placing a user within the Administrators group, the user obtains the rights to do whatever an administrator can do (basically, control the entire machine).

You can leverage groups in ASP.NET by using the Framework's role-based security infrastructure. Role-based security is a powerful technique that allows you to control access to an application on a group basis. For example, you can prescribe that all administrators should be able to access an application without having to specify each individual member within the group. Thereafter, you can manage access to the application through the OS's group infrastructure without having to modify the application's code. Effectively, this allows you to manage access to an application administratively instead of programmatically.

Topic: Authentication

The process of authentication is central to web development because HTTP requests are inherently anonymous. By default, it is impossible to differentiate between the various users accessing a web application. Although such anonymity is frequently acceptable for public Internet sites, establishing a user's identity is important when you want to allow only certain users to access an application (or portions of an application).

Although authentication is frequently associated with user identification, the term is actually more encompassing. More precisely, authentication is the validation of credentials against an authority. This authority can be an encrypted text file (as in Unix), an SQL Server database, the IIS metabase, or the Windows 2000 Active Directory. The actual process of authentication can be performed by IIS, ASP.NET, or the OS itself. In addition, authentication is a Boolean operation. Either the user's credentials are validated successfully, in which case access is allowed; or the validation fails, in which case access is denied. If the request is accepted, then Authorization policies (the next topic in this chapter) come into play, where access to resources can be granted at varying levels of granularity (for example, certain users may only be allowed to read specific files).

The first Authentication technologies we examine in this topic are those exposed by IIS. Remember that IIS processes requests before they are received by ASP.NET. Therefore, the Web Server's authentication policies will always supersede those of ASP.NET. The three authentication schemes we will examine in this topic are:

1. Integrated Windows Authentication, which establishes user identity based on a Windows Operating System Account. When anonymous users access the application, they are queried for their domain IDs and passwords. If the authority verifies them (i.e., if the UserID/password is correct), then access is granted. The actual protocol and authority that are used for verification depend on the underlying OS. For Windows 2000 and XP, Kerberos/Active Directory is used; for NT4, NTLM and the SAM database are employed.
2. Forms-based Authentication, which determines a user's identity based on a custom Web Form that you design. Anonymous users are redirected to this form, where they must (presumably) enter information that will be checked against a data store. This data store can be an XML file, a database, or, as we will see, the project's configuration file itself.
3. Passport Authentication, which obtains the user's identity by means of Microsoft's Passport technology. We will explore this option in greater detail at the end of this topic.

In the examples that follow we will see how we can use these Authentication technologies to determine who a user is. In the next topic on Authorization, we will see how this identity can be utilized to relegate access to certain aspects of an application.

CONCEPTS

IIS Authentication Technologies
As we learned in the previous chapters, an ASP.NET application is contained within the confines of an IIS virtual directory. Therefore, your first option to authenticate requests is to do so using IIS's virtual directory options. Bring up the Internet Services Menu (Figure 1.1) from your Start menu, right-click the aspTest virtual directory that we created in Chapter 2, and select Properties. Next, click the Directory Security tab, which allows you to configure Authentication settings for the virtual directory. There are three settings in this tab, each of which determines how incoming requests are authenticated:

1. Anonymous access and Authentication control—these settings determine whether IIS allows anonymous users to access files

within the virtual directory, or if the user must log in through a valid Operating System account. We will examine these settings in detail in the next section.

2. IP address and domain name restrictions—these settings allow you to restrict access based on the requesting computer's IP address. For example, you could permit access only from machines with IP address numbers between 192.20.5.0 and 192.20.5.100. You can also take the opposite approach and block access to a range of addresses.

3. Secure communications—these settings allow you to configure IIS so that requests and responses are encrypted and decrypted on the fly by the Web Server (these operations are transparent to ASP.NET). For more information on SSL, see °ᴺᐅAS080001.

Remember that these settings are completely independent of ASP.NET and are applied to incoming requests before the Runtime even sees them.

Integrated Windows Authentication

Integrated Windows Authentication validates users by means of either Active Directory/ Kerberos (on Windows 2000 or XP) or SAM/NTLM (on Windows NT4). This may seem like a complex operation, but it is really quite straightforward: when an incoming request is anonymous (we'll see what constitutes anonymity in a moment), the browser queries the user for his ID and password. If the information he enters corresponds to a valid account in the domain, then the request is granted. If the information he enters is invalid, then the user will receive an "access denied" error. Because Windows Authentication only works on IE browsers, this authentication technique is most suitable in Intranet scenarios where the browser can be standardized.

A concept closely tied to Windows-based Authentication is the operating system account under which the web application runs. For example, when you use an application such as Microsoft Word, the program attempts to access system resources (files, the registry, etc.) using the logged-in account (e.g., CODENOTES\sfernandez). A natural question is what account ASP.NET applications run under, given the various authentication schemes that they employ. We will revisit this important question in the next topic on Authorization. For now, simply bear in mind that Windows-based Authentication allows or denies access based on domain membership.

EXAMPLE–WINDOWS–BASED AUTHENTICATION

Windows authentication must be enabled through the Internet Service Manager. Using this tool, right-click the aspTest virtual directory and bring up the Directory Security tab we examined in the previous section on IIS Authentication. Under Anonymous access and Authentication control click Edit, which will bring up a screen similar to Figure 8.1.

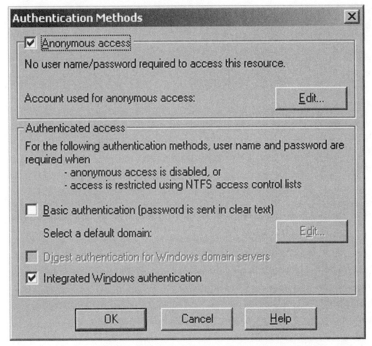

Figure 8.1   IIS's authentication options

As illustrated in Listing 8.1, IIS allows the virtual directory to receive anonymous requests (by default). To enable Windows-based Authentication, simply uncheck the Anonymous Access box in this option page (note that the Integrated Windows Authentication box is selected in Listing 8.1). As a result of these configuration changes, any applications accessed within the aspTest virtual directory will be authenticated according to the following rules:

1. If the request emanates from a computer where the user is already logged in (on the *same domain* as the Web Server), then the request is automatically granted. If not, Step 2 is performed.
2. Internet Explorer prompts the user for his or her domain ID and

password via a login box (Figure 8.2). This information is then transmitted to the Web Server, which verifies it against either the Active Directory or SAM Authorities. If the user's credentials are valid, then access is granted.

Try to access the first timer application that we developed in Chapter 1 by navigating to http://localhost/aspTest/Timer.aspx, and you will observe the effects of the first rule: access is automatically granted (it is as if there were no authentication at all). According to the first rule, if the user is already logged in to the machine (which presumably you are), then access is permitted.

The important point is that the user must be logged in to the *same* domain that the Web Server sits atop of. For example, if the Web Server exists on a domain named CODENOTES, then access is granted only if the user is logged in to the CODENOTES domain (there are ways around this using the Active Directory *trust* concepts). Thus, if you try to access the timer application from another machine on a different domain (the ROARK domain, for example), Internet Explorer will ask for your credentials, as in Figure 8.2.

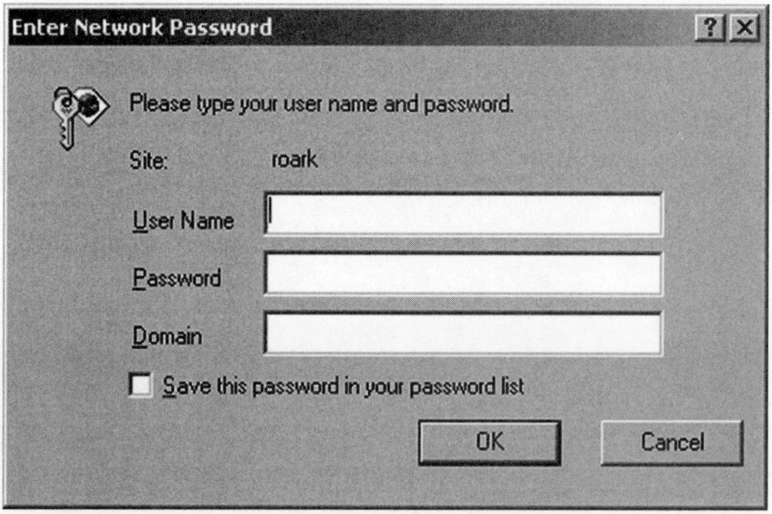

Figure 8.2   IE's login box

A user can enter his or her credentials up to three times using the prompt in Figure 8.2. If all three attempts fail, then IIS returns an HTTP 401 Access Denied error to the browser. Remember that this entire process is completely independent of ASP.NET. With that in mind, consider how you might redirect the Access Denied error that the user receives to a more friendly web page.

You might reason that you could employ the <customErrors> configuration element that we discussed in Chapter 7 (recall that this element can be used to reroute HTTP errors to designated web pages). Remember, however, that this element is only employed if the request is received by ASP.NET. Because unauthenticated requests of this type are rejected by IIS before ASP.NET even sees them, the Framework never has a chance to use the settings in <customErrors>. In order to redirect errors such as these, you must employ IIS's rerouting mechanisms by right-clicking the aspTest directory in the Internet Services Manager and then clicking the Custom Errors tab. Using the options in this screen, you would then direct HTTP 401 errors to a web page of your own design.

Forms-based Authentication

Unlike Integrated Windows Authentication, Forms-based Authentication is performed completely by ASP.NET. The premise behind Forms Authentication is simple. If an incoming request is anonymous, then ASP.NET directs users to a special *login* page of your design. The manner in which this page authenticates users is completely up to you. It could ask the user for a password and ID, which would then be checked against an SQL Server database; or it could query the user for his age, and only allow access to those users older than eighteen (admittedly, an easily foiled scheme). Once you have authenticated a user according to your rules, you redirect him to the original page he requested using a special class in the BCL.

One of the advantages of Forms-based Authentication over the Windows Authentication is that the nature of the authentication scheme and the login screen are completely within your jurisdiction. Whereas the login screen in Figure 8.2 only queries for a UserID and password, a Forms-based login page could ask for considerably more information (such as an e-mail address or credit card number).

EXAMPLE–FORMS-BASED AUTHENTICATION

Create a new project in VS.NET named FormsDemo. As always, the development environment gives the project a default page named Web-Form1.aspx. Add a second page to the project named Login.aspx by going to Project → Add Web Form. We will now configure the project to use Forms-based Authentication according to the following rules:

1. When the user requests any page in the project, he is redirected automatically to the login page (Login.aspx).
2. Login.aspx allows the user to submit his name and password, which are then verified (we'll see how in a moment). If the information he enters is valid, then he will be redirected to the original page, and subsequent requests from the same user will not have to be authenticated again.

In order to enable Forms-based Authentication you must modify the project's web.config file according to Listing 8.1.

```
<authentication mode="Forms" >
  <forms name="LoginForm"
     loginUrl="login.aspx"
     protection="All"
  />
</authentication>

<authorization>
  <deny users="?" />
</authorization>
```

Listing 8.1   Enabling Forms Authentication in web.config

Two configuration elements in ASP.NET control security: `<authentication>` and `<authorization>`. We will examine the `<authorization>` element in the next topic, but basically, the `deny users="?"` line in Listing 8.1 prevents anonymous access to the application and forces requests through Forms-based Authentication (similar to the manner in which we had to disable anonymous access in IIS in the previous section).

Forms-based Authentication is enabled by setting the `<authentication>` element's `mode` attribute to `Forms` (you will notice that by default this attribute is set to `Windows`, an option we will examine in the next topic). If Forms Authentication is enabled, then there must be a `<forms>` element within the `<authentication>` element, which prescribes the web page to which anonymous users are directed. In Listing 8.1 we stipulate that anonymous users should be directed to Login. aspx. To understand the last attribute, `protection`, we need to consider how ASP.NET determines if requests are anonymous in the first place.

Using Cookies for Authentication
Recall from our discussion on Session in Chapter 7 that a cookie is a small piece of information embedded inside the user's browser. When

an incoming request is received by ASP.NET, the Framework looks for a special "Forms" cookie. If one is not found, then ASP.NET classifies the request as anonymous and directs the user to the login page. If the user is validated, then this special cookie is placed inside the client's browser so that subsequent requests (from the same user) won't have to be reauthenticated.

The protection attribute determines the strength to which ASP.NET encrypts and validates the special cookie it uses for Forms Authentication. The setting of All in Listing 8.1 is the strongest and most reliable option, although other parameters can be used (see the MSDN for details).

The Login Page

As a result of the settings in Listing 8.1, anonymous users will be directed to Login.aspx. Using VS.NET, design the login page such that it is similar to Figure 8.3.

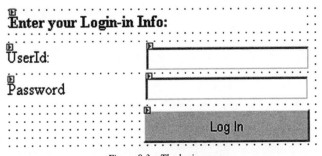

Figure 8.3 The login page

Next, add the following code to the page's CodeBehind file. This code will only allow access to users with an ID of "Steve" and password of "Foo." (Note that the login page would be a good candidate for the Validation controls we examined in Chapter 5).

```
'Required namespace:
Imports System.Web.Security
Private Sub Button1_Click(...)
If TextBox1.Text = "Steve" And TextBox2.Text = "Foo"
Then
  FormsAuthentication.RedirectFromLoginPage( _
    "Steve", False)
Else
  Label1.Text = _
    "Invalid ID, re-enter your Login-in Info:"
```

```
End If
End Sub
```

Listing 8.2   *Login.aspx—Forms-based Authentication*

Listing 8.2 is straightforward. When the user clicks the Log In button in Figure 8.3, the code checks to see whether the user is "Steve" with password "Foo." If this is the case, then the user is directed to the original page requested, by means of the FormAuthentication class's RedirectFromLoginPage() method. This method accepts two parameters. The first is the UserID, which is passed to the application's Authorization policy (as we will see in the next topic). The second is a Boolean variable, which determines whether authentication should be reperformed in the event that the same user attempts to access the application from another browser instance (this parameter actually has to do with the special Form cookie ASP.NET uses—for more information, see ⚫⥈AS080002).

Having written the Login page, add the following code to Web-Form1.aspx, which prints out the UserID that was obtained during authentication.

```
Imports System.Web.Security
Private Sub Page_Load(...)
  Response.Write("Welcome...")
  Response.Write(Page.User.Identity.Name)
End Sub
```

Listing 8.3   *WebForm1.aspx*

The Page.User.Identity class provides access to all of the information stored about a particular authenticated user. Run the application by pressing F5, and because WebForm1 is the default page of the project, VS.NET will navigate to http://localhost/FormDemo/WebForm1.aspx. Because the call is anonymous (i.e., the browser does not yet possess the special Form cookie), ASP.NET directs the request to Login.aspx. Enter in a UserID of Steve with password Foo, and you will be redirected to WebForm1, which prints out "Welcome . . . Steve". If you enter in any other UserID and password, however, the request will not propagate.

Storing User Information Inside web.config
Listing 8.2 is unrealistic. In practice, you should never hard-code UserIDs and passwords into the project itself. More often, you would query a data store such as an SQL server database or an XML file. A third option is to store usernames and passwords inside a project's

web.config file. This is accomplished by adding a <credentials> element within the <form> element, as shown in Listing 8.4.

```
<authentication mode="Forms" >
  <forms name="LoginForm"
    loginUrl="login.aspx"
    protection="All">
    <credentials passwordFormat="Clear">
      <user name = "Steve" password="Foo"/>
      <user name = "Bill" password="Bar"/>
    </credentials>
  </forms>
</authentication>
```

Listing 8.4   Storing UserIDs/passwords in web.config

Information that is embedded into the configuration file via the <credentials> element can then be extracted by means of the FormAuthentication class's Authenticate() method, as shown in the login page's new code in Listing 8.5.

```
'Replace the Button1_Click method in Listing 8.2
'With this modified version

Private Sub Button1_Click(...)
If FormsAuthentication.Authenticate(TextBox1.Text, _
  TextBox2.Text) Then
  FormsAuthentication.RedirectFromLoginPage(_
    TextBox1.Text, False)
Else
  Label1.Text = "Invalid ID, Enter your Login-in Info:"
End If
End Sub
```

Listing 8.5   Extracting data in web.config

The Authenticate() method accepts a name and password, and returns True if it finds a corresponding UserID/password pair inside the web.config file. Therefore, based on Listing 8.4 and Listing 8.5, the only users who will be authenticated are Steve and Bill with passwords Foo and Bar, respectively.

The primary shortcoming with this technique is that passwords appear as clear text inside the configuration file. The passwordFormat attribute makes it possible to encrypt these passwords such that they are unreadable. This technique is illustrated online at ⌇AS080003.

Passport-based Authentication

A third way to authenticate users is to employ Microsoft's Passport technology. This option, which requires the Passport SDK, is similar in concept to Forms-based Authentication, except that it directs users to Microsoft's Passport sign-in site, rather than a custom-designed Web Form. More information on Passport Authentication can be found at ᵒ⁻ᶜᴺ✓AS080004.

Mixing Authentication Schemes

Integrated Windows Authentication is performed by IIS; Forms-based Authentication is performed by ASP.NET. You can combine these two schemes and have each authentication technique performed by its respective engine. For example, if you use the Internet Services Manager and disable anonymous access to the FormDemo virtual directory from the previous example, authentication will proceed in the following fashion when the project is accessed:

1. The incoming request is processed by IIS, and if the user is not logged in to a valid domain, he is presented with the login box in Figure 8.2.
2. If IIS validates the user's credentials, then it forwards the request to ASP.NET. If the user's credentials are rejected, the browser receives an HTTP access denied error.
3. ASP.NET detects that the browser does not contain a special Form cookie, and thus considers the request anonymous (even though IIS authenticated it). It directs the request to the Login.aspx page depicted in Figure 8.3.
4. The user must enter his credentials a second time (which could differ from the UserID and password he or she used for Windows Authentication). If ASP.NET validates the second set of credentials, then it (finally) forwards the user to the page originally requested.

Although mixing Authentication models can be a complex procedure, you could use the preceding setup to ensure that: (1) only users within a given domain can access the application; and (2) all users must log in through your specially designed login form. For example, if you were writing an application for the company's Intranet, you could use Windows Authentication to ensure that the application was accessible only to members of the corporation's domain. Then you could use Forms-based Authentication to restrict accessibility to a subset of users within the company. As we will see in the next topic, however, if you decide to intermix Authentication schemes, you must take certain precautions when setting the application's Authorization policy.

SUMMARY

Authentication is the process of establishing a user's identity. This is accomplished by comparing the user's credentials against an Authority. The three authentication schemes in ASP.NET differ in the Authority against which credentials are checked and the entity that performs the authentication.

Integrated Windows Authentication validates a user's credentials against either Active Directory (Windows 2000, XP) or the SAM database (NT4). This authentication scheme is facilitated by IIS and requires that anonymous calls to the application's virtual directory be turned *off* in the Internet Services Manager. When a request is anonymous (if the client is not logged in to a valid domain), then Internet Explorer queries the user for his ID and password. If the information the user enters is valid, then the request propagates to ASP.NET. If the information is invalid, then the user receives an Access Denied error. This Authentication scheme is best employed in Intranet scenarios, as it only works on an IE browser.

Forms-based Authentication allows developers to implement custom validation solutions. Developers must design a special login Web Form, to which anonymous users are directed. This login page can query for any type of information (e-mail, credit card, age, etc.) and check it against any Authority (a database, a text file, the registry, etc.). In other words, the type of validation that is carried out by Forms-based Authentication is completely up to the developer. After validating the user's credentials, the login page directs the request to the original page, using the FormAuthentication class's RedirectFromLoginPage() method. Forms-based Authentication is enabled by setting a project's <authentication> element to Forms. The <authentication> element must also contain a <form> element that specifies the login page that is used for authentication.

The premise behind Passport authentication is similar to Form authentication, except that users are directed to Microsoft's Passport sign-in site rather than to a custom-designed Web Form. Utilizing this Authentication scheme requires the Passport SDK, which can be downloaded from the Microsoft website (www.microsoft.com).

Topic: Authorization

Whereas Authentication is the process of determining a user's identity, Authorization is the process of determining which resources a user can access once their identity has been established. In this topic we will examine the various Authorization techniques in ASP.NET.

CONCEPTS

NTFS File Authorization

Every time you use Windows NT4, 2000, or XP, you are, in fact, already employing a form of authorization. Whenever you access a file, the Operating System consults the file's protection settings to determine whether access should be permitted. You can examine a file's protection settings by right-clicking the file in Windows Explorer, selecting Properties, and then clicking the Security tab. This tab allows you to control what users can and cannot do with the file. For example, you could institute a policy stipulating that only users in the Administrators group could write to the file, whereas all other users could only have read access. This Authorization mechanism is referred to as NTFS file protection, as it is only available on the NT File System format (which is supported by Windows NT, 2000, and XP).

You can employ NTFS file authorization directly on a Web Server. Consider the timer application that we wrote in Chapter 1 (Listing 1.3). You could apply NTFS protection settings on Timer1.aspx, which stipulated that the file could only be accessed by CODENOTES\Steve. Such a policy is enforced by the OS and is completely independent of IIS and ASP.NET. Employing NTFS file protection, however, raises an important consideration in ASP.NET security: Under what Operating System account does the ASP.NET Runtime execute? We investigate the answer to this important question later in this topic.

The <Authorization> element

One of the most powerful Authorization schemes in ASP.NET is the ability to declaratively prescribe application accessibility based on user (or group) identity. This is accomplished by using the <authorization> element in the project's web.config file. Consider the FormsDemo project that we wrote in the previous topic (Listing 8.2 through Listing 8.5). This application identified users according to the IDs they provided in Login.aspx (Figure 8.3). Once this ID has been ascertained, the application's authorization policy is applied in accordance with the <authorization> element. Consider Listing 8.6.

```
<authorization>
   <allow users = "Bill"/>
   <deny users="*"/>
</authorization>
```

Listing 8.6   Authorization in web.config

The policy in Listing 8.6 specifies that Bill is an allowed user and that ASP.NET should deny access to everyone else (in ASP.NET, "*" represents everyone, while "?" signifies anonymous users). This policy is applied *after* authentication has been performed. Thus, after the user enters his credentials and the login page validates him or her, ASP.NET consults Listing 8.6 to determine whether the user is allowed to access the application. Because of Listing 8.6, even though Steve is granted access by the authentication process, he will be denied access because of the Authorization policy (only Bill is given access).

The preceding process may seem redundant and counterintuitive. After all, what's the point of granting Steve access during the Authentication phase, only to revoke it during the Authorization period? The answer to this question involves the following considerations:

1. Frequently, applications will share one data store for Authentication (they do not use information embedded inside their own web.config files). A separate Authorization step allows an application to be configured specifically, even though Authentication information is shared. For example, you may perform Forms-based Authentication against a company database outside your jurisdiction (i.e., you don't control which users are added to it). Because the project's web.config file is within your jurisdiction, however, you can still delegate access to the application based on your own rules (i.e., even though both Steve and Bill are in the company database, you can grant access only to Bill).
2. Authentication is a Boolean operation—access is either granted or denied. Users can be compartmentalized into various levels of access. For example, certain users may be allowed to perform only certain operations.
3. Authorization allows you to grant access to a collection of users very easily using Roles, a topic we will discuss in the next section.

The second point above (varying access according to the user) is demonstrated in Listing 8.7.

```
<authorization>
   <allow users = "Bill" verbs="POST"/>
```

```
<allow users = "Steve" verbs="GET"/>
<deny users="*"/>
</authorization>
```

Listing 8.7   Varying access using the verbs attribute

Listing 8.7 prescribes that Bill can only perform HTTP POST actions, whereas Steve is limited to HTTP GET actions (these settings can have destructive consequences for ASP.NET-based applications; see ☞AS080005 for details). This is in contrast to Authentication, whereby a user is either granted access or denied it.

Machine.Config and deny users="*"

One aspect of Listing 8.7 that may seem confusing is the `<deny users="*"/>` line. After all, isn't it enough to simply allow access to Bill and Steve? Why must we explicitly deny access to all other users? To understand the necessity of this line, we must recall the interplay between the web.config and machine.config files, which was detailed in Chapter 7.

Consider what occurs if the `deny` line is removed from Listing 8.7. ASP.NET first reads the project's web.config file, which grants access to Bill and Steve. However, it then consults the globalwide machine.config file and finds the following line, which grants access to *all* users: `<allow users="*"/>`.

As a result, you must negate this line with `<deny users="*"/>`, which revokes access to *all* users. Although we now have conflicting configuration settings, as we learned in Chapter 7, those in web.config prevail (and hence, only Steve and Bill are permitted access).

Integrated Windows Authorization

The `<authorization>` settings in Listing 8.7 grant access to Bill and Steve. These identities were established by means of `FormDemo`'s login page, which uses Forms-based Authentication. Another option in ASP.NET is to perform authorization based on the user's Integrated Windows Account (i.e., his or her domain account). This technique is illustrated in Listing 8.8.

```
<authentication mode="Windows"/>
<authorization>
  <allow users="CODENOTES\sfernandez;
    CODENOTES\asomani"/>
  <allow roles="CODENOTES\Administrators">
  <deny users="?" />
</authorization>
```

Listing 8.8   Windows-based Authorization

Note that in Listing 8.8 the `<authentication>` element's mode attribute has been set to Windows (also note that there is not a `<forms>` element as with Forms-based Authentication). The Windows setting instructs ASP.NET to obtain the user's identity from the IIS Windows Authentication procedure, which we examined in the previous topic (whereby IIS queries the user for his or her domain account).

Listing 8.8 only allows access to the `sfernandez` and `asomani` users in the `CODENOTES` domain, as well as any users who belong to the domain's Administrators group. Recall from the Concepts section in this chapter that the Windows OS allows you to create groups that encapsulate a set of users. To allow access to an entire group in ASP.NET you must use the `roles` attribute, as illustrated in Listing 8.8 (also note that the group must be prefixed with the domain name: `CODENOTES\Administrators`).

deny users="?" versus deny users=""*
An important setting in Listing 8.8 is the `deny users="?"` line. Unlike `deny users="*"`, which denies access to *all* users, this line revokes access to all *anonymous* users (recall that in ASP.NET, `"?"` refers to all anonymous requests). The difference between these two lines has a subtle but substantial effect on the operation of Listing 8.8, because in ASP.NET the `users` attribute is given preference over the `roles` attribute.

With this fact in mind, consider what would happen if you replaced the `"?"` with a `"*"` in Listing 8.8. As a result, any members of the Administrators group (other than `sfernandez` and `asomani`) will be denied access, even though the `roles` attribute includes them. Because the `users` attribute takes precedence over `roles`, the `deny users="*"` line will be applied to all Administrators members, thus denying them access. Therefore, when using the `roles` attribute in ASP.NET, always deny access by using the anonymous (?) specifier instead of the global specifier (*).

Role-based Security
The Authorization policy in Listing 8.8 utilizes the predefined Administrators role. You can define your own roles on the Operating System by using either the `Computer Management Console Tool` or the `Active Directory Computers and Users` tool (depending upon whether you are utilizing Active Directory). For example, you could create an OS group named `Managers`. After adding certain users to the `Managers` group, you could then use the `<authorization>` attribute to allow only those members in the group to access an application. In addition to specifying roles on the OS level, you can also employ CLR role-based security, which allows you to define roles separate from the Operating System. We detail this procedure, as well as some programmatic techniques you can use with roles, at ᴄᴺ AS080006.

Mixing Authentication Schemes

In the previous topic we explained that one could intermix authentication schemes, using IIS for Windows Authentication, and then ASP.NET for Forms-based Authentication. A question that often arises when this technique is employed is: Which ID does ASP.NET use for Authorization? In other words, if the user logs in through Windows Authentication as CODENOTES\asomani, but then logs in as Steve by means of Forms Authentication, which ID does ASP.NET apply to Listing 8.8? The answer to this question is determined by the mode attribute of the <authentication> element. If it is set to "Windows" then the Windows Authentication UserID (CODENOTES\asomani) is used; if it is set to "Form", then the Form UserID (Steve) is applied.

What Domain Account Does ASP.NET Runtime Execute Under?

By default, applications execute under the logged-in account (which, for my machine, is CODENOTES\sfernandez). Thus, whenever an application I'm running tries to open a file, consult the registry, or access any other resource on the system, the OS ensures that CODENOTES\sfernandez has the proper permissions to do so. Every running application must execute under a valid domain account, including the ASP.NET Runtime. The natural question, of course, is: What account does the Runtime execute under? This is an important question, because any entity that ASP.NET (and hence a web application) attempts to access—a file, a database, the registry, etc.—is performed under the context of this account. If you are familiar with SQL Server, for example, you know that a database can be configured such that it is accessible to only certain domain accounts. Likewise, the NTFS security system, which we discussed at the beginning of this chapter, can be used to employ the same restrictions on a file.

To begin our investigation into this far-reaching question, create a new project in VS.NET named WhoAmI. Add the code in Listing 8.9 to the project's Page_Load() event, which prints out two important pieces of information.

```
'Import a required namespace:
Imports System.Security.Principal
Private Sub Page_Load(...)
  Response.Write("The User's ID: ")
  Response.Write(Page.User.Identity.Name)
  Response.Write("<p> ASP.NET Runtime account:")
  Response.Write(WindowsIdentity.GetCurrent().Name)
End Sub
```

Listing 8.9   Determining the ASP.NET Runtime account

We'll explain the operation of Listing 8.9 in a moment, but run the application by pressing F5, and the program will output something similar to the following:

```
The User's ID:
ASP.NET Runtime account: YourDomain\ASPNET
```

Listing 8.10   WhoAmI output

As you can see, the ASP.NET Runtime executes under a special account named ASPNET. This account was added to the OS automatically when you installed the Framework. Thus, any resource utilized by the application must be configured to allow access from this special account. Listing 8.9 determines this "host" account by using the WindowsIdentity class located in the System.Security.Principal namespace.

We'll return to the host account in a moment, but notice that the program doesn't print out a value for the user's ID. Remember that Page.User.Identity.Name is the ID ascertained during the authentication period. However, as we learned in the previous section, the type of authentication performed in ASP.NET is configured by means of the <authentication> element's mode attribute. Look in the project's web.config file, and you will see that this attribute is set to Windows (by default), which means that ASP.NET obtains the user's ID from IIS's Windows Authentication scheme. Furthermore, as we observed in the beginning of this chapter, the default behavior of IIS is to allow anonymous requests. Thus, IIS doesn't perform any authentication when you run the application, which results in the empty UserID value.

Using the Internet Services Manager, disallow anonymous requests to the WhoAmI virtual directory (see Figure 8.1). Rerun the application, and the output will now read:

```
The User's ID: YourDomain\YourUserID
ASP.NET running account: YourDomain\ASPNET
```

Listing 8.11   Revised WhoAmI output

Because IIS disallows anonymous requests, it performs Integrated Windows Authentication on the incoming call. As discussed at the beginning of this topic, if the call emanates from a machine with a valid logged-in account, then the request will be granted. If not, then Internet Explorer will query the user for their account information. In either case, the user's ID propagates to ASP.NET, which prints the information in the browser.

User ID versus Host Account

It is imperative that we understand the difference between the two accounts displayed by the WhoAmI application. The first account, Your Domain\YourUserID, is the one that ASP.NET uses for Authorization purposes. For example, if we gave the application an Authorization policy similar to Listing 8.8, then ASP.NET would only grant access if YourUserId were in the Administrators group. Assuming that access was granted, the application would then execute and utilize OS resources under the second account, YourDomain\ASPNET. In other words, whereas the user's domain account is used to identify the user and apply authorization, the second account (ASPNET) is used to access resources when the application runs thereafter.

Impersonation

In practice, you may want Runtime to run under the user's account. That is, in the previous example you might want the ASP.NET host account to be YourUserId instead of ASPNET. There are several reasons why this scenario is desirable. First, OS operations such as registry and file access will be performed under the context of the user's account, which allows you to employ techniques such as SQL Server database protection and NTFS security. Second, because the default account used by ASP.NET (ASPNET) is granted only a limited number of privileges by the system, you may wish for the Runtime to execute with a greater amount of latitude. Third, any components spawned from the web application (such as Class-Library assemblies or COM components) will also run under the more capable user account. This is an especially important consideration for COM+ developers who leverage COM+ role-based security, as this technology depends on components running under distinguishable accounts.

You can implement the described behavior (i.e., the masking of the ASPNET account with a user account) by adding the following line to the project's web.config file, which instructs ASP.NET to execute under the *account* that IIS authenticates (add this line after the `<authentication>` element).

```
<identity impersonate="true"/>
```

Listing 8.12   Impersonating another user

This technique is referred to as impersonation, because ASP.NET impersonates the domain account of IIS rather than using the default ASPNET account. Run the application a third time, and it will now output:

```
The User's ID: YourDomain\YourUserID
ASP.NET running account: YourDomain\YourUserID
```

Listing 8.13   Impersonation output from WhoAmI

As you can see, the ASP.NET Runtime now executes under the user's account. You might apply this setting for special "Administration" portions of an application, which must access vital system resources such as the registry, system files, etc. Another option is to have the Runtime execute under an account that you specify by means of the userName and password attributes:

```
<identity impersonate="true"
   userName="CODENOTES\sfernandez"
   password="Pablo"
/>
```

Listing 8.14   Configuring ASP.NET to run under CODENOTES\sfernandez

As a result of Listing 8.14, the Runtime will always execute under the CODENOTES\sfernandez account. At the time of this writing there appear to be some problems with specifying the host account in this fashion. See ᴄᴺAS080007 for details.

Anonymous Access in IIS

You may wonder what occurs if you employ impersonation when an incoming request is anonymous. In other words, what happens when you instruct ASP.NET to impersonate IIS, if the Web Server permits anonymous calls, and thus doesn't run under a user account itself?

Using the Internet Services Manager, turn on anonymous access for the WhoAmI virtual directory, and rerun the application. The output will now read:

```
The User's ID:
ASP.NET running account: YourDomain\IUSR_MachineName
```

Listing 8.15   Anonymous access

As you might expect, the user's ID is not reported, as IIS does not authenticate incoming calls (and thus an ID is not available to ASP.NET). However, when an incoming call is anonymous, IIS runs under a special account named IUSR_MachineName (where MachineName is the name of the machine). Think of this account as the IIS equivalent of the ASPNET account that we saw earlier—it is added to the system when the Web Server is installed. In this example, because ASP.NET is configured to impersonate IIS (by means of the `impersonate` attribute), it, too, runs under `IUSR_MachineName`.

Host Process Review

As you can see from this example the host account of the ASP.NET Runtime depends on two main factors: first whether IIS allows anonymous requests, and second, whether ASP.NET is configured to impersonate IIS. The host account that results from the combination of these factors is given in Table 8.1.

	ASP.NET Impersonate= "false"	ASP.NET Impersonate="true"
Anonymous requests (IIS)	**DOMAIN\ASPNET**	**DOMAIN\IUSR_ MACHINE**
Authenticated request (IIS)	**DOMAIN\ASPNET**	**The user's account**

Table 8.1   ASP.NET host account table

Changing Default Accounts

There are two default accounts in Table 8.1: `IUSR_MachineName`, which is used by IIS when an incoming request is anonymous, and `ASPNET`, which is used by ASP.NET when impersonation is turned off. You can change the default accounts used by IIS and ASP.NET by using the Internet Services Manager and by modifying the machine.config file, respectively. We illustrate how to change default accounts at °⤷AS080008.

Domain Accounts and Forms-based Authentication

Unlike Integrated Windows Authentication, Forms-based Authentication is completely independent of IIS. A requirement that frequently arises when you employ Forms Authentication is to have the ASP.NET Runtime execute under different domain accounts, depending upon the UserID that is established during the authentication phase.

Consider the `FormsDemo` application that we developed in the previous topic (Listing 8.2 through Listing 8.4). This application grants access to two users: Bill and Steve. In this case, we may wish to specify that when the user is Steve, then ASP.NET should execute under the `CODENOTES\Manager` account. Conversely, if the user is Bill, then the Runtime should use `CODENOTES\NotManager`. Unfortunately, "mapping" accounts in this fashion requires manual code that goes outside the managed world of .NET. We illustrate this more complex procedure online at °⤷AS080009.

The Forbidden Handler (HttpForbiddenHandler)

As we learned in the previous chapter, an HttpHandler is a low-level ASP.NET entity that is capable of handling raw HTTP requests. Open machine.config using a text editor, look under the <httpHandlers> element, and you will find the following lines:

```
<add verb="*" path="*.cs"
  type="System.Web.HttpForbiddenHandler" />
<add verb="*" path="*.vb"
  type="System.Web.HttpForbiddenHandler"/>
```

Listing 8.16   The ForbiddenHandler configuration

These lines direct requests for files with .cs or .vb extensions to the HttpForbiddenHandler class. You may recognize that files with these extensions house a project's source code. By directing users to the forbidden handler (which simply denies access) when these files are requested, users are prevented from downloading a project's source code. You can utilize this handler to protect other types of files from being downloaded by the user. For an example that employs the forbidden handler, see ⨀AS090010.

HOW AND WHY

Why Do I Get the Following Error?

Access to the path "%winroot%\Microsoft.NET\Framework\version\ Temporary ASP.NET Files….\somefile" is denied.

At the end of the day, any resource that an ASP.NET application attempts to access is subject to the Operating System's policies. As we saw at the beginning of this topic, you can employ NTFS security to restrict access to a particular file. Recall from the end of Chapter 3 that ASP.NET must perform a number of steps in order to respond to a request. One of these steps is the compilation of the application's Page class, which is placed in the Temporary ASP.NET Files directory. You will receive the error in question if the host account of the Runtime does not possess the NTFS rights to access this directory (or files within it). For example, if you instruct ASP.NET to impersonate IIS and the authenticated user only has Guest privileges on the Web Server, then ASP.NET will be prevented from producing the Page class, thus producing this error.

To correct this problem you must ensure that the domain account in question has NTFS privileges to write to the system directories that ASP.NET accesses. For more information, see ⨀AS080011.

SUMMARY

Authorization is the process that is applied after a user's identity has been established through Authentication, and it allows developers to manage access to an application's resources. In ASP.NET, Authorization is enabled by means of the <authorization> configuration element, which can be used to grant access either to a particular user or to a collection of users within a group. A group (also known as a role) can be defined on the OS level (such as the Administrators group) or on the CLR level, which exists independent of the OS.

Resources that a web application utilizes, such as files, databases, and COM+ components, frequently have their own Authorization schemes. Often, these policies are based on the OS account under which the ASP.NET Runtime executes. By default, ASP.NET applications execute under a special account named ASPNET. Via the Framework's impersonation options, however, it is possible to have the Runtime execute under the user's account that is established by Integrated Windows Authentication.

Chapter Summary

The thorny issue of security has always been a prime concern for web developers. The ASP.NET Framework exposes powerful Authentication and Authorization options that allow you to easily establish a user's identity and manage resource access with this identity. There are three entities that enforce security in ASP.NET:

1. The Windows Operating System, which uses OS-level Authorization policies to determine which users can access the resources on the Web Server. These resources include entities such as files and the system registry, and they are regulated by well-known Windows security features such as NTFS protection.
2. Internet Information Server, which can leverage the Operating System's network Authority (Active Directory or SAM) in order to limit application access to only those members within a Windows Domain (Integrated Windows Authentication). These settings are independent of ASP.NET and are akin to those features that you used in traditional ASP.
3. ASP.NET, which allows you to easily develop custom-based solutions to validate a user's credentials against a custom Au-

thority, such as a text file or database (Forms-based Authentication). ASP.NET security options are configured in a project's web.config file.

These three entities can also leverage one another's features. For example, ASP.NET can apply role-based security against the user's domain account that is obtained by IIS, whereas the Windows OS utilizes ASP.NET's "host" account (the account under which the Runtime executes) to regulate access to OS entities.

The ASP.NET host account plays a crucial role in application security, as it is not only employed by the OS itself, but by other entities such as COM components that leverage COM+ role-based security and databases that utilize OS accounts for security purposes. The ASP.NET host account depends upon the configuration settings in both IIS and ASP.NET. The Runtime can execute under default accounts such as ASPNET and IUSR_Machine, the user's account, or a specific account that you designate.

Indeed, writing secure applications in ASP.NET requires mastering the security features offered in these different realms. Although the interplay among the participating entities can become complex, the combination of the features afforded by the Windows OS, IIS, and ASP.NET allow web applications to be thoroughly secured.

Chapter 9

—

MIGRATION, LEGACY CODE, AND

ENTERPRISE SERVICES

The virtues of a new technology are often counterbalanced by migration efforts; a new Framework may be more feature-rich than its predecessor, but is of little value if the price of transitioning to it outweighs its bene-fits. Such is the concern with ASP.NET.

As with most new technologies, the most thorough path to ASP.NET migration is to completely rewrite an application in the new Framework. For ASP.NET, this involves porting older ASP code written in VBScript and JScript to typed languages such as VB.NET or C#. In addition, components used by the ASP application (such as COM components written in VB6) must be converted to Class-Library Assemblies.

In practice, migration usually takes on a more gradual approach. In this chapter we examine the technologies designed to ease the transition from ASP to ASP.NET:

1. COM Interop, which allows ASP.NET applications to call COM components that you may be utilizing in ASP.
2. Platform Invoke (PInvoke), which allows you to call Win32 DLLs from ASP.NET. Although you did not have this capability in ASP (and should only employ this technology in special cases), it is invaluable in situations where you want low-level functionality (security debugging, for example).
3. Special <@%Page directives that allow you to move existing ASP scripts to ASP.NET with minimal effort.

The first two technologies are significant because they allow you to call pre-.NET (native) components from managed ASP.NET applications. Although this a powerful capability, calling native code from ASP.NET has some drawbacks (see the following Cautions section).

The last topic in this chapter illustrates how ASP.NET developers can leverage COM+ services using special classes in the BCL. If you are unfamiliar with COM+'s role in the realm of web development, consult the following Core Concepts section.

CORE CONCEPTS

Native Code Cautions

Recall from our discussion of the .NET Framework in Chapter 3 that the presence of the CLR creates a dichotomy between applications running on the Windows Operating System. Applications that run within the CLR (such ASP.NET applications) are said to be managed. Entities that predate .NET and execute outside the CLR (such as COM components) are said to be unmanaged.

There are many differences between the managed and unmanaged worlds. For example, unmanaged applications use native Operating System types, with cryptic names such as DWORD, WCHAR, LARGE_INTEGER, and so on (you were completely abstracted from these details in ASP). Managed applications, on the other hand, use types in the Common Type System such as System.String, System.Int64, etc.

Much like communicating between different languages, moving between the unmanaged and managed worlds requires a translator. For COM components, this translator is called a Runtime Callable Wrapper (RCW); for Win32 DLLs, it is the CLR that does the translation. In either case, translation comes at the price of performance.

Calling native components from ASP.NET applications forces the CLR to suspend its execution and give way to code that operates outside its boundaries. This process is further compounded because the CLR must translate data between both sides of the fence using a process called marshalling. When you call a native component that accepts a string, for example, the CLR must convert the managed System.String into an unmanaged equivalent and reverse the process when the function returns.

For performance reasons, it is good practice to avoid the use of native components wherever possible. As we saw in Chapter 3, the .NET Framework exposes hundreds of services through the Base Class Libraries, which house evolved versions of many technologies that you have used in the past. For example, as we discuss at ⟨CN⟩AS090008, ADO.NET is a newer managed version of ADO.

Another reason to avoid the use of native components is their lack of stability. As explained in Chapter 3, the CLR conserves resources by allowing multiple ASP.NET applications to execute within one Operating System process. Although the CLR can protect concurrently running managed applications from one another by using AppDomains, native code that is invoked from ASP.NET is not granted such protection. Because native entities execute outside the CLR, they have no concept of AppDomains; if a COM component does something illegal, it will bring down the entire host process (aspnet_wp.exe) and any other ASP.NET applications within it.

Finally, when calling native code from ASP.NET, you must ensure that the ASP.NET Runtime account (which was examined in the previous chapter) has the proper rights to invoke native code. Ensuring this condition is not always intuitive; for details see ⟨CN⟩AS090009.

Nevertheless, there are times when calling native code from ASP.NET is unavoidable. Thousands of COM components exist for which there are no managed equivalents. As we will see in this chapter, VS.NET's menu options make calling native components from ASP.NET extremely straightforward. Simply bear in mind that calling native code is costly, and consider .NET alternatives wherever possible.

Three-tier Architecture, Application Servers, and COM+

Enterprise applications are often divided into logical units of functionality. A common model is the "three-tier" architecture setup, which consists of the following units:

1. The presentation layer, which houses the logic and design behind the graphical interface the user sees. This layer is written in whatever web technology you are using, be it ASP.NET/ASP, JSP, or PERL.
2. The business layer, which processes client requests and determines the information that must be written and read from the third layer. The business layer validates the user's requests against business rules, such as whether or not a credit card is valid, etc.
3. The data layer, which stores all the information for the system, usually inside a relational database such as Microsoft SQL Server, ORACLE, or IBM'S DB2.

Typically, Enterprise applications house their business logic (sometimes referred to as middle-tier logic) inside software components, which themselves reside within an application server. With traditional ASP, such software components were usually COM components written in either Visual Basic or Visual C++ and were housed in Microsoft Transaction Server (MTS) on NT4, or in COM+ on Windows 2000. Among other services, application servers such as COM+ provide components with important infrastructure for security, transactions, and object pooling (whereby a single component can be utilized by multiple applications in order to avoid initialization overhead).

You can leverage COM+ services from ASP.NET by using the classes found in the System.EnterpriseServices namespace. These classes are not used directly by ASP.NET applications, but are employed by Class-Library Assemblies (components) that web-based applications would utilize. For more information, see ⚭AS090012.

Topic: COM Interop

COM Interop technology allows you to use COM components from ASP.NET. As discussed in the Core Concepts section in Chapter 1, COM was the standard mechanism behind component communication on the Windows OS prior to .NET.

You have, in fact, already used a COM-based entity from ASP.NET in this book. In the CLR topic in Chapter 3, we used a COM component to determine the host process of an ASP.NET application by utilizing the CreateObject() function (Listing 3.5). Although it is still usable in ASP.NET, CreateObject() is undesirable for two reasons:

1. As discussed in Chapter 3, objects created through this mechanism are late-bound. If you call an object incorrectly (e.g., by invoking a method that doesn't exist), the error will not be caught until the application executes inside the browser.
2. Because CreateObject() does not make use of a COM component's type library (also discussed in Chapter 3), user-friendly features such as IntelliSense are not available on objects created through this mechanism.

As we will see in the upcoming example, both these limitations are removed when you use VS.NET's Add Reference option to leverage COM components from ASP.NET.

EXAMPLE–USING TRADITIONAL ADO FROM ASP.NET

One scenario where you are likely to utilize COM Interop technology is when you call ADO from ASP.NET (since ADO is exposed through COM). In traditional ASP, ADO is the standard library for communicating with databases. As we have previously stated, .NET offers a new database technology called ADO.NET, which differs considerably from its predecessor. In fact, the models are so different that developers familiar with the intricacies of ADO are likely to continue using it in ASP.NET (just remember that calling native code from ASP.NET incurs a performance hit).

Caution aside, we now demonstrate how to use "traditional" ADO from ASP.NET. Begin by creating a web application project in the VS.NET, using VB.NET as the language. Next, go to the Project menu and select Add References. Click on the COM tab and select the ADO library (version 2.5), as shown in Figure 9.1.

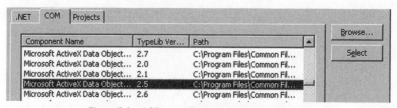

Figure 9.1   Adding a reference to a COM component

Click Select and then OK, at which point VS.NET will import the COM component into the project (it performs a lot of underlying operations during this time, which we will examine in a moment). After VS.NET completes its work you'll notice that it has added a new reference named ADODB to the Solutions Explorer.

We have now added a reference to the ADO library, which can be accessed through the ADODB namespace. Add a button to your application, and then add the following code to its event handler, which extracts and prints out the result of a database query.

```
'Need this namespace:
Imports ADODB

Private Sub Button1_Click(. . .)
  Dim mConnect As New Connection()
  Dim mRecord As New Recordset()
```

```
Dim mCmd As New Command()

'Open Connection (change to reflect you Database)
mConnect.Open("DSN=CodeNotes")

'Obtain an ADO recordSet of the Companies Table:
mCmd.CommandText = "Select * From Companies"
mCmd.ActiveConnection = mConnect 'No Set
mRecord = mCmd.Execute   'No Set

'Print all the StockIDs in the TradeTble Table
mRecord.MoveNext()
Do While Not mRecord.EOF
  'No default properties, so explicitly use value:
  Response.Write(mRecord("CompanyName").Value & "<p>")
  mRecord.MoveNext()
Loop
mConnect.Close()
end sub
```

Listing 9.1   Using ADO from ASP.NET

There are some notable differences between the ASP.NET code in Listing 9.1 and equivalent ASP code that uses ADO. First, note that there are no CreateObject() statements. Rather, by importing the ADODB namespace at the top of the listing, we can explicitly dimension variables as ADO RecordSets, Connections, etc. This alternate technique has the added benefit of providing IntelliSense in the development environment. Additionally, COM objects accessed in this fashion are early-bound, which means that they can be type-checked at compile time. Thus, if you try to call an inappropriate method on an ADO RecordSet (such as rs.Foo()), VS.NET will catch the error when you try to compile the application.

Our ASP.NET code differs from traditional ASP code in two more respects. As illustrated in Chapter 3 (Listing 3.5), the Set keyword is no longer used in VB.NET, hence its exclusion from Listing 9.1 Second, default properties are no longer supported in the traditional VBScript/ VB6 manner. In ASP we could have written the following:

```
Response.WriteLine(mRecord("CompanyName"))
```

Listing 9.2   Default properties in ASP (VBScript)

In ASP.NET we must write the more verbose:

```
Response.WriteLine(mRecord("CompanyName").Value)
```

Listing 9.3   Default properties in ASP.NET (VB.NET)

Because Value is the RecordSet's default property, it is used automatically whenever a RecordSet is referenced ambiguously, as it is in Listing 9.2. Default properties were an unwieldy syntax element in VB6 and VBScript. VB.NET, however, does not support the default property syntax, so you have to explicitly reference the property name. Although more succinct, default properties make code difficult to read. This is one syntax change that you will have to perform repeatedly as you migrate ASP code to ASP.NET.

Run the application by pressing F5, click the button, and the application will print the results of the query on the screen. You should modify the connection string in Listing 9.1 to reflect the database you are using. In our case, we used a Data Source Name (DSN) called CodeNotes. Alternatively, the connection string could specify an SQL Server or an Oracle database.

Interop Assemblies

Using COM components in ASP.NET is extremely straightforward thanks to an entity called an Interop Assembly. When you added a reference to the ADO library in the previous example, VS.NET created an Interop Assembly for you behind the scenes.

An Interop Assembly is one that "wraps" the COM component you are trying to use. In fact, in ASP.NET you never directly communicate with a COM component. Instead, you invoke the Interop Assembly, which does the communication on your behalf. Thus, in Listing 9.1, the application is really making calls against an Interop Assembly, which, in turn, communicates with the *real* ADO library. As you might imagine, there must be some type of buffer between the "managed" Interop Assembly and the "native" ADO library. This entity is called a Runtime Callable Wrapper, or RCW for short.

Runtime Callable Wrappers

As we learned at the beginning of this chapter, to invoke COM components from .NET the CLR must convert method parameters into their proper COM representations. To this end, the CLR constructs an entity called a Runtime Callable Wrapper. In addition to performing data-type conversion (marshalling), the RCW invokes the COM component and controls its lifetime. You will not have to work directly with RCWs. The .NET Runtime takes care of the RCW behind the scenes.

TLBIMP and TLBEXP

Interop Assemblies are generated automatically by VS.NET whenever you reference a COM component within its environment. It is also possible to create Interop Assemblies manually, using a Framework tool called TLBIMP. This tool examines a COM component and generates an Interop Assembly that can then be referenced in ASP.NET; Visual Studio.NET simply saves you an extra step by performing the conversion implicitly. Keep in mind that the Interop Assembly is not a functional replacement for the COM component. If you deploy the ASP.NET application to a Web Server, you must copy both the assembly and COM component to the target machine (and register the COM component).

Interestingly, .NET also permits the reverse process. That is, you can call managed Assemblies from pre-.NET applications using a utility called TLBEXP. For example, with TLBEXP you can call a Class Library written in C# from traditional ASP. An example that demonstrates this approach can be found online at ⚙CN⟩AS090001.

ADO/COM Interop Caveats

Although calling COM components from ASP.NET is straightforward, there are a few caveats we should point out. In Listing 9.1 we had to account for VB.NET's syntax changes (such as default properties) before our code would compile. In addition, we must account for a few behavioral changes that result when a COM component is converted into an Interop Assembly.

Consider the following line of code, which changes a RecordSet's cursor type (the manner in which its records can be viewed):

```
myADORecord.CursorType = adOpenDynamic
```

Listing 9.4   Setting RecordSet cursor type in ASP

This line, which works perfectly in VB6 and ASP, will not compile under VB.NET. This is not a shortcoming of VB.NET, but rather a difference between the visibility of types in COM components versus Assemblies. The adOpenDynamic constant is part of the CursorType enumeration, and, although ADO makes the enumeration globally accessible to clients, assemblies require that you fully qualify the constant value:

```
myADORecord.CursorType = CursorTypeEnum.adOpenDynamic
```

Listing 9.5   Setting RecordSet cursor type in ASP.NET

Provisions for Threading and COM+

In addition to addressing the characteristic differences between COM and Assemblies, you must also make a special provision for the following types of COM components:

1. Components written in Visual Basic 5 and 6.
2. COM components with Single-Threaded Apartment affiliation (more on this below).
3. COM+ components that attempt to access their object "context." If you are unfamiliar with the term, context is a concept specific to COM+. Only component developers have to worry about this situation. (This provision does not apply to MTS components, however, as you cannot use MTS components directly from ASP.NET. Remember that ASP.NET only runs on Windows 2000 and XP, whereas MTS is specific to NT4.)
4. Components that attempt to use ASP-intrinsic objects, such as Response and Request (it is possible, for example, for COM objects to use these objects explicitly to write directly to the browser).

To use these types of components in ASP.NET you must add the following attribute to the .aspx file's Page directive:

```
<%@ Page  ASPCompat="true" …
```

Listing 9.6   Setting compatibility

Without getting into too much detail, the ASPCompat="true" attribute is required because of certain assumptions that ASP.NET makes about a component's threading capabilities. Those well versed with the underpinnings of COM will recognize concepts such as Multithreaded Apartment (MTA) and Single-Threaded Apartment (STA). The majority of COM components fall into one of these two categories, which determine whether the COM runtime protects components against concurrent access.

By default, ASP.NET assumes that you are calling more capable MTA components, which can only be written in C++. Because VB6 produces only STA components, the ASPCompat attribute is required whenever you call VB6 components. Note that this directive can degrade performance, and you should use it only when it is required. This slowdown is a byproduct of intricate COM details, which are beyond the scope of this book. For more information, see ⊶AS090002.

Processes and Protection

By default, COM components execute within the ASP.NET Runtime process (aspnet_wp.exe). This is a potentially dangerous situation as problematic components can bring down other ASP.NET applications running within the same process (recall that multiple ASP.NET applications execute in a single process via AppDomains). You can avoid this precarious situation by using COM+ to configure components such that they run in dedicated "surrogate" processes, which are separate from aspnet_wp.exe. Details on employing this option can be found at AS090003.

SUMMARY

Using COM components in ASP.NET is very straightforward. Simply use VS.NET's Add References menu option, click the COM tab, and then select the component you wish to use. VS.NET will import the component into the project, and after you reference the appropriate namespace, the component can be used as if it were a regular .NET assembly.

Behind the scenes, VS.NET creates Interop Assemblies that communicate between the managed world of the CLR and the native world of COM. The Interop Assembly, in turn, creates a Runtime Callable Wrapper (RCW) that manages the underlying COM component. You can also generate Interop Assemblies manually by using the TLBIMP tool that ships with the Framework.

To use STA COM components (such as those produced by VB6), as well as COM+ components that attempt to access object "context," you must include the ASPCompat="true" attribute in the application's Page directive.

Topic: Migrating ASP Scripts

Given the syntactical similarities between VBScript and VB.NET, it seems reasonable to conclude that porting older ASP scripts to ASP.NET is simply a matter of renaming files with an .asp extension to .aspx. Although this is true in the simplest of circumstances, porting more complex ASP scripts requires more work.

In ASP you programmed in either JScript or VBScript. With ASP.NET, these languages have evolved into JScript.NET and VB.NET, respectively. Because VBScript is more commonplace, we'll consider some of the issues that arise when you migrate an ASP application written in VB-Script to an ASP.NET application written in VB.NET.

CONCEPTS

Porting the Timer.asp Application

In Chapter 1, we wrote a simple ASP timer application (Listing 1.1) to contrast ASP.NET with its predecessor. Porting this application to ASP.NET is very simple. Go to the aspTest virtual directory we used in the first chapter and rename Timer.asp to Convert.aspx. Next, in the renamed file, we need to modify the script declaration and <form> tags.

```
<%@ Language=VBScript %>
<FORM NAME="timerForm" ACTION="Timer.asp" METHOD="post">
```

Listing 9.7   Modifying the form and language settings

Change the lines from Listing 9.7 into the following:

```
<%@ Language=VB %>
<FORM NAME="timerForm" ACTION="Convert.aspx"
METHOD="post">
```

Listing 9.8   VB.NET language and ASPX <form> tags.

The first change switches the language from VBScript to VB.NET, and the second change reflects the new name of the script file.

Run the application by navigating to http://localhost/aspTest/Convert.aspx in your browser, enter in a sum size of 5 million, and the application will function identically to the ASP application developed in Chapter 1. The program times how long it takes to perform the summation. Because of the new file extension, however, IIS directs the request to ASP.NET Runtime rather than ASP's Runtime.

Unfortunately, our migration efforts bear little fruit. Results will vary, but based on our testing there isn't much of a performance difference between the converted ASP.NET application and the original ASP one. To understand why, we must examine the application's script code (reproduced here from Listing 1.2):

```
dim TimeStamp
dim i, output, total, count

If Request.Form("num") <> "" then
  count = Request.Form("num")
```

```
  TimeStamp = timer
  for i = 1 to count
    total = total + i
  next
  TimeStamp = CStr(timer - TimeStamp)
End If
```

Listing 9.9   Application code

Note that in typical script fashion, the variables in Listing 9.9 are typeless. Recall from Chapter 3 that typeless variables in VBScript are really Variants. Also recall from Chapter 3 that, in VB.NET, the Variant data type has been supplanted with the Object type. Thus, when ASP.NET compiles Listing 9.9, it implicitly turns all the variables into generic Objects. Because an Object is generic, the .NET Runtime must perform extensive runtime type-checking, which degrades performance.

You can increase performance dramatically by taking advantage of VB.NET's strong-typing features. In Listing 9.9, modify the second line such that it reads:

```
dim i, output, total, count as Long
```

Listing 9.10   Declaring typed parameters

Listing 9.10 illustrates a syntactical improvement in the newest version of Visual Basic. In previous versions of the language only the last variable in such a declaration would be of the specified type. In other words, in VB6 and earlier, only count is dimensioned as the Long type whereas the other variables are turned into Variants. Thankfully, in VB.NET this counterintuitive convention has been eliminated—all four variables in Listing 9.10 are of type Long.

Rerun the application, and the performance will equal that of the ASP.NET timer applications we developed in Chapter 1. By declaring the variables as Long integers, we can let the runtime bypass all of the generic type-checking that must be performed on an Object. In other words, the computation will take a fraction of a second, as opposed to several seconds. As you can see, even the simplest change in migrated scripts can increase performance dramatically.

Page Compatibility Directives
Listing 9.9 declares variables without specifying their types. This is made possible by a Page attribute called Strict, which is implicitly set to False by ASP.NET. In other words, Listing 9.9 is permissible in VB.NET because of the Strict attribute that ASP.NET embeds into the Page behind the scenes:

246 · CodeNotes® for ASP.NET

```
<%@ Language=VB Strict=False%>
```

Listing 9.11   The Strict attribute

You can force ASP.NET to disallow typeless declarations by setting the `Strict` attribute equal to `True`. If you make this change, then ASP.NET will refuse to compile Listing 9.9 (variable types must be explicitly declared), and you must convert it as per Listing 9.10.

An attribute similar to `Strict` is `Explicit`, which determines whether variables must be declared before being used. By default, this attribute is set to `True`, which means you must always `Dim` a variable before using it. Setting the `Explicit` attribute to `False` allows variables to be used without declaration (it is recommended that you don't use this option, as it leads to unreadable code). Those familiar with Visual Basic should know that this attribute equates to the `Option Explicit` directive in code. Similarly, the `Strict` attribute correlates with the `Option Strict` directive, a new feature in VB.NET.

SUMMARY

Although the ASP timer application was migrated to ASP.NET with relative ease, in practice things are rarely as simple. When converting more complex scripts you must account for the many syntax changes between VBScript and VB.NET. Changes in variable scope, parameter passing, error handling, and default parameters must all be accounted for. Furthermore, when you use COM components, you must account for the changes illustrated in the previous topic (enumeration visibility, etc.). Finally, there are also subtle differences between the intrinsic objects of ASP (Request, Response, etc.), and their equivalents in ASP.NET. See ᶜᴺ➤AS090004.

Keep in mind that although migration may be costly, benefits such as superior performance due to ASP.NET's compiled languages usually make such efforts worthwhile.

Topic: Platform Invoke

With ASP.NET it is possible to call functions found in plain Win32 DLLs using the CLR's PInvoke mechanism. This capability will be new to many web developers, as this was not directly possible under traditional ASP. In this topic, we will examine the Win32 API, identify some areas where its use may be appropriate in ASP.NET pages, and show you how to make calls directly against the API using PInvoke.

CONCEPTS

The Win32 API

Before the days of object-oriented paradigms and component frameworks such as COM, developers programmed against functions. To communicate with an application, a developer utilized its Application Programming Interface (API), which was an assortment of functions that exposed the core functionality of the program. The Windows Operating System was no exception.

In the early days of Windows, developers wrote applications in C using the Windows API. As its name suggests, the Windows API is the Application Programming Interface for the Windows Operating System. Any service performed by the OS, be it memory management or File I/O, can be accessed using one of the thousands of functions in this library. If you peer inside the `%winroot%\system32` directory, you will find hundreds of DLLs that contain these functions. Technically, PInvoke can be used against *any* DLL, but it is most often used against Microsoft "system" DLLs, including those that house the Win32 API.

The problem with the Windows API is that it is a C-style library that is cumbersome to use. For example, to open a text file with the API you must use the Win32 `CreateFile()` function, which accepts seven parameters that specify the file name, access mode (read/write), whether the file is to be shared, and more. This mode of access is more verbose and difficult than using the `FileSystemObject` or `TextStream` components available in ASP.NET. For this reason, the Win32 API is usually spurned in favor of frameworks such as Microsoft Foundation Classes (MFC) and Visual Basic.

All these frameworks do, however, is wrap the Win32 API in a more intuitive manner. Any Windows application that attempts to open a file, regardless of the technology in which it is written, implicitly uses the Win32 `CreateFile()` function underneath. In fact, every program on the Operating System, be it a device driver or ASP application, is, for the most part, a collection of Win32 API calls.

Why Use the Win32 API Directly?

Given that the Win32 API is wrapped by more intuitive frameworks, you may wonder why you would ever want to call it directly. Because the Win32 API is the most direct method of communicating with the

Operating System, situations may arise when you need to call a Win32 function for which no "wrapper" exists. One such situation occurs when dealing with security. As we learned in Chapter 8, security under ASP.NET can become quite convoluted given the interchanging roles of IIS, the ASP.NET Runtime, and the CLR. Functions in Win32, such as GetTokenInformation() and LookupAccountSid(), allow you to "poke around" and discover what the Operating System is really doing (e.g., determining the NT account under which the application is running, probing the low-level NT security entities that come into play (such as Security Identifiers [SIDS] and Discretionary access-control lists [DACLs]).

As we have cautioned repeatedly in this chapter, however, you should only resort to unmanaged components such as Win32 DLLs when you cannot find a managed equivalent.

EXAMPLE

In this example we will consider calling a very simple Win32 function (found in kernel32.dll) from ASP.NET—Sleep(). Predictably, Sleep() delays program execution for a period of time. In practice, you will want to use the Win32 API for more complex operations. A more involved example can be found online at °CN>AS090005.

Calling Win32 functions from ASP.NET requires using the DLLImport attribute found in the System.Runtime.InteropServices namespace. Recall from Chapter 3 that attributes are nonprogrammatic code statements that affect application behavior by embedding metadata into an assembly. When using the DLLImport attribute, you specify the function you wish to call and the DLL in which it resides. Thereafter, the function will be invoked in the same manner as any other function in the application. Behind the scenes, the DLLImport attribute informs the CLR to use PInvoke technology to call into the DLL.

Create a new VB.NET web application project in VS.NET, add a button to your project, and then add the following code to the CodeBehind file.

```
'Need this namespace:
Imports System.Runtime.InteropService

Public Class WebForm1
  Inherits System.Web.UI.Page
  <DllImport("kernel32.dll")> _
```

```
Public Shared Sub Sleep(ByVal msec As Integer)
End Sub
Private Sub Button1_Click(. . .)
  Sleep(5000)
  Response.Write("Finished Sleeping")
End Sub
End Class
```

Listing 9.12   Using the DLLImport attribute

As depicted in Listing 9.12, the DLLImport attribute is used to specify both the function name (Sleep) and the DLL it is located in (kernel 32.dll). As a result of this line, when the ASP.NET application calls Sleep(), the CLR loads kernel32.dll and calls the "real" function behind the scenes. During the process, the CLR takes care of the thorny details associated with calling unmanaged code (parameter marshalling, etc.).

Run the application by pressing F5, click the button, and after delaying for five seconds, the application will print "Finished Sleeping" in the browser.

Parameter Marshalling and Error Handling

DLLImport exposes additional parameters that control how the CLR marshals data and handles errors when DLL functions are invoked. Using these parameters requires the knowledge of low-level Win32/COM concepts such as BSTRs, HRESULTs, Unicode, etc. Such parameters are intended only for those developers who want fine-grained control over the CLR's native invocation mechanisms. For details on these parameters, see ⊶CN AS090006.

SUMMARY

In order to access DLL functions from ASP.NET, you must use the DLLImport attribute found in the System.Runtime.InteropServices namespace. This attribute is placed before the declaration of a function and specifies the DLL in which the function resides.

Calls to functions marked with DLLImport are intercepted by the CLR, which marshals parameters and returns values between the managed and native realms, and calls the real DLL. DLLImport exposes several parameters that assist the CLR in its conversion efforts and error-handling characteristics.

Chapter Summary

The .NET Framework exposes two technologies that allow web developers to leverage unmanaged code from ASP.NET applications. Platform Invoke (PInvoke) allows you to call functions residing in Win32 DLLs using the DLLImport attribute. Using this attribute, ASP.NET developers can leverage the Win32 API or any other DLL file.

With VS.NET, developers can use COM components directly from the IDE through its Add Reference menu option. Behind the scenes, VS.NET constructs an Interop Assembly that "wraps" the COM entity through the CLR's COM Interop technology. COM Interop technology is based on Runtime Callable Wrappers (RCW), which communicate between the managed world of the CLR and the native world of COM.

Although the native invocation mechanisms illustrated in this chapter allow you to call legacy COM components and Win32 DLLs, you should try to leverage the BCL for similar functionality whenever possible. Calling native code from .NET incurs a performance penalty, as the CLR must step outside the managed world of .NET. Additionally, if an application utilizes a COM component, it is subject to the annoying stipulation that existed with traditional ASP—the Web Server must be shut down in order to update the component.

Index